*When Miners March* is a volume not to be missed by labor historians, scholars of Appalachian Studies, and persons interested in West Virginia history. A primary source written in easily accessible style, William C. Blizzard's work provides a dramatic account of West Virginia miners' struggle to build the UMW.

James J. Lorence, Professor Emeritus,
Department of History
University of Wisconsin
Marathon County

This is a very accessible and salt-of-the-earth review of what West Virginia miners confronted on their march toward winning dignity and respect in their profession. A real treasure for anyone looking to understand the struggles of labor in the mining industry.

Mark A. Martinez, Professor and Chair
Department of Political Science
California State University
Bakersfield

I urge every person who believes in justice for working families to read Bill's work. He understood that the fight for a better life for the working class did not end at Blair Mountain.

Cecil Roberts, President
United Mine Workers of America

William C. Blizzard's *When Miners March* should be studied at every college and university level. There are lessons to be learned.

Ross Ballard II, Professor
Department of Education
Johns Hopkins University

This engaging book, by the son of a leader of one of the fiercest moments of coal miner struggles in the United States, is a valuable contribution to the preservation of a history that should be honored and never lost. Read it and weep, and cheer.

Each morning when I arise early to write, the Postscript to *When Miners March* posted above my desk, serves as my mission statement:

"Some readers, some scholars, may protest this writer's method of departing from academic 'objectivity', and rooting enthusiastically for the coal miners.

"That is too bad, but we have no apologies. We want our writing to be read, not grow musty in the library of any elite coterie. This is a people's history, and if it brawls a little, and brags a little, and is angry more than a little, well, the people in this book were that way, and so are their descendants."

Current events – notably the struggle for unions to remain relevant and empowered, and coal's role in the climate change crisis – make the writings both relevant and remarkable.

*Full texts of reviews as well as information on ordering books, audio dramas, music sound tracks, or scheduling the When Miners March Traveling Museum can be found at our web site,* **whenminersmarch.com.**

*Photo taken in the mid-1950's By William C. Blizzard*

Coal operators used this cannon against Union miners in what became known as the Battle of Blackberry City. In the early 1950's, Bill Blizzard and lifelong friend, Charley Payne, "talked away" the cannon from a coal operator without firing a shot. After the capture for the Union, it was placed in Bill's yard until he died in '58. It then went to Charley and several generations of his family. They have made it available for display in the *When Miners March Traveling Museum*.

"That thing was once the coal operators' substitute for collective bargaining."

Bill Blizzard and Charley Payne
*Charleston Daily Mail*, 2/10/1954

# WHEN MINERS MARCH

William C. Blizzard

**PM PRESS**

# WHEN MINERS MARCH

## William C. Blizzard

Copyright: © Appalachian Community Services 2010
All Rights Reserved
**ISBN: 978-1-60486-300-0**

Library of Congress Control Number:  2009912466

PM Press
PO Box 23912
Oakland, CA 94623

Cover Design,
Front Photo Art,
and Book Layout
by Tom Rhule
Charleston, WV

# CONTENTS

# Foreword

"It is strange to me that no one has written this book before."

Thus begins *Thunder in the Mountains*, Lon Savage's now classic 1984 treatment of the West Virginia mine wars of 1920-21. Twenty years later, Robert Shogan begins his 2004 work, *The Battle of Blair Mountain* as follows: "When I first became interested in the Battle of Blair Mountain in the early 1960's, I thought it remarkable that so little had been written about this unprecedented episode in our development as a nation." Incredibly, the book you now hold was written more than thirty years before Savage's book and predates Shogan's work by more than half a century. William C. Blizzard penned this definitive history of coal miners in West Virginia in the 1940's and early '50's.

The 1921 Battle of Blair Mountain in which thousands of miners formed an army to unionize the southern West Virginia coal fields is a story oft told. Introducing his work, *The West Virginia Mine Wars*, David Alan Corbin cites Mother Jones, Frank Keeney, Fred Mooney, and Sid Hatfield as heroes of the miners' struggle – and rightfully so. Yet looking at the crisis on Blair Mountain, we find Mother opposing the march; Kenney and Mooney necessarily absent due to trumped up murder charges; and Sid Hatfield, murdered before the march, also missing the big event. Bill Blizzard was the chief official protagonist in the drama played out around Blair Mountain. He led the Red Neck Army as they marched toward Logan County in 1921, hoping to bring the U.S. Constitution and the UMWA to the scab mines of Logan and Mingo counties. His eventual service to the Union spanned more than 40 years – from the early battles on Cabin and Paint Creeks (1912-13) until his retirement from the Union as President of District 17 in 1955. In that year he asked John L. Lewis for permission to retire from "the greatest Union in the world." Bill Blizzard was the lead defendant in the trials following the miners' march on Blair Mountain. Coal operators sought to hang some 200 miners and literally pronounce a death sentence on both the UMWA and the labor movement across our nation. Bill Blizzard was to be the first to swing, but he did not comply.

This work was originally offered in serial form titled, *Struggle and Lose...Struggle and Win!* in the newspaper, Labor's Daily, of late '52 and early '53. The political climate of the time ensured scant attention would be paid to articles in any such publication. Further, as an employee of Labor's Daily, William C. Blizzard was not given a byline. Later scholars simply did not know that their books had already been written. The earlier text is published here in book form for the first time. The only changes from the original are essentially cosmetic and made by William C. Blizzard following publication of the first edition and his successful eye surgery. More than half a century in existence, this work is not only a history of coal miners in West Virginia; it is an important piece of American history. For Bill Blizzard's son to have written this book is of tremendous import to scholars, but we must not let a fancy pedigree shade the life of William C. Blizzard himself. While long ago a UMWA member, William C. Blizzard spent his life primarily as a writer and photographer. Learning his trade at Columbia University, the author was a skilled craftsman. This meticulously researched work is a smooth read; never is there a doubt as to where Blizzard's sympathies lie. Perhaps here the genes do come into play. Opinion, supported by the facts of the situation and humor to lighten many grim realities, are spices that add zest to the entrée served herein.

The text focuses on the miners and their Union. Yet this story must be told in context. Despite national political winds whispering silence, the author offers a thorough economic analysis shedding light of day on systemic inequities. The personal troubles of the miners are linked to broader public issues. While their paths did not cross at Columbia, the author writes in the tradition of C. Wright Mills and goes boldly where the facts lead.

William C. Blizzard's life has mirrored his work. Those who read this amazing book are not merely introduced to the thoughts of a safe and secure academic; the author lost more than a few jobs for his stubborn adherence to principle. A popular writer whose verbiage has been repeatedly entered into the Congressional Record by Senator Robert C. Byrd, William C. Blizzard was last heard from by the people of our state when he was fired by the *Charleston Gazette* for not crossing a picket line. William C. Blizzard did not cross picket lines....

Photos included are largely from the collection of the author and provide a glimpse into the many twists and turns of the intertwined lives of the elder Bill Blizzard and his beloved Union.

Subsequent to the publication of the first edition, the full import of Bill Blizzard to the miners' Union and broader labor movement has become more evident. For that reason and to counter the many falsehoods offered by others  regarding his role, we have chosen to include numerous photos of Bill as well as the entire Blizzard family of Union supporters. Bill Blizzard was the archetypical grass roots leader. As such, he is generally written out of history by those who view power as based on organizational authority. Additional text offering a biographical sketch of Bill Blizzard will hopefully assist in making this American hero more real to coming generations.

For this edition, an informal and perhaps irreverent review of the existing literature is included to enable readers to expand a bit. Supplemental materials include abbreviations ACS (Appalachian Community Services) and WCB (William C. Blizzard).

Academic texts often claim impartiality but such is a fantasy. The very questions one asks – or leaves unasked – contain and reveal an author's bias. In keeping with the spirit of William C. Blizzard's original work, added materials are offered here with an open and proud bias in favor of those who work for a living rather than those who live from the value created by others.

# Acknowledgments

Time has moved on since this work was first assembled. Any reasonably complete list of those meriting thanks for assisting in this book's original creation is lost both to memory and to history. A tip of the hat to those gone on will have to suffice. Several libraries were of service in the compilation of the original text. Most notably: Kanawha County Public Library; Library of Congress; Marshall University Library; West Virginia State Archives; and the West Virginia Supreme Court of Appeals Law Library.

After more than half a century, many others were needed to enable the resurrection from scattered sources and the addition of photos and documents to the original text. This project was made possible in no small part through the kind assistance of James M. Cain; Douglas Estepp; Eric George; Heather George; Leesa McVay; Marguerite (Blizzard) Nekoranec; Harry O'Rourke and the Magnificent Seven from St. Louis University; Princeton University, Firestone Library; Tom Rhule; Rutgers University, John Cotton Dana Library, Roberta Tipton; Dana Spitzer; Jean Thomas; West Virginia Division of Culture and History, Greg Carroll and Gordon Simmons.

This second, expanded edition would not have been possible without support and encouragement from literally hundreds of miners and their families. Ross Ballard, former miner from Boone County, saw the import of *When Miners March* and transformed it into an eight CD audio drama that includes a powerful sixteen-cut music sound track. Kathryn Bowles (great granddaughter of Bill Derenge), Tracey Hughes, Paul Kees, Kenny King, Betty and

Elwood Maples, John Payne (grandson of Charles "Tuck" Payne), Billy Rose, Dwight Siemiaczko, and Terry Whitlock (grand daughter of C.E. "Red" Jones) are among those who have provided both histories and artifacts that have confirmed the validity of WCB's work and aided Appalachian Community Services in developing a traveling museum to share when peddling books.

The boost we received from Moore-Huntley Productions in selecting both Ross Ballard and William C. Blizzard to appear on the History Channel was much appreciated. William Cleaver has served as technical advisor for computer matters.

Finally, a parting thanks to William C. Blizzard (1916-2008). He was busy signing books up until the day before his death.

## Author's Note

Readers may observe that in *When Miners March* a few factual errors may occur as well as the usual typos and mechanical blunders common to unedited text. This in part, was not accidental. My publisher's desire was that my *Labor's Daily* text remains unchanged in this version so that the book could appear as an unedited historical document. Errors may also be due to the lack of careful proofing of my text as it appeared in *Labor's Daily*, in serial form, for no person on that staff was assigned proofing duty. Such errors, if any, are retained in this version.

During the first half of my workday at *Labor's Daily*, I was allowed to prepare a text version of this manuscript in my home, the same text to appear in that newspaper on the following day. I occasionally proofed the text from hot type galleys, but rarely. The second half of my busy workday was spent in the newspaper office or outside with routine journeyman tasks such as editorial writing and news gathering. This original serial-printed book was based upon several years of research and experience prior to the existence of *Labor's Daily*.

Finally, for this current edition of *When Miners March*, I was unable to do much proofing because of an irritating eye condition. *When Miners March* now appears before you (figuratively) unshaven, uncombed, in time-worn garb and with coal dust on almost every page.

William C. Blizzard – Dec. 20, 2004

*Photo by Lou Raines*

Author photographed shortly after *Labor's Daily* ended publication.

An old typing instruction book reads: "If you would not be forgotten when you are dead and rotten, do something worth writing about or write something worth reading."

My father and other coal miners have lived the most important part of this advice. In this book, I try to accomplish the other.

William C. Blizzard

# STRUGGLE AND LOSE…
# STRUGGLE AND WIN!

*Above is the title of the following work as originally pub-lished in* Labor's Daily.

# Chapter One: Turner Finds Coal

11/18/1952 (First)

John P. Turner was excited and so might be forgiven for applying his willow switch a bit too hard to the rump of his bay stallion. The stallion quivered and his hoofs struck the rutted road to the salt mill at a frantic gallop. Turner patted the horse's neck and grinned at the speeding scenery. "Sorry, old boy," he said, "I guess I got too anxious. We're on mighty important business."

Turner swung off the foam-flecked animal at the office of the salt mill superintendent. He reached into a saddlebag and brought forth a head-sized chunk of something wrapped in an old sack. For a moment he looked at the chunk, eyes gleaming. Then he turned and strode rapidly into the clapboard office.

The superintendent was startled by the wide grin and flushed face of Turner. "Hell!" he said, "What's up?"

"Plenty," said Turner, holding out his mysterious bundle. "Look!"

"I'm looking," said the superintendent, "and all I see is a sack – a damn dirty sack – that looks like it might have a head of cabbage in it. What is it, Turner?"

Turner said nothing, but walked to the desk and turned his burden upside down. There was a thud as something black and dully gleaming fell out, rolled over on the desktop and stopped.

"My God!" said the superintendent. "It's coal!"

Turner nodded. "That's right. I've got a big seam of it right up the river, and I didn't even know it. I've had a contract to give your salt mills all the wood you burn. I guess you wouldn't object if I sold you coal instead."

"You bet we wouldn't," said the superintendent. "I'll call a conference and we can dicker. And don't look so excited. You make me worry about your terms."

John P. Turner had a right to be excited. Of course it had been known for years that coal was in the hills. It was even being mined commercially in what is now West Virginia, and had been since 1810 by Conrad Cotts. But that was at far-away Wheeling. And no one else had bothered with the coal deposits in the Kanawha Valley. Most everybody burned wood, even for large operations such as the salt mills which dotted the area. John Turner and those who followed him changed that.

For his discovery in 1817 was important not only for himself. The fact that coal was present in the Kanawha Valley was to affect the way of life of thousands of people, give impetus and strength to great organizations, be the basis of huge fortunes and grinding poverty, force some men to become merciless rulers and others rebellious slaves. Over this black bone of contention men were destined to fight with fist and guile, batter with club and blackjack, kill with rifle and machine gun. John Turner had made a portentous discovery.

The conflict over coal in the Kanawha Valley is interesting in itself, but it becomes much more so when it is appreciated that in this struggle can be found all the elements present in the many battles which coal miners and other workingmen have fought. The fight is unceasing, and it continues today. But it progresses in an uneven manner, at times outwardly calm, then exploding volcanically. The major explosion in this particular industrial battle happened in 1921. Both periods will be treated herein in some detail.

## West Virginia Fight Typical

Certain features of the West Virginia battle, which are typical, are as follows: Huge combines of capital move from exploited to unexploited territory. Coal operators of one section war among themselves, then combine to fight coal operators of another section, then all together make a common front against the coal miners' Union. The coal miner attempts to build himself an organization so that he can have something to say about his own life – and is beaten, jailed, starved and shot.

It sounds like war, and it is. The only time this battle ceases, oddly enough, is when the United States Government is at war. Then a halt of sorts is called and it becomes a violation of the law for the coal miner to engage in any sort of industrial battle to improve his conditions, no matter how serious the provocation.

Pledged not to strike, the miner sees his plight worsen because of increased prices, while the coal operator wallows in super profits and bathes in the blood-money which flows into his coffers during every foreign war.

The coal operators like to have the technical state of war exist as long as possible, so that the miners' Union is powerless. This was true after both World War I and World War II, when the United Mine Workers of America was subjected to censure and penalty because the "war" was still going on. This was a silly state of affairs, as not a shot had been fired in many months, and "business as usual" was being resumed. But it happened – twice.

## Always the Same

In a passage of touching beauty, Mother Mary Jones, the miners' great champion of another era, had this to say. "The story of coal is always the same. It is a dark story. For a second's more sunlight, men must fight like tigers. For the privilege of seeing the color of their children's eyes by the light of the sun, fathers must fight as beasts in the jungle. That life may have something of decency, something of beauty – a picture, a new dress, a bit of cheap lace fluttering in the window – for this, men who work in the mines must struggle and lose, struggle and win."

And a life of danger and struggle it was for the men born and yet unborn who were destined to burrow into the earth for the great natural resource which John Turner had discovered. But the great giant of energy which lay sleeping beneath the round green hills of West Virginia was not to be awakened until over his head was heard the whistle-toot and rumble of the locomotive. Coal, except for slow river shipments from convenient points, could not be sent to market until there were rails to ship it over.

And the rails came. In 1873 the Chesapeake & Ohio Railway was completed to Huntington and made steady progress toward tidewater. The Capitol City of Charleston, then a thriving village of about 3,200 population, had a wagon bridge across the Kanawha connecting it to the railway. The Kanawha & Ohio Railroad came to Charleston in 1884, while the Coal & Coke Railroad, later bought by the B. & O. was built to Sutton in 1893. The West Virginia Central Pittsburgh (later the Western Maryland), was built to Davis in Tucker County in 1884 and extended to Elkins by 1891.

Production, however, remained relatively small scale until shortly before the turn of the century. In 1875 there were only nine mines in the Great Kanawha Valley. But in the following twenty-five years many schemes were hatching, much planning was taking place, and the stage was being set for bloody, ruthless, industrial war. West Virginia's potential was obvious to many men and these men were dreaming and acting. The eyes of great corporate combinations, full of lust, were intent on rape of the virgin state.

11/19/1952 (Second)

In 1879 Edmund Kirke wrote a little book about West Virginia titled *The Workman's Paradise, Hints To New Settlers.* If the state, with its comparatively untouched coal and virgin timber, was an Eden at that date, the idyll was soon to be shattered by the advent of that venomous, but wealth-producing serpent, Industrialism. A foretaste of this is given in Kirke's remarks: "...in about 5 years it (West Virginia) has sent to market products which have paid the Chesapeake and Ohio Railway a freight which may be roughly stated at five million dollars. This had been done during five years of great business depression."

Exceedingly primitive mining legislation was on the West Virginia statute books as early as 1879. According to Mary Elizabeth Hennessey, a Legislative Act of March 10, 1879 authorized the Judge of the Circuit Court of any county to appoint an inspector of mines upon presentation of a petition verified by the affidavit of any credible person and signed by 100 voters of the county. The number of such inspectors appointed is not on record, but it will be guessed that they were few.

## Mine Department Created

In the same year the state authorized the appointment of a mining inspector and a mine boss was supposed to look out for the safety of the miners. In 1887 two mining districts were created with an inspector for each and a "fire boss" was authorized to check the miner's working places. The inspection system was enlarged again in 1897, and on Feb. 24, 1905 the Act was passed which created the West Virginia Department of Mines.

The above measures were without doubt created because of coal miner pressure for some kind of safety precautions. How well they were enforced may be deduced from the fact that on March 7, 1891 it was declared unlawful for any corporation or company to pay its men in script. The issuance of script, a token money which is good only in the company store, still goes on today, although wages may not be paid directly in this manner.

Patterns of industrial conflict were set very early in the Valley. What was apparently the first major dispute was at the Marmet mines in Putnam County in January, 1891. The men went on strike and the company imported Negroes as strikebreakers. This vicious practice accomplished two things: It brought the miners to terms, and it divided the labor movement by setting the Negro against the white and vice-versa. In this manner good workingmen, black and white, were blinded to their common interests. A great deal of the so-called "race" problem in the United States is due to such company practices.

## Private Thugs Hired

This strike also saw the hiring of private "detectives" – this time the Pinkertons – to protect the strikebreakers and company property.

As early as 1894 the National Guard was called upon as a strike-breaking agency. This was at Eagle, in Fayette County and at Boggs Run in Marshall County, where the strike lasted only 8 days. The operator tactics were effective. In 1897 there were only 206 Union men of the 18,000 coal miners employed in West Virginia.

To the north, by 1898, was a society which had already traveled much of the road which West Virginia was to follow with so much hardship and brutality. Coal had been mined in huge quantities for many years in the states of Ohio, Pennsylvania, Indiana and Illinois, and in lesser quantities in several others.

The coal miners of these sections had early found that in order to obtain a decent living it was necessary to do more than petition their employers. In 1849 the first Union of coal miners was formed by a miner named John Bates in the anthracite region of Pennsylvania. Its career was short and it died with its first unsuccessful strike. A much larger organization came into being at St. Louis, Mo., on Jan. 28, 1861. This was the American Miners' Association, which did a great deal of organizing in all states which then produced coal and put out the first official journal of the American coal digger called the *Weekly Miner*.

## John Siney's Union

In 1864 the Workingmen's Benevolent Society, headed by John Siney, was formed by anthracite miners. This organization had as its aim not only the organization of miners, but of all workingmen. As it happened, it outlasted the American Miners' Association, which fell victim to the post-Civil War slump. To John Siney goes the credit for negotiating the first wage agreement with a coal operators' association. This was signed at Pottsville, Pa., on July 29, 1870, between the Workingmen's Benevolent Association and the Anthracite Board of Trade. But there was an economic panic in the mid-seventies and Siney's organization also fell by the way.

On May 15, 1883 the miners again formed a union, this one known as the Amalgamated Association of Miners of the United States. It was in a strike almost before it was formed and was badly defeated, but the miners met again in 1885 and established The National Federation of Miners and Mine Laborers. About the same time the Knights of Labor set up National Trade Assembly No. 135 as a miners' branch of that organization. And the National Federation changed its name to the National Progressive Union of Miners and Mine Laborers.

The next step in this process of struggling and losing, struggling and winning, was marked by an event which has become a landmark in American Labor history. At a convention in Columbus, Ohio, on Jan. 25, 1890, Master Workman John B. Rae of the Knights of Labor announced that the National Progressive Union of Miners and Mine Laborers and National District Assembly 135, K. of L., had voted to unite their ranks into one big union.

## UMW Is Formed

That Union was to be called the United Mine Workers of America. It had a membership of 20,912 and a treasury of $139.00. President John B. Rae was to receive a salary of $1,000 a year and the dues to the national Union were 20 cents a month.

The infant which was destined to become a mighty giant very nearly perished in its diaper days. First came the failure of the Connellsville coke strike in 1891, and then a mixed-up situation wherein the miners were supposed to strike for the eight-hour day on May 1 of that year. But the strike order was countermanded and the strike fizzled. Sixteen thousand men dropped from the UMW rolls.

Then came the panic of 1892, with consequent poverty, unemployment, and cutting of wage scales. After that was an unsuccessful strike in 1894. These were the days of the famous march of "General" Coxey's army and the use of the Sherman Anti-trust Act of 1890 to jail Eugene Debs. Individual workingmen whose total wealth might be a pair of pants and a mule were penalized under a Sherman Act which was to have been used, the politicians claimed, against great corporations.

By 1897 there were fewer than 10,000 members of the UMW in the whole United States – probably a whole lot fewer. The treasury contained something less that $600. The infant UMW seemed in bad need of an oxygen-tent. But none was available and there must have been many who had mentally engraved R.I.P. on the Union's headstone. Except the operators, of course, who were probably, with great glee, engraving the initials R.I.H.

11/20/1952 (Third)

A new president, Michael D. Ratchford of Ohio, was elected in 1897. The prospect could hardly have been more dismal. The UMW was cashless and very nearly member-less. Ratchford's thought processes at this time have not been recorded, so it can not be said by what line of reasoning he called a strike on July 4,

1897. Certainly he must have felt that matters could be no worse, come what may.

In any event, he shot at the moon and hit it. The miners came out and stayed out. Three long months it took. But the operators capitulated. And this was the magic medicine the puny UMW needed for survival. At the 1898 convention, Ratchford was able to report that the Union now had 33,000 members and $11,000 in the treasury.

In 1898, and for many years prior thereto, the principal coal-producing area in the United States was composed of Western Pennsylvania, Ohio, Indiana, and Illinois, generally called the Central Competitive Field. The effects of the panic of 1892 were still felt by the coal industry in this area, and many miners were working as little as one and a half to two days a week. The operators in the Field, as the name implies, were certainly competitive, all of them trying to sell in the same market, cutting one another's throats.

## West Virginia Looms

And by 1898 these coal operators saw the threat of another major competitor – nonunion coal from West Virginia. It took no seer to forecast that the stream of coal from the Mountain State would soon turn into a river which might easily sweep away the shaky financial structure of the northern operators. The Union miner in the Competitive Field was just as worried as his boss. He was hardly making a living, while in non-union West Virginia his fellow miners were working around the clock six days a week – and knocking him out of a job while making only a pittance for themselves. Also, the northern coal miner had seen the scab from West Virginia break his strike of 1894.

Something had to be done. So, on Jan. 26, 1898, a joint conference of Union representatives and coal operators from the Central Competitive Field met in Chicago, Ill. The UMW, of course, was aware of its own grievances and anxious to help its miners and increase its membership. The operators had two things in mind. One was to sit down and agree to quit underselling each other, to establish a regulated and stabilized program to which all members would adhere. In this way all could live. The other important point on the agenda was West Virginia.

Being coal operators they could profess no love for unionism, but they saw little chance to shake off the UMW in the Central Competitive Field. So there was only one thing to do – encourage the Union to organize West Virginia. If the Union succeeded it would mean increased costs to the southern operators, which would help to keep West Virginia from underselling. If the Union failed it would still give the C.C.F. temporary relief, for southern production would be cut in the event of a strike, and the W.Va. operators would have to spend money for guards and rifles and machine guns.

## Wins 8-Hour Day

The UMW certainly wanted to add to its membership by organizing miners everywhere, and was quite agreeable to the operators' proposal – which was never formally incorporated into the conference proceedings.

But it did not make an agreement without certain concessions, especially with its new-found strength after the 1897 victory. It demanded and got a 10-cent increase, so that miners in the Central Competitive Field now made the handsome sum of 66 cents a ton for screened coal. And there was another concession so startling that it was hard to believe – Union soft-coal miners after April 1, 1898 were to work an 8-hour day!

Only a few years before, agitators for the 8-hour movement had been called wild-eyed anarchists, public enemies and fit objects for hanging or deportation. The press had intimated that such a short workday would in all likelihood wipe the coal industry off the map. Somehow, though, the coal industry did not expire, and has managed to struggle along until this day. Actually, in 1898 the northern miners would be lucky to get two to three days work a week at any hours, so the concession was not too costly to the operators.

For the operators the most important point in the inter-state conference was the agreement to civilize their commercial warfare to the extent that prices would be uniform and no backstairs chicanery would be permitted any single operator.

T.L. Lewis, the vice-president of the UMW, summed up the inter-state conference of 1898: "As I understand it, it is for the purpose of wiping out competition between us as miners first, viewing it from our side of the question; next, for the purpose of wiping out competition as between the operators, in these four states."

## Operators Yell

Down in West Virginia the local coal operators were eyeing these proceedings with nervous and indignant mien. They were quick to cry "conspiracy!" and they kept yelling it for at least 22 years, taking it to court in attempted Union death blows in 1913 and again in 1920. They forgot that the Kanawha Coal Operators Association might have been called a conspiracy just as easily as the Confederation of Northern Operators. The UMW was merely serving its own interests by utilizing the competition between the two employer groups.

Newspaper and official propaganda sources painted a horrible picture for the West Virginia public of Union and alien northern forces combining to swoop down upon the Mountain State. Meanwhile the coal barons of the South laid in rifles and ammunition and contacted the proper sources for mine guards and strikebreakers.

It is true that part of the picture was a war for coal markets between the Unionized Central Competitive Field and the nonunion West Virginia territory. For the northern coal operators it was a question of economic survival. They used what weapons they could to prevent pilfering of their markets by the underselling southern operators. They were closer to the Great Lakes markets, and they tried to get their freight rates lower and West Virginia's higher. The West Virginia operator was out to make as much money as he could – he saw millions in the offing – and if the northern operator was forced into bankruptcy that was too bad.

The quality of mercy is more apparent in a shark's attack than in these economic forays.

11/21/1952 (Fourth)

The mine owner in West Virginia had several advantages over his Central Competitive Field rivals. He had "high" coal, seams of six feet or over, highly adaptable to mechanized mining, and free from impurities. The coal was soft, high grade, and easily mined. Production cost was a fraction of that of his rivals. His men were not unionized, so he could pay what he pleased, pay attention to safety as he pleased, maintain living conditions as he pleased. His labor overhead was low. For instance, as late as 1912 he was paying his men less than 25 cents a ton. At this time the C.C.F. was paying 90 cents.

In addition the "company town" plan was stronger in West Virginia than elsewhere. The company owned the store, the houses, the recreation, if any, the blacksmith – everything. And each thing it owned was made to show a profit. No wonder West Virginia operators could undersell the C.C.F. in their own backyard!

It was not true, however, that the Union was in collusion with the operators of the Central Competitive Field. The UMW was aware of the vast industrial potential of the Mountain State, and organizing attempts had been made before the Interstate Conference. When the UMW was formed in 1890 a convention was called in Wheeling by M. F. Moran to form a West Virginia branch called District 17, and Moran was elected president.

## First District 17 Convention

The first annual convention of District 17 was held at Charleston on April 14, 1891. President Moran reported that the total income for the year had been about $1,000 and the cash on hand amounted to $48.21. The miners at Raymond City, W. Va. were on strike at the time, and aid was pledged to them.

The first great organizing drive in West Virginia was in 1897, when the UMW won its life-giving victory in the Northern coal fields. Such celebrated figures as Samuel Gompers, Eugene V. Debs, Mother Jones, Chris Evans and Michael Ratchford organized and addressed mass meetings in Fayette and other counties.

In an admirable spirit of unity, representatives of many trades helped the UMW in its fight. Aside from AFL President Gompers, also organizing were Henry Lloyd, President of the United Brotherhood of Carpenters and Joiners of America, President Mahon of the Street Railway Employees, Joseph Vitchenstein, a Pittsburgh newspaper Union representative, President Rae of the Painters' Union, James O'Connell, President of the International Machinists' Union, William A. Carney, Vice-President of the Amalgamated Association of Iron and Steel Workers, and James Wood, Vice-President of the Cigar Makers International Union. Organizers from other trades, not officially recorded, were without doubt also present.

## Gompers Heads Committee

A committee headed by Samuel Gompers called on West Virginia Governor G. W. Atkinson, asking that they be accorded the privilege of holding public meetings for "the discussion of matters concerning the welfare of the said miners." The word "privilege" is the language of the Governor. It seems to be taken for granted that miners had no constitutional rights in West Virginia. The committee also complained about an injunction issued by the Circuit Court of Marion County, and asked that the Governor do something about the injunctive coercion.

Governor Atkinson, like many governors since, replied in an evasive letter which used a lot of words and said nothing. Between the lines it said, of course: "Get out of West Virginia or I'll throw the book at you."

The Governor's exact words are as follows: "So long as the working men of this state conduct their cause in a lawful and peaceful manner it will be my duty, as it will be my pleasure, to protect them; but if they should, in an ill-advised hour, violate the laws by interfering with the rights of property of others it will be my sworn duty to repress energetically and speedily all lawlessness, and to see that the public peace is maintained at all hazards, and that the property of our people is protected; for we must all, whether rich or poor, employer or employee, high or low, respect and obey the law."

Federal injunctions, the first to be used in the West Virginia coal struggle (as far as can be determined), fell like snowflakes. They temporarily, then "perpetually" enjoined from organization and agitation. L.V. G. Morris, a Federal Deputy Clerk in the Circuit Court at Parkersburg, W. Va., wrote a letter on Aug. 15, 1897 to J.T. Waters, Deputy Clerk at Charleston, which gives an idea as to just how prepared the West Virginia operators were to use the injunction weapon:

**Letter Is Quoted**

"The attorneys were very anxious to have the injunctions issued from here to last night, but I could get no printer to print them. My idea was to have about 100 spas, and 1,000 injunctions printed with the name of the plaintiff blank (as all the injs. are alike) and fill in name of plaintiff with pen on as many copies of each as were required."

From the above it would appear that the Union printers could find better work to do than set up injunction forms! The injunctions were made on a typewriter, most of them carbons. The Marshal's return shows that Sam Gompers received his copy in Fayette County on August 17, 1897 at 2 p.m.

The Kanawha County Circuit Court, not to let the Federal courts outdo it, also issued its first injunctions in the case of "The Winifrede Coal Company vs. Chris Evans, Frank J. Weber, et als., signed Grant P. Hall, Clerk," on August 17, 1897.

The coal diggers fought the injunctions with what was to become in West Virginia the most potent organizational weapon of the miners: the mass march. Union men would congregate at one point in a ragged "army" and go on a march through unorganized fields, speaking and organizing as they went. As men joined the Union the army grew larger, morale grew higher, and non-union mines shut down.

## The Miners March

In his *Volume II* of the *History of the UMW* Chris Evans quotes a letter from Frank J. Weber, an American Federation of Labor organizer then working for the UMW:

"Montgomery, W. Va.
"Aug. 25, 1897

"Friend Chris Evans:

"R. L. Davis is here. I had him speak to the colored men. I went to Powelton without the Army. As no one appeared yesterday, I will visit Powelton again in the morning. We start at 12:30 a.m., in order to be on the field early. A few men went in at Boomer's Branch, and another army will arrive there at 4 a.m. I have not heard from Mason since Sunday. I wish you would notify him to gather all men west of Handly and march to Ace. I have appointed committee to visit the St. Clair Coke miners and ask them to lay down as we must close down. I have not heard from New River.

"I will march in two divisions to Powelton – one up the railroad, and the other through Morris Creek over the mountain. As soon as I return I will report. If I am successful at Powelton I will try Ansted or the Gauly Mountain mine.

"With best wishes, I remain,

"Yours fraternally,

"F.J. Weber."

The strike continued and on October 14, 1897 Chris Evans, Michael Ratchford and others met at Charleston with coal operators Morris O. Brooks, Enoch and John Carver, T.E. Embleton and J.D. Harris to discuss the situation. Two miners and two operators were appointed as a committee to meet at 2 p.m. The miners arrived at the specified hour, but the operators failed to appear. President Michael Ratchford published a statement in a Charleston paper, part of which follows:

"Chris Evans and myself will meet any two operators in the Kanawha Valley, in this city, and there discuss the merits of the case, that we may go before the public in a proper light....

"From this it will be seen that the responsibility of the present conflict is not with us, but with the operators, and if either or both of these propositions are rejected, the public will surely rest the blame where it properly belongs."

It is not known where the public rested the blame, but the operators knew their own power. Organization in West Virginia was for the time defeated. In 1893 there were only 375 UMW members in the entire state.

11/22/52 (Fifth)

After 1898 the operators of the Central Competitive Field found they had a wonderful talking point when the UMW asked for a raise. "Why," they would shout, "haven't you organized West Virginia? We can't give you any increase up here until you do. We're being ruined by nonunion coal." The Union would reply that it was doing its best but West Virginia operator tactics, plus the isolated and rugged terrain, made the task difficult. And the northern operator would sit on his point triumphantly.

But many operators in the Central Competitive Field had decided that this West Virginia proposition was too good to overlook. So they secretly bought into the West Virginia coal lands, so that they actually had a finger in both pies and it was impossible to lose. This didn't keep them from yelling about organizing West Virginia, even though in that field they were buying machine guns and hiring armed guards to shoot the Union to pieces.

Another complicating force was the railroads. They were necessary for the shipment of coal and they were tied up with the mine ownership in many devious ways almost impossible to prove. Naturally, they made their freight rates favor those coal lands in which they had the heaviest interest. Just a glimpse of the situation will give an idea of its complexity. The Pennsylvania Railroad owned most of the stock in the Norfolk and Western, and shortly before had a large interest in the C&O, but sold out to the Hawley interests. The C&O, in turn, owned half the Kanawha & Michigan, the Lake Shore & Michigan Southern owning the rest. But there was a suit filed in 1912 by the United States Government charging that the C&O and Lake Shore & Michigan were a combine, and that the C&O also controlled an apparently competing line, the Cincinnati, Hamilton & Dayton.

## U. S. Steel Arrives

This is not the entire West Virginia situation. To make it complete it is necessary to know that in 1901 a really huge corporate interest moved into the state – United States Steel. A syndicate of E. H. Gary, William Edenborn and Isaac T. Mann bought up 300,000 acres of coal land, four-fifths of the Pocahontas Field. This they turned over to the Norfolk & Western Railroad, which was, as has been pointed out, a subsidiary of the Pennsylvania. And the Pennsylvania Railroad was connected with the Girard Trust Company of Philadelphia, a connecting link with the Morgan financial empire of New York. Very big guns indeed were interested in blasting out West Virginia coal.

The railroad owners were anti-union and old hands at strikebreaking. They were quite happy to give advice and personnel to the West Virginia operators who wanted no part of the UMW. The railroads, the coal companies and the corporate interests formed one family, not an especially happy family, but one welded together by mutual economic advantage.

Every year the miners and operators of the Central Competitive Field sat in joint conference. And every year the northern operators wailed about the increased competition of West Virginia coal and accused the UMW of not attempting to organize that field. The Union was trying, without a doubt. Vice-President T.L. Lewis told the 1902 conference: "Some of the things that could be related about the happenings in West Virginia would be a shame to go into print. It would certainly make the hair raise on some of your heads."

## W. Va. Production Mounts

But it was true that the northern operators were more feeling the southern competition. In 1901 Pennsylvania bituminous coal decreased in sales to Chicago markets by 39,262 tons; Ohio coal to the same markets decreased by 54,734 tons, Illinois by 238,000 tons; and Indiana by 22,000 tons.

West Virginia showed an INCREASE in sales to the Chicago markets of 80,987 tons. The giant in the southern hills had not yet attained his full growth, but he was becoming a mighty strapping youngster.

While most coal miners in West Virginia were not then formal Union members, it became clear as to where their sympathies lay. When the great anthracite strike was called by John Mitchell on May 15, 1902, the soft coal miners in the Kanawha Valley and elsewhere struck in sympathy, although this was not a part of the

UMW national policy. At a meeting of District 17 and UMW international officials in Huntington, it was decided to call a strike in that area on June 7, 1902. The strike was eventually smothered, but the fact that it was effective proved that the West Virginia coal miner was ready for organization and that it was not "outside" pressure that forced him to walk off his job, as the coal operators contended.

According to George Wolfe, then secretary of the Winding Gulf Operators' Association and president and manager of the Atlantic Smokeless Coal Company, the 1902 West Virginia shutdown covered the counties of Mercer, McDowell, Mingo on the Norfolk & Western Railway, and Kanawha and Fayette on the C&O In testimony in later litigation Mr. Wolfe said that

> "It was along in the fall of 1902 before there was any resumption of work generally in the New River field, and the effect of that strike in the Kanawha field lasted some time longer.... So far as the Chesapeake & Ohio was concerned, there was an almost total cessation of production of coal for quite a time."

**Union Leaders Arrested**

Thirty-six leaders of the 1902 strike in West Virginia were arrested under an injunction and as many as 2,500 miners assembled and marched in large mass meetings. It was evident that the miners of West Virginia were interested in becoming Union men. It is also evident that mine guards, injunctions and other devices were used to break the strike. Baldwin-Felts gunmen, notorious in later years, were imported for the first time, replacing the Pinkertons. The National Guard camped in Fayette County for almost three weeks. The operators of West Virginia were just getting warmed up for later showdowns.

The UMW did, however, get a slight toehold in the Kanawha field. Most of Cabin Creek was organized and there was some organization along the Kanawha River. There was much seesawing after this, the miners sometimes winning, sometimes losing. The operators killed the Union on Cabin Creek in 1904, but it was established on part of adjacent Paint Creek.

And still West Virginia production mounted. By 1903 it was the third largest coal producer. From that year to 1912 its production increased five times, while that of Ohio and Pennsylvania barely doubled. From 1900 to 1910 the population of West Virginia increased only 27 per cent, while the number of mine employees jumped 143 per cent.

## Company-Owned State

From 1898 to 1912 West Virginia increased its coal production by 350 per cent – and still, the UMW had been unable to organize the miners, despite their apparent willingness. The West Virginia operators sat in their company towns in a company-owned state, behind impregnable legal barriers. If legalisms failed, guns seldom did, and the operators had plenty of guns and men to use them. In 1912 there were only 1,136 card-carrying coal diggers in West Virginia and there were 69,611 miners in the state.

On paper the situation looked bad. As a delegate to the 1913 interstate conference said, West Virginia was "a dagger in the heart of the United Mine Workers of America." Did the miners of West Virginia really want to remain scabs, as the operators insisted? Or did they remain quiet because talk is not so effective when a gun is aimed at your head? The answers to these questions came with the strike of the West Virginia miners in 1912, and the subsequent senatorial investigation.

# Chapter Two: King of the State

11/25/1952 (Sixth)

In 1912 the miners' met as usual with the operators of the Central Competitive Field, first at Indianapolis and then on March 20 at Cleveland, Ohio. The Union asked for an increase of 10 cents on the ton and 20% more for day men. The strong opposition of the operators may be seen in the fact that the settlement was for about 5 cents increase per ton and 5.26% for day labor. The District men from West Virginia then went home to bargain with their own operators (who were apparently unwilling to have anything to do with these conferences) on the basis of this agreement.

Not so very many of the mines in the Kanawha Valley were then organized. And the operators in the area had taken a lesson in strategy from those of the Central Competitive Field. Whereas the C.C.F. operators had argued against an increase so long as West Virginia remained unorganized those operators in West Virginia who WERE organized argued against a raise for their men until the local nonunion men were also brought into line.

The Union and the mine owners who operated Union mines met in the Ruffner Hotel at Charleston on April 1. There was a great deal of haggling; the procedure being somewhat like this: The miners offered a series of demands, and the operators countered with an offer to renew the old contract with no increase and the 9 hour day. Then the miners withdrew all their demands except for the "Cleveland advance" of 5.26%. The operators refused. Will England, chairman of the joint scale committee, offered to go back to the old contract provided the miners could have the check-off. The operators interpreted the check-off as a demand for the closed shop (even the Union mines operated on an open-shop basis), and refused.

## Conference Breaks Up

The miners then said they would not demand the check-off if they could have the Cleveland advance. There was no agreement on this and the conference broke up April 20, 1912.

The miners and operators met again on May 1, and the Kanawha River operators agreed to give an increase on both tonnage and day labor, but a little less than the basic increase granted at Cleveland. But Quinn Morton, chairman of the operators' scale committee, would make no such agreement for his Paint Creek mines. He discovered that there was no point in his arguing at all because he had made a contract in 1909 for five years and he was going to stick to that contract.

It may be that Morton's individual obstinacy was genuine. And it may be that his refusal was merely the signal for a concerted operator walkout. It is impossible, at this date, to know. In any case, Morton had some little notices printed and went home and stuck them up in various places.

These notices ran as follows:

"NOTICE

"To Our Employees: May 3, 1912

"Neither our surrounding conditions nor the market warrant an advance in wages.

"We offer to you work at the scale of wages in effect prior to March 31, 1912.

"Any of our employees who don't wish to accept this offer and resume work will please vacate our houses at once."

To see that his men obeyed, Morton brought in 10 Baldwin-Felts mine guards with high-powered rifles and borrowed a machine gun from the New River District. The miners left their houses without causing themselves to be shot, but only a few worked. So Morton proceeded to haul in scabs with the cooperation of the railroads.

And this was the beginning of the great Paint Creek strike of 1912-13. It is a well-documented strike, as these struggles go, and we owe its documentation primarily to Mother Jones, who smuggled a message to the United States Senate from her place of confinement at Pratt, West Virginia, asking for an investigation. Mother at the time was jailed by the military authorities in the home of B. S. Carney, a coal company official.

Over the ridge and parallel with Paint Creek is Cabin Creek. Here the miners had organized a Union in

1902, only to have it broken two years later. For eight years the miners on Cabin Creek had worked under armed guard, and no stranger was allowed up the narrow valley without being questioned by company-hired thugs. If he wasn't approved he was told to get out, and it was the part of wisdom to obey the edict. It is impossible to prove this point, but it is an actual fact no less that a number of bodies have been consumed in coke ovens in the State of West Virginia.

By 1912 the Cabin Creek miners were ready for a chance to throw off their oppressors. They quit their jobs in support of the Paint Creek strikers. And the strike continued to spread. Up and down the Kanawha Valley men put down their tools – "poured out their water." The spark on Paint Creek, thrown into an explosive situation, had produced a conflagration. The UMW was now battling for its life in West Virginia.

The demands of the striking miners were these:

1.  Abolition of the mine guard system.
2.  A reform in the system of docking. (A miner might be docked a thousand pounds of coal for loading a few pieces of slate.)
3.  The employment of checkweighmen on the tipples to represent the miners and to be paid by the miners. (The law provided for these checkweighmen, but this law was ignored by the coal companies.)
4.  Permission for the men to trade where they pleased, without discrimination for so doing. (A man might find himself fired for not trading

at the company store.)

5. The payment of wages in cash every two weeks and not in script or credit cards. (Also part of West Virginia law, but ignored by the operators.)

6. Improved sanitary conditions, with the requirement that the companies remove garbage and keep the houses in condition.

7. Payment for mining coal on the basis of the short ton on which the coal is sold, and not on the basis of the long ton, on which it was mined. (In other words, at that time the miners loaded 2,240 pounds of coal for a ton.)

8. Rentals of houses based on a fair return on their cost, with allowances for upkeep and electric lights on the same basis. (Rentals were checked out of a miner's pay before he got his money, as was his light bill. Both amounts were purely arbitrary sums.)

9. The nine hour day – they had been working ten.

10. Recognition of the UMW and the check off.

11. An increase in pay. (The least important of their demands. In unorganized fields pay was 25 to 35 cents a ton, in the Kanawha Union Field 49 cents. In the Central Competitive Field it was 90 cents!)

## A Mighty Battle

It was to be a mighty battle for the coal operators, who from a governmental point of view, WERE West Virginia. One U.S. Senator was Clarence W. Watson of

Fairmont, whom the miners accused of being "king" of the state. He was president of the Consolidated Coal Company in northern West Virginia, owning 100,000 acres of land and employing 15,000 nonunion men.

Prime minister to the "king" was the other United States Senator, William E. Chilton. Chilton was owner and manager of the *Charleston Gazette* and a law partner of William McCorkle. McCorkle was a Democratic leader in the State Senate and their law firm represented, by some estimates, four-fifths of corporate interests in West Virginia. The UMW could be sure of being fought by the press – with the exception of the two labor papers in the Kanawha Valley – and, more important, by every official governmental agency in the state.

11/26/52 (Seventh)

If the operators had not expected the strike it was amazing how fast they got into action with the traditional strike-breaking methods. By 1912 a remarkable sort of human being had been created by the demands of employers for methods to "handle" their rebellious workers. This was the so-called labor agent. It was his job to give advice to well-paying companies as to the best methods of breaking strikes, and furnishing scabs to take the jobs of striking workers secured his main income.

One such man was George Williams of the "Industrial Corporation" of New York. He was hired to bring in men by the Cabin Creek Coal Association, an operator group. The agreement was verbal and the association promised him $3,000 for supplying scabs for a year. When he got the word that he was hired he put the following ad in newspapers in New York, New Castle, PA., Chicago, Cleveland and other cities:

> "Miners and laborers for coal mine – black-smiths, track layers, drum runners, motor runners, motor helpers, trappers, greasers, slate men, tipple boys, mule drivers, tipple bosses, and men. Good steady job all the year around; family men of all nationalities preferred. Transportation furnished; long contract; also strong men used to pick work can make $6 per day. Strike on. Homes all furnished. All the coal you want, $1 per month. Here is your chance to make money and a good home. Apply early. Call Mr. Williams, 548 Broadway."

**Scabs Answer Call**

It will be noted that Mr. Williams does state that there is a strike on, but the information is buried in the body of the ad so that even a literate person might miss its significance. And many of the scabs were barely able to read English. It seems that there was a large response from men anxious to "make money and a good home." As the great-hearted Williams says: "In the wintertime I can get a half-million men for any kind of work – strikes or any kind – because outside work is closed and people are starving in the big towns."

Vultures of this type were employed by M. T. Davis of the Cabin Creek Coal Association. A. W. Laing and his brother John, principal operators on Cabin Creek, must have been very proud of their cohort.

It seems, however, that they were hardly less heartless. While throwing miners out of their miserable little shacks, A. W. Laing lived in a 20-room brick mansion at 1416 Kanawha Blvd. in Charleston. John Laing was not only a Cabin Creek coal operator but head of the West Virginia Department of Mines at the time this strike started.

He had been appointed on Dec. 22, 1908, despite the fact that a District 17 convention at Montgomery on August 8, 1899 introduced a resolution condemning the "brutal assault and abuse by Superintendent John Laing and his confederates that inflicted bodily injury on organizer George Scott."

## Laing Is Example

John Laing is a good example of how men change. Before the turn of the century he was a UMW vice-president, but shortly thereafter quit the Union and beat up organizer Scott, then, in 1913, hired Baldwin-Felts gunmen to terrorize his former brother-miners. When asked his opinion of miners by the investigating committee he stated that they were "illiterate, a lower element of labor," and as to labor leaders: "They are absolutely beneath recognition in my judgment." Laing himself had been both.

Other examples of turncoats in the miners' movement were unearthed by this Senatorial committee of 1913. This is interesting only as an object lesson: What a man is today is not necessarily what he will be tomorrow. This, unfortunately, makes life complicated. But it is true. There was John Nugent, for instance.

When the United Mine Workers of America was formed in 1890 at Columbus, Ohio, John Nugent was there. He had been a leader in the old Knights of Labor. Chris Evans, UMW historian, gives the following quote from a contemporary newspaper by an eyewitness of the formation of the UMW: "John Nugent and Alexander Johnson who led the rival organizations (the K. of L. and the National Progressive Union of Miners and Mine Laborers) in the Hocking Valley, shook hands and swore allegiance to the miners' Union, and to show his sincerity, Mr. Johnson kissed Mr. Nugent in the mouth."

## Nugent Changes Sides

This seems to be a reverse on the old Judas story, for in 1907 Nugent went to work for the West Virginia coal operators, after having for a time been president of District 17. His post in 1907 was an odd one, and at first glance he did not seem to be employed by the coal owners, for he was appointed by the governor and had the title of State Commissioner of Immigration.

But the post carried no salary. He was paid by the coal companies to bring in labor, was even sent to England and Wales for that purpose. In other words John Nugent became a labor agent, different in degree only from George Williams, the New York scab specialist.

Another was T. L. Lewis, associated with the UMW for many years, once its national president (1908-1910), who was a commissioner for the Ohio Operators at the time of the senatorial investigation, and an apologist for their tactics. Still another was D. C. Kennedy, president of District 17 from about 1902 to

1904, who quit in the latter year to become a commissioner for the Kanawha Coal Operator's Association. Yet another was Phil R. Penna, UMW national president from 1895 to 1896, commissioner for the Indiana Coal Operators' Association as late as 1939. These are major examples of an easily perceived trend: The coal operators always tried to purchase the most intelligent and aggressive of the miners in order to cripple the Union movement.

Sadly enough, they sometimes succeeded. If the giant beneath the hills of West Virginia had been a beautiful wanton, she could have led no more men astray.

By mid-summer of 1912, the friction between the striking coal miners and the coal operators had developed a great deal of heat. The operators of both Paint and Cabin Creeks had, since 1902, imported Baldwin-Felts "detectives" to guard the scabs brought in by men like George Williams. On Paint Creek, the Baldwin men had established a sort of nonunion headquarters at Mucklow, a camp armed to the teeth with rifles, pistols, and machine guns. Near the mouth of the creek was Holly Grove, the miners' encampment. Men, women and children lived there in tents, having been evicted from their homes to make room for strikebreakers.

Duels between Holly Grove and Mucklow continued throughout the approximate 12 months of the strike. (The strike actually lasted some months beyond its official settlement, however, the miners struck intermittently because of dissatisfaction with the terms of the new agreement.) The miners hated the armed guards and the "loyal" employees at Mucklow, and fervently wished them in Hell. The strikers had been treated with brutality and they were facing guns. So they got their own guns. O.J. Morrison, among other Charleston merchants, took advantage of the sudden demand by displaying old Springfield rifles in his store window at the bargain price of $1.98.

Morrison stated that he sold some guns to jobber H. Galperin, then seemingly a pawnbroker, which he bought from Cal Hirsch & Sons of St. Louis, Mo. From March to August of 1912 Morrison sold 1,000 rifles and 14,500 rounds of ammunition. The Charleston merchants, like the Charleston newspapers, were for "law and order," but they did not mind making a little money while the making was good. The miners bought hundreds of rifles, perhaps thousands. They refused to be cowed by privately hired gunmen.

**People for Miners**

In Charleston, grand juries convened, but the people were on the side of the miners. On June 5, 1912 there was a battle near Mucklow in which the guards killed an Italian and wounded a Negro miner. To add insult to homicide the Baldwin men had a number of miners arrested and asked the grand jury to indict. But the grand jury refused and instead indicted the Baldwin men for the murder of the Italian! The case was not pushed by the prosecuting attorney, however, as it is a fact confirmed by a statement of Governor William E. Glasscock that not a single mine guard served a day in jail for any activity during the strike!

On July 26, 1912 there was another big Muck-low-Holly Grove battle and Governor Glasscock called in the National Guard. At one time he had the entire National Guard on Paint and Cabin Creeks. Then he asked both the miners and the operators to submit the names of two men to investigate the situation, saying that he would appoint a fifth. Glasscock later testified that operators refused, saying it would "cause trouble." The Governor then appointed his own commission – which, except for finding fault with the inexcusable mine-guard system, did a beautiful whitewash job for the operators and blamed the striking miners for everything.

11/28/52 (Eighth)

About the middle of August, Glasscock issued a call for a "peace conference," asking people to gather in the House of Delegates chamber to work out a way to arbitrate the strike. A conference of about 500 or 600 hundred people met, but broke up when an operators' attorney named Taylor Vinson said that his employers would be glad to cooperate provided there was no mention of recognition of the United Mine Workers of America! This meant, of course, that they would not cooperate at all.

Meanwhile the miners were still living in tents and the scabs were pouring in over the railroads, at least 1,200 to one coal company on Paint Creek. By mid-August the 5,000 striking miners on Paint and Cabin Creeks also had as company several hundred assorted railway policemen, Baldwin guards and special constables, plus 1,300 militiamen. The narrow valleys must have been overflowing with men, and two-legged animals resembling same.

Being a "transportation" man scab was no easy life. They were hated by the miners and despised by their employers; they were simply unemployed workers who had no idea where they were going when they got on the train. It is significant that the ordinary men got white cards, but there were others who were issued blue cards. These were the professional toughs, killers and gunmen. They kept the others in line, and were paid a small sum for so doing.

## Scabs Under Guard

Once you got on a scab labor train to West Virginia you didn't change your mind and get off. There were generally two guards with pistols and blackjacks at each end of the coaches, and the doors were locked. The labor agent wanted to be sure that the Cabin Creek and Paint Creek coal operators got their man. Some of these men later told pitiful tales. Others joined the Union after they arrived. One boy of 22 named Philip Cajano stated that he did so one night on Cabin Creek and the next morning was fired from his job. Later that day he was beaten by three guards while M. T. Davis, superintendent of the Cabin Creek Consolidated Coal Company, looked on approvingly. The illiterate Cajano weighed only 125 pounds and could hardly see through the heavy compound lenses of his spectacles.

It is touching just how fond the coal companies were of their "transportation." They liked them so well that they kept them under armed guard to see that they didn't leave. But a carpenter named George Lawson and some other scabs decided they couldn't stand their life and tried to escape from a house on Cabin Creek. Lawson tried to crawl through a window and a guard knocked out two of his teeth. But he ran a goodly distance before they caught and beat him again. By this time the other "transportation" was running away and the guards had to leave to catch them. So Lawson took to his heels and walked about 15 miles to Montgomery where he caught a train to New York.

William Rayner a 19-year-old orphan boy from New York, had been a cook, but on his arrival far up Cabin Creek at Decota he was told that he was going to shovel coal at $2 a day. If he stayed 60 days the company in its goodness would not charge him his fare from New York. But they wouldn't pay him until the end of the month. He stayed in a two-room house with seven other men, all of whom slept on a bare mattress with a comforter for warmth. After five days he was paid one dollar in company script.

## Scabs Flee West Virginia

He had been told by the company that the Union miners would shoot him if he tried to leave, and he stood it for 16 days before quitting. It was December, but he escaped one midnight and spent the night in the woods. Then he walked to Charleston, over 30 miles distant, wearing out his shoes and stockings on the way, and reported to the office of District 17 of the UMW. Mother Jones listened to his story and gave him 50 cents and the Union fed him and gave him a place to sleep. Then he walked 23 miles to Handley and hopped freight to New York.

James Kane was a machinist but was told to mine coal when he arrived on Cabin Creek at Kayford. He refused and was kept prisoner in a house for four days by rifle-carrying guards. One day guards went to lunch and he and two other men slipped out of the house and kept to the hills until they came to Eskdale, where the Union miners saw that they were allowed to get the rest of the way out of the creek.

On August 28, 1912 Governor Glasscock appointed his commission to look into the strike. It was composed of three men: the Right Rev. P.J. Donahue of Wheeling: Captain S.L. Walker of Fayetteville, and the Hon. Fred O. Blue of Charleston. These gentlemen sallied forth into the coal fields and returned with some marvelous discoveries. They found that the nonunion miner had no reason to want a Union because he was making just as much money as his fellow miners in the organized West Virginia fields. The average annual wage frequently soared to six or seven hundred dollars!

## The Commission Reports

The sole reason they didn't earn more was because they were lazy. The distinguished commission reported: "A minute examination of the payrolls disclose... that 16 or 17 (work) days in the month constitute a high average, and that many engaged in the mines decline to labor more than 12 or 14 days. This is particularly true of the native-born miners and many colored men..."

Living conditions were idyllic: Operator Charles A. Cabell of Decota on Cabin Creek "provided for his men a swimming pool fed by mountain springs with water crystal clear: a library and reading room, a bowling alley and even a miniature theatre." The democratic thinking of the operators was shown by the alleged fact that "Mr. Cabell joined in the games when the day's work was done." The certain fact that several thousand of these pampered miners were on strike was clearly a case of mass insanity.

The inevitable conclusion of the commission was as follows: "We find that the operators in this state are within their rights in declining to recognize a Union which would place them in a helpless minority when joined to those of the four competitive states; and by the operation of the freight differential of 19 cents per ton to the lakes and other points would, all other conditions being equal, render them absolutely unable to find a profitable market for the 90 per cent of the total output."

In other words, if West Virginia coal operators were forced to recognize the UMW they would go out of business. As at this date almost every coal miner in the state does belong to the Union, and as West Virginia under such conditions has retained its place as a world leader in soft-coal production. It would seem that the commission was either a victim of error or coal operator pressure.

11/29/52 (Ninth)

The later testimony of Bishop Donahue is interesting. He commends the "personal bravery and even recklessness" of the Baldwin-Felts guards, but admits, "They were not the grade of men who should be representing the rights of property and justice." By this last statement the Bishop implies that he sees justice to be with the coal operators, but that they should hire a different class of men to uphold it.

Bishop Donahue quotes the beatitudes freely, pointing out that "our Lord does not say 'Blessed are the poor.' He says 'Blessed are the poor in Spirit.'" He reminds the Senatorial body before which he is testifying that his commission found "that if a man in W. Va. chose to work with ordinary industry he could make his $3 or $4 a day without any trouble."

Senator Martine then asks: "Do you mean that net…?"

And Bishop Donahue replies: "Why no, Senator.... The net would be nothing in most cases, or the net would be about $25 a month debt."

It can be seen that if Martine had not had the keenness to ask this question the Bishop might have left a false impression. It may not be polite to accuse the distinguished Bishop and his commission of deliberately misrepresenting the truth in their report, but Martine's question seems to have convicted the Bishop with his own tongue.

## Bishop Is Frank

The good churchman is frank in his bias. The idea of Unions of workingmen is appalling to him and he says so thusly: "It is the function of the Church to get some of these horrible ideas worked out of them (the miners) like whiskey and beer are worked out of a man at Carlsbad. They have the most horrible leaders in the State, and other States in the Union, and I think this strike, unless some radical remedy is applied, only represents the first indications of the awful storm that is coming in this country." The envisioned storm, it will be noted, has not yet arrived.

To cure the West Virginia miners of striking the Bishop said that "first of all I would make them all go to Church twice on Sunday." Then he would make them hang up the eight beatitudes in their houses, with emphasis on "Blessed are the poor in spirit for theirs is the kingdom" and "Blessed are the meek." "And what would be the consequence of following such a program?" asks Senator Borah. "If," says Borah, "these men were not struggling and contentious and aspiring, the reverse of it would be, finally, industrial slavery, would it not?"

"Yes", answers Bishop Donahue. "It would."

Let it be noted before going further that the writer of this little history is in no sense any sort of religious bigot, and is not attacking the Bishop because he is a Catholic, any more than he would attack anyone else because he is Protestant, Jew or Shintoist. But an individual member of any religion, or none, is fit subject for attack if he proves himself the enemy of workingmen fighting to improve their living standards. That is the writer's touchstone and high position in religion or lay hierarchy has no bearing on the matter.

## Commission Overlooks Facts

This commission, while engaged in lyric praise of the W. Va. coal miner in 1912, overlooked a few figures which are interesting. The table below shows a comparison for a four-year period of the number of employees per thousand killed in coal mines in four states. During these years the states of Illinois, Ohio and Pennsylvania were, by and large, unionized. West Virginia was overwhelmingly nonunion. Note the West Virginia figures:

|              | 1909 | 1908 | 1910 | 1911 | 1912 |
|--------------|------|------|------|------|------|
| **Illinois**     | 2.53 | 6.60 | 1.97 | 2.27 | 2.04 |
| **Ohio**         | 2.43 | 2.94 | 3.45 | 2.40 | 2.92 |
| **Pennsylvania** | 3.45 | 3.13 | 3.07 | 3.09 | 2.65 |
| **W. Va.**       | 5.43 | 6.06 | 4.79 | 5.21 | 5.26 |

For a ten-year period ending in 1912 West Virginia had a coal miner death rate per thousand of 5.71, Illinois 3.04, Ohio 2.89, and Pennsylvania 3.39. It was almost twice as likely that you would have been killed in those ten years if you had worked in a W. Va. mine instead of a mine in another state. Percentage-wise, in that 10-year period the West Virginia mining death rate exceeded Pennsylvania by 68.4%, Illinois by 87.8% and Ohio by 97.6%. By these figures Unionization is proved to be, quite literally, life insurance for the coal miner. Governor Glasscock's commission did not mention this.

## Baldwin Brutality Cited

Nor did the Bishop attempt to recite to the Senatorial body the numerous instances of the brutality of the "brave" Baldwin-Felts guards which were recorded by his own commission. They are many, but just one will give the reader an idea: This is the testimony of Gianiana Seville, the wife of a Union miner, as it was taken by the Glasscock commission:

"Q. Have you had any experience with the guards on Paint Creek?

"A. I know that there were guards up there and they beat me up.

"Q. Explain to the Commission the circumstances attending this beating?

"A. My husband was going down to the store and then he got arrested by the guards and the guards were going to take him away. I went close to tell the guards to let my husband alone; that I thought he had an excuse. My husband had never hurt anyone or done anything. When I went close and told them, they beat me up and threw me down on the track. They tore my shirtwaist from my arm.

"Q. What else occurred?

"A. About the 5th of June, I was washing in the house early in the morning and the guards came to the house and broke in the house and they punched me in the face and then went and threw the things upside down in the house searching for firearms. They were all mad. On the bed there was a little baby and they kicked me in the stomach and they called me bad names and used profane language.

"Q. What other assaults were made on you or what other blows were struck, if any?

"A. When they kicked me, I fell down on the floor and they picked me up and said: 'give me the keys to the trunk."

"Q. Did they strike you only once?

"A. I was pretty near fainted and I do not know. They were dragging me around.

## Woman Was Pregnant

"Q. What was your condition at that time?

"A. I was pregnant six months.

"Q. What effect did those blows have upon your condition; what was the result?

"A. The effect was that since that time I felt sick all the time until my baby was born dead. I never heard my baby since the blow was struck.

"Q. How long was it after the assault before the child was born?

"A. I was struck on the 5th day of June (1912) and the baby was born dead in the hospital on the 19th day of August. The doctor told my husband that the baby was dead nine weeks before it was born.

"Q. What was the name of the doctor?

"A. It was two doctors. One is G.S. Schafer at Cannelton and the other at the Paint Creek Hospital, but I don't know his name.

"Q. Was it Dr. Hunter?

"A. I do not know.

"Q. Was the birth a natural one?

"A. No. I felt awful sick and they called the doctor and the doctors gave me some medicine, morphine of something and they carried me to the hospital on a cot."

Is it any wonder that the coal miner hated the guards and that some of them were found shot through the head in circumstances that did not look like suicide?

12/2/1952 (Tenth)

The Baldwin-Felts men were also spies and snoopers, who for years had built up files of the names of Union men which went to all operators. If you opened your mouth to talk Union in West Virginia you were not only fired but you couldn't get a job in the mines anywhere in the state. Below is a copy of one of the shorter letters blacklisting only one man, evidently considered a dangerous character:

"General Manager, Or Superintendent.

"Dear Sir:

"James L. Taylor, white, age about 29, height 5 ft. 10 in., weight about 170 lbs., smooth shaven, sandy hair, blue eyes, was dismissed by the Mill Creek Coal & Coke Company a few days ago account of shooting coal on the solid and being a strong Union man.

"This is the same party who was dismissed from the Empire Coal & Coke Company in June, 1906, on account of being a Union man and writing articles to the *United Mine Workers Journal*, at which time all operators were notified.

"Yours truly,
"/s/
"Sept. 20, 1909."

While this humanitarian commission with the Bishop at its head was in the coal fields, Governor Glasscock had decided that not even the army of private thugs and state militia could cope with the situation. Iron law and iron enforcement were needed to keep the coal miner from winning his strike. As has been stated, the civilian population in general was favorable toward the strikers. Capt. S. B. Avis of the National Guard, later a coal operators' attorney, was then prosecuting attorney of Kanawha County and was complaining that he couldn't get a grand jury to indict or a petit jury to convict the miners.

The obvious answer was martial law, although this had never before been used in West Virginia. So martial law was proclaimed for the Paint Creek-Cabin Creek area on Sept. 2, 1912.

## Miners Dislike Militia

Glasscock maintained that Tom Cairnes, the president of District 17 of the UMW, was agreeable to the imposition of martial law when told that it was the only way to get rid of the mine guards. There is no way to check this, but the attitude of the coal miner in general toward the militia, with or without martial law, is pretty plain. As a Captain Levy of C Company, Second Infantry, National Guard, said under questioning:

"I think they thought us just about as bad as Baldwin guards."

The miners had every reason to think so. The Baldwin men did leave when martial law was declared. But there were three periods of martial law, and just as soon as a period was declared ended the militia would change their uniforms and hire themselves to the company as private guards. Frequently they didn't even change uniforms. This procedure was advised by state officials, and was approved by the Governor.

Confronted with the above charges, Adjutant General Charles Douglas Elliott said plaintively: "An officer buys and pays for his own uniforms, yet we are not supposed to wear them in our other avocations!" With this setup, no Baldwin men were needed, and it was probably less expensive for the coal operator to break the strike in this manner.

Captain Levy testified that when the first martial law was lifted he was "practically ordered" by Adjutant General Elliott to take a job as a "watchman" for a coal company on Paint Creek. He worked under a Captain Lester of the National Guard, and they chose the other militiamen who were to remain as privately-hired guards. Then when martial law was declared again on Nov. 15, 1912, Captain Levy changed his shirt and pay-roll connection (the latter was a very slight change), and was back with the "yellowlegs!"

## Militia Were Strikebreakers

It was an efficient system but not one that endeared the militia to the miners. It was quite clear that the National Guard was being used as a strike-breaking agency. A mine guard under any other name smelled just as much like gunpowder.

On the same day that Governor Glasscock proclaimed martial law he set up a military commission to serve in lieu of the civil courts. George S. Wallace, a Huntington lawyer and lieutenant colonel in the National Guard, was made the judge advocate of the military tribunal. That is, he acted in the capacity of a prosecuting attorney. A newspaper report quotes the Governor as saying of his commission: "For this duty I have selected men in whom I have the highest confidence, because their power is almost limitless, and they may impose such punishment, including death, as they deem proper in the situation." Yes, indeed, the Governor said "including death!"

Whatever the military tribunal "deemed proper" was not disclosed to the public. The trials were held in secret. But some of it came out later. A miner named Frank Nantz swore at Capt. A.C. Wood, who attempted to arrest two miners who had a fist fight. This was eight days before the second martial law was declared, so the Guardsman was a privately-hired coal company policeman at the time. Nantz swore and told the officer that he had no right to arrest anybody. Then when martial law went into effect a few days later Nantz was arrested and sentenced to five years in the penitentiary on the technical charge of interfering with an officer. He was tried by a military court and sentenced to the penitentiary for a "crime" committed before martial law was in effect!

## Courts Call It Legal

The Nantz case was appealed to the State Supreme Court by Attorney Harold W. Houston in an attempt to invalidate the whole proceeding. But Governor Glasscock was upheld by a decision of four to one. Judge Ira E. Robinson had the courage to dissent in both this and a similar case involving Mother Jones:

> "That the Governor has constitutional and statutory power to so use the militia and thereby arrest persons so far as reasonably necessary, no one will deny. But because the Governor has this power, must judicial construction run random and thrust upon the citizens of this state military courts for the trial of civil offenses, in the very face of the direct inhibitions against such procedure contained in our constitution, and regardless of constitutional guarantees?"

Judicial construction, despite Judge Robinson, did just that. Nantz was killed in late 1914 by a man named Matt Jarrell whom he was trying to arrest while serving as a Socialist Marshal at Eskdale. He had filed suit on Sept. 16, 1913, against Governor Glasscock for $50,000 because of his arrest and sentence, but it was still pending at his death.

Lawrence Cepreant, an Italian miner who scarcely understood English, was found guilty of perjury and sentenced to the penitentiary for seven and one half years. The severe sentences were usual and miners were tried in groups of 80 or more, being confined without bond while awaiting trial in an impromptu "bullpen" at Pratt, near the mouth of Paint Creek. Until the defendant was taken to jail, he didn't even know the decision of the so-called court. Parenthetically, this writer would like to note that his own grandmother, a miner's wife, was hauled before this tribunal.

**Martine is Correct**

Senator Martine put the matter correctly when he asked in amazement. "You did not apprise him – you gave him no opportunity or knowledge to know whether you had convicted him of a felony, and the first the poor devil knew was when he was gobbled up and went to the penitentiary?" Major James I. Pratt of the Second Infantry, an employee of the adjutant general's office, had to admit that this was true.

The military court was ruthless and highhanded. Union organizers – including the octogenarian Mother Jones – and an undetermined number of striking coal miners fell victim of the Glasscock dictatorship and were arrested and summarily thrown into jail. The right to bond, to habeas corpus, was suspended, the state and federal constitutions ignored and flouted. And the State Supreme Court gravely pronounced the whole procedure legal!

It is an inescapable conclusion that the coal operators owned the state machinery of West Virginia, – executive, legislative and judicial – almost in total, and that this machinery was being used in its full power to break the strike of the miners. The West Virginia coal miner, despite his proud state motto, was just about as free as a serf in Czarist Russia. He knew it, too – recorded speeches are full of comparison – and he was determined that there was going to be a change.

So he was beaten up and saw his family hungry and went to the penitentiary, but the strike continued. So, too, did the drumhead court, grim terror weapon of coal operator oppression.

12/3/52 (Eleventh)

In connection with this military court there was set up a system of "conditional pardons." Here is the way it worked: A man was put in the penitentiary for a trivial offense, as has been described before, the military tribunal's decision being secret, known only to the Governor and subject to his approval. Somewhat later Governor Glasscock would grant the miner a pardon, providing he would sign his name to a contract stipulating that he would, in effect, no longer associate with the strikers or help their cause.

If the miner signed the pardon and was released he could not again participate in Union activity. If he did so, the pardon was automatically revoked and back to the penitentiary he went. This was indeed a new twist on the "yellow-dog" contract!

Here is the "yellow-dog" clause in one of the pardons signed by Glasscock. (The prison term here was mild – only six months in the Mason County jail – as the victim was tried during the first period of martial law. The second military tribunal, as Glasscock himself said, used lengthy penitentiary terms as more effective "correction.")

> "This jail sentence is remitted, however, upon these terms and conditions only, to be assented to hereon in writing by the said Archie Tyler: That if the said Archie Tyler shall by threat, force, menace, or otherwise intimidate, or attempt so intimidate, any miner or other person who desires to work or who is seeking employment, or if he shall combine or conspire, together with any other person or persons for said purpose, or for any unlawful purpose, or if he shall violate any of the laws of this state, or fail, or refuse to conduct himself as a peaceable and law abiding citizen, or for any cause satisfactory to the governor, the governor may cause him to be arrested and returned to the jail of said county to serve out the remainder of the sentence imposed upon him aforesaid."

The victim signed this contract, and if ever a man was tied hand and foot that man was Archie Tyler!

## Hatfield Grants Pardon

When Governor Henry D. Hatfield succeeded Glasscock, he pardoned some of the men sent to prison by the military tribunals. We quote one of these pardons in full in order that the facts may be made clear about the "pardon" system.

"To All to whom these presents shall come, greeting:

"WHEREAS, in November, 1912, Dan Chain, alias Few Clothes, was arraigned before a military commission convened at Pratt, Kanawha County, West Virginia, charged with obstructing a railroad company in the use of its property in violation of section 31, Chapter 145, Code of West Virginia, 1906; was tried upon charge before the said military commission and found guilty, where upon the said military commission sentenced him to confinement in the penitentiary for the period of five years, and

"WHEREAS, on the 3$^{rd}$ day of January, 1913, William E. Glasscock, governor of the State of West Virginia, granted and issued to the said Dan Chain, alias Few Clothes, a conditional pardon, the terms and conditions of which were assented to in writing by the said Dan Chain, releasing him from further confinement in the penitentiary by reason of said sentence imposed by said military commission, and

"WHEREAS the said Dan Chain, alias Few Clothes, having violated the term and conditions of said pardon, William E. Glasscock, governor, on the 19$^{th}$ day of January, 1913, issued a warrant addressed to Bonner H. Hill, sheriff of said Kanawha County, revoking the said conditional pardon and directing said sheriff to re-arrest the said Dan Chain, alias Few Clothes, and return him to the penitentiary to serve out the remainder of the sentence imposed upon him as aforesaid, and "WHEREAS, I am of the opinion that the said Dan Chain, alias Few Clothes, should again be granted a conditional pardon:

"Now, therefore, be it known that I, Henry D. Hatfield, governor of the State of West Virginia, in consideration of the premises, divers other good and sufficient reasons me thereunto moving, do hereby grant unto the said Dan Chain, alias Few Clothes, a conditional pardon, releasing him from further confinement in the penitentiary by reason of said sentence, and I hereby order and direct the warden of the penitentiary to immediately, upon receipt of this proclamation, release the said Dan Chain, alias Few Clothes, from further confinement therein.

## The Conditional Clause

"This pardon is granted, however, upon these terms and considerations only, to be assented to hereon in writing by the said Dan Chain, alias Few Clothes: That if the said Dan Chain, alias Few Clothes, shall violate any of the laws of this state, or fail or refuse to conduct himself as a peaceable and law abiding citizen, or for any other reason satisfactory to the governor, the governor may cause him to be arrested and returned to the penitentiary to serve out the remainder of the sentence imposed upon him as aforesaid.

"The governor reserves to himself and successors in office the right to determine when and whether the terms and conditions of this pardon have been violated."

"In testimony whereof I have hereunto signed my name and caused the seal of the State to be affixed.

"Done at the Capitol in the City of Charleston, this 17th day of May, in the year of our Lord one thousand nine hundred and thirteen, and of the State the fiftieth.

"By the governor

HENRY D. HATFIELD."

Let it be respectfully noted in passing that Dan Chain, alias "Few Clothes," was a tall, rangy Negro, one of the fighten'st Union men on Cabin and Pain creeks.

## Guilty Before Trial

Sometimes, in their zeal to rid West Virginia of the abhorrent UMW, the uniformed flunkies of the coal operators tripped over their own feet. One case is recorded in which Major James I. Pratt, a member of the National Guard, also a member of the military court, and, incidentally, an employee in the office of the adjutant general of the State of West Virginia disqualified himself by trying too hard.

Two Union organizers and the editor of a Charleston labor newspaper had been arrested by the military. They fought for a writ of habeas corpus. It was denied and the matter was finally carried to the West Virginia Supreme Court of Appeals. Major Pratt, of course, did not want to release such valuable guests from his bullpen and he made a return to the writ as follows:

> "Respondents deny that the petitioner is wholly innocent of the charges against him, but on the contrary are informed and believe, and so aver, that the petitioner is guilty thereof."

Pratt signed his name to this, which meant that he was judging these people guilty before he tried them. If the habeas corpus was refused, the defendants had the melancholy knowledge that they would be tried by a judge who had declared their guilt before the evidence was in! By so signing his name, Pratt disqualified himself in the case.

This incident merely points up the fact that the "trials" before the tribunal were quite unnecessary and in many cases did not even occur. When a miner was arrested by the military he knew that he was going to be found guilty on the testimony of a variety of loathsome stool-pigeons, or no testimony at all. And with no opportunity for defense, he simply wondered how long his sentence would be.

# Chapter Three: Bloody Bull Moose

12/4/52 (Twelfth)

The drumhead court at the mouth of Paint Creek was naturally much discussed, though only the Governor, who approved the sentences and the tribunal itself, knew its actual proceedings. There were in addition, two lawyers who had supposedly been designated to "defend" the accused, for the sake of form. The regular Union attorneys refused to recognize the tribunal as anything but an unconstitutional device for the railroading of Union men, and would not join the farce. Finally public opinion forced the opening of the "court" to the public gaze. This was during the third period of martial law.

William Bruce Reid, a Charleston newspaper reporter, took advantage of the chance to see the military court in action. He saw 98 prisoners – including Mother Jones – tried in three days. And while trying to get a statement from Mother he was himself arrested! He was told to photograph nothing and to talk to no prisoners.

Shortly thereafter Governor Henry D. Hatfield came into office and was supposed to review the findings of the commission. Most of the charges against the miners were for "conspiracy," but it was never determined what the sentences of the third commission were. Hatfield did not make them public, but simply released the strikers in small groups – a tacit admission that the whole procedure had been extra-legal.

The days of martial law were not yet ended, but with the senatorial investigation the eyes of the nation were on West Virginia, and house had to be cleaned somewhat. Even the military flunkies were sick of it. Adjutant General Elliott at Governor Glasscock's farewell dinner on March 3, 1915, said "that if men, possessors of wealth and education and opportunities, would always have the same consideration for human beings as they did for bank mules we would have less trouble."

## Governor Quotes Record

But the record is not complete without quoting from Governor Glasscock's official version of the matter. In his biennial message to the Legislature of 1913, he had this to say:

> "This military commission had much work to do and performed their duties fearlessly and impartially. During their term of service they tried and sent to the penitentiary and to jail something like one hundred persons for violation of law.... No such complaint was made after the military commission was organized.... It had been the great complaint of the people who had resided on these creeks that had had no law.... During the first reign of martial law the most of the violators were sent to jails and as was demonstrated by future events that did not seem sufficient punishment to cause these people to respect the law and I determined to use still more drastic methods than were used during the first martial law period.... Quite a number of people were tried by

the last commission, the majority of who were found guilty and sentenced to the penitentiary."

The Governor does not say how many coal operators were sent to the penitentiary. None, of course, were even arrested. It does seem very odd that when you buy a coal mine you automatically buy virtue and that when you work in a coal mine you automatically acquire a criminal bent and may confidently look forward to a trip to the penitentiary.

## No Legal Equality

It may just possibly be that there was no equality before the law. That is, if you were a miner, and carried a gun or pulled a trigger your chances of becoming a convict were excellent. But if you represented the coal operators – as did DE FACTO if not DE JURE, the Baldwin-Felts guards, the railway detectives, the variety of special police officers and the state militia – and carried a gun or pulled a trigger, your chance of getting a good salary, a promotion, and praise from the Governor, were excellent. Both sides in the struggle, certainly, used guns. But for one side there were penalties. For the other, none.

Opinions at the time concerning Governor Glasscock varied, of course, depending upon the attitude of the opinion-bearing toward the coal miners. Certainly the miners agreed wholeheartedly with U.S. Senator Stuart Felix Reed of West Virginia, who said in reply to West Virginia Senator Nathan Goff's remark that West Virginians tended to place their governor upon a pedestal: "Instead of stand upon a pedestal, he stands in the pillory. In my opinion he will stand there as long as men revere liberty in West Virginia."

The episode of the "Bull Moose" train is an excellent example of the terroristic methods of the operators – who were not only not punished but continued to live as solid "respectable" citizens. If, like Lady Macbeth, they later worried about the blood on their hands, and went around shouting "Out, out damned spot!" it is nowhere recorded.

The Bull Moose consisted of an engine fitted with sheet iron to protect the engineer, and an ordinary passenger car, an armored baggage car. It had been designed by the C&O Railway for the benefit of the coal operators. It was run into any spot in which there was trouble, but its main function was the transportation and protection of strikebreakers. There was a better-equipped armored train called the Woodrow Wilson, but the Bull Moose itself was formidable.

The baggage car had thick iron plates on the inside across the doors for the protection of the occupants and was equipped with two machine guns and about 15 rifles. On the night of Feb. 7, 1913, when the most famous, or infamous, of the Bull Moose battles took place, there were 30 additional rifles on the train. Coal Operator Quinn Morton had just purchased them in Charleston from Lowenstein's, a hardware store.

At this time there was some confusion as to martial law – very understandable confusion. The first martial law had been lifted Oct. 14, and the second period instituted Nov. 15, 1912. Governor Glasscock had never officially ended the second period of martial law, as he wanted the miners to think it was still in effect, but there had been a verbal understanding between the Governor and his officers, and there was actually no martial law anywhere in West Virginia in February, 1913.

## Sheriff Gets Word

About three or four o'clock in the afternoon of Feb. 7, Bonner Hill, sheriff of Kanawha County, got word from a company official at Mucklow that another battle was taking place between that town and the miners' tent colony of Holly Grove. Hill had no way to get up there that he cared to take, but when he phoned Glasscock about the matter he was ordered to go. He thought immediately of the Bull Moose, which happened to be sitting at Cabin Creek Junction. The train offered a safe method of travel, so he went to the Ruffner Hotel to ask Quinn Morton to get it for him. Morton, it will be remembered, was the Paint Creek operator whose adamant refusal to negotiate precipitated the 1912 strike in West Virginia.

Morton called the C&O and the C&O sent the Bull Moose down to Charleston to pick up Hill. The sheriff then had Morton make out a John Doe complaint, and a sheaf of John Doe warrants was typed up so that Hill was empowered to arrest anyone in sight. Then Morton went out and bought 30 Winchesters and the ammunition. The two machine guns and 15 rifles already on the Bull Moose were evidently considered insufficient.

12/5/1952 (Thirteenth)

Sheriff Hill did not go up Paint Creek alone. There were 15 or 16 men on the Bull Moose, all heavily armed. This included five or six special deputies. Quinn Morton, another coal operator named McClenahan, and George Lenz, who was a special policeman for the C&O Railway, trained in the use of the machine gun. The Bull Moose came to Holly Grove about 11 o'clock p.m. It was running slowly and it did not speed up as it shot its way through the town.

There are many conflicting stories as to who shot first – whether the miners fired on the train and the train merely replied, or vice-versa. But Harvey S. Campbell, a C&O special policeman who traveled with "transportation", testified as to the general company policy: "I was ordered to shoot if there was rocks or any crooked moves made." The C&O naturally left the definition of a "crooked move" up to "lexicographers" who were more at home with guns in their hands than dictionaries.

Whoever shot first, it is clear that the men in the Bull Moose sat in comparative safety and turned loose a machine gun and rifles upon women and children. And the train continued its slow pace, spraying lead as it went.

## Coal Miner Shot

Heavy armor protected the men in the train, and by a miracle there were few casualties in Holly Grove. In the wretched little shack of Francis Francesco the shooting was heard and he ran outside and was killed instantly. His wife, pregnant and with a child in her arms, ran into the kitchen with Francesco's cousin, who was shot in the leg. A neighbor, Annie Hall, the mother of five children, was shot through both feet as she lay in her bed. The Bull Moose, meanwhile, pulled into Mucklow, where plans were made for the arrest of the miners at Holly Grove! It was taken for granted that shot-up miners had no legal redress. They were fair game for coal operators, sheriffs, and C&O policemen.

This happened on a Friday, and on Monday the "arrest" actually turned out to be a pitched battle. Two of the operators' men, named Vance and Bobbitt, were killed. The miners hauled away their dead and injured, so their casualties were not determined. Four days later Governor Glasscock issued the third and last proclamation of martial law.

A few weeks later a new Governor, Henry D. Hatfield, took office. It might be noted that Glasscock was from Monongalia County, a coal mining area, and that he was a Republican. Hatfield was from McDowell County, another large coal producer, and was also a Republican. One might draw the conclusion that the election had changed matters little, for the coal operators, of course, were the ruling powers in both counties.

Nevertheless, the demands of the miners could not be ignored forever, and Hatfield released a number of the men imprisoned under the Glasscock regime. He did not, however, lift martial law until June, 1913. Three days after he took office, on March 7, 1913, the last drumhead court was held at Pratt, the defendants being Mother Jones, Socialist leader John W. Brown, and other plain miners.

Hatfield also made an agreement with the UMW national officials which became known as the "First Hatfield Agreement", in April of 1913. This settlement was evidently verbal at first, but its enemies said that it provided no increase in pay, no abolition of the mine-guard system, and no recognition of the UMW.

From extant historical records it would seem that the miners themselves didn't like the agreement, for they continued to strike, off and on, for some little time. They were not willing to surrender without concessions after more than a year of grueling hardship. Other "Hatfield Agreements" followed until finally both the Paint Creek and Cabin Creek miners went back to work in late July, 1913.

A letter from East Bank of August 6, 1913 had this to say: "The terms of the settlement, if carried out faithfully, will be a slight improvement on the old system, but the workmen have little faith in the sincerity of their greedy masters and that is what prevents the signing up at all the mines."

**What Was Won?**

In the belief that miners may be interested in just what was won after this major struggle, it will be noted that the UMW was recognized as bargaining agent and that the mine-guard system was ameliorated, if not abolished. As a matter of comparative and historical interest the pay scale which the miners finally had to settle for on Paint Creek is reproduced herewith: "Mining, 29 cents a ton; machine runners, $2.25 per day of 9 hours; machine runner helpers, $2.00 per day; motor men,

$2.25; motor men helpers, $2.00; track layers, $2.43; team drivers (two mules) $2.16, (one mule) $2.05; pump runners in mine, $2.10; all other inside labor, $2.00; drum runner's helper, $1.95; slate and timber men, $2.22; car repairmen, $2.50; blacksmiths, $2.50; tipple men, $2.05; helpers, $1.85; trappers, $1.00; driver boss, $2.50; oilers, $1.08; common labor, $1.75.

It was not, after such a battle, a large victory. And neither coal operator nor coal miner believed that their little war was over. On September 19, 1913, a group of operators met in Huntington and formed the "Coal Operator Protective Association" with a capital of one million dollars. The first plank in its platform was "to oppose the spread and growth of Socialism", just as the first plank of reactionary organizations of today is allegedly to oppose the spread and growth of Communism.

In actuality the Coal Operator Protective Association was formed to continue the battle against the Unionization of the coal miners. The miners, in their turn, rested from the fight and nursed their grievances.

In Europe a vast storm was about to break, a mighty conflict, which was to dim all lesser struggles: A world war was in the offing. And the miners had a contract that was supposed to last until April 1, 1916.

12/6/52 (Fourteenth)

The Senatorial commission to investigate West Virginia mining conditions sat in Charleston and Washington, D.C. and heard a great deal of evidence. They learned, for instance, that Pratt, the little town near the mouth of Paint Creek where the military trials were held, was named for the firm of Charles Pratt & Co., organized in 1901 with headquarters in New York City.

Charles Pratt testified that he owned about 21,000 acres of coal lands in West Virginia, which he had bought not for the development of coal, but "I should say, broadly, for speculation."

Part of this property was leased to the operators involved in the 1912-1913 strike: The Paint Creek Collieries Co., the Imperial Colliery Co., and the Standard Splint & Gas Co. Pratt, living in Brooklyn, received 8 cents a ton royalty for every chunk of coal dug on his property, an average of about $60,000 a year. With part of this money from West Virginia miners he built the Pratt Institute in Brooklyn, where 3,000 children were taught to earn their livings.

Senator Kenyon told Pratt that part of the trouble in West Virginia seemed to be that men of great wealth put in money, collected royalty, and considered their responsibilities ended. Pratt answered that he thought he was doing "a very kind and sensible thing" in leasing his property and added: "I do not suppose that the children of the class of people who are doing this hard work as miners are prepared for any such kind of work as we are doing in Brooklyn."

**Writer Is Irked**

In other words the children of West Virginia miners, according to Pratt, are too stupid to learn anything! Let it be noted that the writer of this series, the son of a coal miner, was born not many miles from Pratt only three years after Charles Pratt uttered these silly, defamatory words. And the writer resents the hell out of his statement! It is a terrible irony that coal miners of West Virginia broke their backs to educate children of other states, while their own offspring suffered from lack of schools. Even in 1952 West Virginia ranks not very high in the national scale as regards educational facilities.

The reason for this is obvious. West Virginia was and is a comparatively backward state for the simple reason that its tremendous wealth was stolen by outside interests. Pratt is only one example, and the ramifications of absentee ownership are far too complex to be analyzed in this short history. But it can be pointed out that Pennsylvania operators who were also owners of the Scranton Correspondence Schools owned the Paint Creek Collieries Co.. The Christian Collieries Co. and the Imperial Collieries Co. (also on Paint Creek) were the property of a Judge Christian of Lynchburg, Va., and other out-of-state wealth-reapers.

The only money that remained in the West Virginia vaults after the looting got well under way was the tiny sum paid the coal miners. More than that, only a fragment of this sum remained, for most of the miner's wages returned to the companies through the check-off for rent, groceries, electric lights, blacksmithing, tools and other items.

## West Virginia Robbed

The native West Virginia operator, of course, made such money as he could – and sometimes this was a fortune – but as it lined his own pockets it did not contribute to the general welfare of the state. The wealth of a Croesus was in the West Virginia hills, but it did not enrich West Virginia. Such a situation, to put it as mildly as possible, is criminal.

As has been stated before, on March 4, 1913, Governor Henry D. Hatfield, a Republican from McDowell County, took office. He had in his campaign promised the miners concessions and relief from the oppression of coal company guards. It is true that he did almost immediately conclude the first "Hatfield Agreement" with the UMW international officials – Thomas "Dean" Haggerty and others.

It is also true, as has been stated above, that the miners hardly welcomed the settlement with open arms. Many old miners whom this writer spoke with felt that Hatfield was really their friend. This writer most respectfully disagrees. That Hatfield was a friend of the coal operator is shown by his support in 1914 of coal operator Edward Cooper of McDowell County in the race for United States Congressman. The Huntington Trades & Labor Assembly had denounced Cooper as a founder of the before-mentioned "Coal Operators Protective Association."

And Cooper was also supported by Taylor Vinson, who, it will be remembered, was the coal operator attorney who broke up the "peace meeting" called by

Governor Cornwell in August, 1912, by declaring that the operators would never hear of recognizing the UMW. Another supporter of Cooper, it is fairly well confirmed, was Ernest Gaujot, the meanest, most murderous, most infamous of the Baldwin-Felts thugs in the 1912-1913 strike! Cooper won the election, but it must have been no day of rejoicing for the miners of the state.

## Hatfield Stops Press

Besides this defection Hatfield was guilty of two acts which were as dictatorial and hateful as any of Glasscock's. Martial law was continued after his inauguration, and was still in effect at the time of the first "Hatfield Agreement." At that time there were two labor papers in the Kanawha Valley. Both had Socialist editors, and both had supported the striking miners with great energy.

But they differed with Governor Hatfield and international UMW representative "Dean" Haggerty as to the excellence of the first "Hatfield Agreement." They said so in print and in no uncertain terms. One of the newspapers was the *Labor Argus*, published in Charleston and edited by Charles H. Boswell. Boswell, in the spring of 1913, had just completed four months in jail. He had been sentenced by the military regime along with Mother Jones and other UMW organizers, and his allegiance to the miners' welfare could not be doubted.

Shortly after Boswell denounced the first "Hatfield Agreement", he was visited at his printing plant by Adjutant General Charles Douglas Elliott and several National Guard members. His office was searched and a squad of soldiers later took 106 of his mailing galleys, not bringing them back until late June, when martial law was ended.

12/9/52 (Fifteenth)

The other labor paper was in Huntington, but it, like the *Labor Argus*, had a large following in the coal fields. It was called the *Socialist and Labor Star* and its editor, W. H. Thompson, also attacked the Hatfield settlement, as has been before explained. The Friday, May 30, 1913 issue of this paper sets forth the reasons why the "little truth teller" had not appeared for a few weeks.

It seems that on May 9, 1913, at one o'clock in the morning, Thompson was awakened to find his house surrounded by deputy sheriffs. He learned later that four other owners of the paper were also entrapped like desperate criminals. The deputies showed him a typewritten order from Governor Hatfield directing that he be arrested and placed in the Cabell County jail. He was then taken to his printing plant where he found a squad of militia under Major Tom Davis. All this happened in Huntington, more than 70 miles from the zone governed by martial law! As Thompson describes it:

> "Some of the type in the newspaper pages was beaten to a shapeless mass of mashed metal. After the types and plates had been beaten and broken the "forms" were hurled from the composing stone and their contents scattered over the office and street. Portions of the wrecked material were found the next morning two squares from the *Star* office."

## Editor Is Jailed

Account books, files and records were confiscated and other soldiers went back to Thompson's house and looked through desk drawers for more "incriminating" material. Thompson, meanwhile, had been thrown into jail at Huntington. He stayed there until that afternoon, presumably under civil authorities, and was then turned over to the military. The military, headed by Major Tom Davis, took him to Charleston to the Kanawha County jail, where he was confined for 13 days and nights, sleeping without mattress on the jail's steel floor. He was never charged with anything, never given a trial, and finally, released.

Governor Hatfield later denied some details of Thompson's statements, but even giving Hatfield's denials full credence the essence of the truth is as above. All credit to a brave labor editor! All shame to a newspaper-suppressing governor! Thompson, in addition to being editor of the *Socialist and Labor Star*, had been for six years a member of the UMW, was at the time of his arrest a member of the International Typographical Union, where he served as a member of his local's scale committee, was a delegate to the Huntington Trades & Labor Assembly, and had served two terms as president of Huntington ITU Local No. 533.

## Justice Is Denied

There is an interesting sequel to the Hatfield-Thompson feud. Thompson sued the Governor in the Circuit Court of Cabell County, alleging clear violation of his constitutional rights and demanding charges.

There were many delays, but at length the trial was set for Feb. 9, 1914. And on March 30, 1914, the West Virginia Supreme Court issued a writ of prohibition against the Cabell County Court, forbidding it to proceed with the case against Hatfield!

That this was a perversion of the law, with the connivance of the state's highest judicial body, seems obvious. The Supreme Court decision that Governor Hatfield had been right in suppressing the newspaper was not unanimous. One judge dissented, and his name should be revered by all who value freedom of expression. He was Judge Ira Robinson. Once before he had dissented in a civil rights case of major importance. This had been when the court majority had refused the habeas corpus petition of Mother Jones, John W. Brown, and others, imprisoned by the military court at Pratt.

Judge Ira Robinson had given as his opinion that they had a right to bond, despite the hysteria of the time. And he dissented in the Thompson-Hatfield incident with vigor:

"This decision (Judge Robinson wrote) permits a governor to deal with private rights and private property as he pleases. He has only to answer that he does so officially, and an action, though alleging facts showing that his act is wholly without his political province, will be prohibited. Such a view is wholly un-American and inconsistent with constitutional government. Reason and authority condemn it, and the administration of even-handed justice cries out against it."

## The 'Red Man' Act

Good for Judge Robinson! But the law under which Hatfield jailed Thompson is still on the statute books of West Virginia. And many a Union man has gone to jail because of it. This is the infamous "Red Man Act". This law was taken from the code of Virginia and incorporated in the West Virginia code by the Wheeling Convention which formed the new state in 1861. It is given in Sections 5, 6, and 7 of Chapter 14, Code of West Virginia:

"Sec. 5:    The Governor may cause to be apprehended and imprisoned or  may compel to depart from this state all suspicious subjects, citizens agents, or emissaries of any foreign state or power at war with the United States.

"Sec. 6:    He may also cause to be apprehended and imprisoned all who in time of war, insurrection, or public danger, shall willfully give aid, support, or information to the enemy or insurgents or who, he shall have cause to believe, are conspiring or combining together to aid or support any hostile action against the United States or this state.

"Sec. 7:    In order to obtain information in such cases the governor may send for the person and papers of anyone whom he shall believe to be subject to these last two sections."

The old Virginia lawmakers did not, of course, have labor Unions in mind when they drafted the above Act. But coal miners have learned that their enemies will use any legal stick to beat a miner's head. Certainly the Red Man Act has been so used. As the State Supreme Court has not ruled it unconstitutional, every Union member should see that it is wiped from the statute books.

12/10/52 (Sixteenth)

Laws are frequently perverted by reactionary employers from their original purpose. The Sherman Anti-Trust Act was passed in 1890 in response to the demand of the people for a limitation upon the great economic monopolies which had been born as capital had gathered control of whole industries into one gold-plated, steel-cored fist.

It may be stated flatly that the Sherman Act never accomplished its avowed purpose, as the monopoly of yesterday has swollen into the cartel of today – that is, corporations now act on an international scale, affecting the futures of millions in entire nations. Comparatively mild civil – not criminal – charges were brought in some cases against large corporations but the teeth of the law were most effectively plucked. Not only did these huge interests nullify this law, insofar as they were concerned, but they turned around this legal weapon and used it to shatter the organizations of the people, the labor Unions! You may be sure that the teeth of the law, by a financial magician's trick, were then reinstated!

An instance of this occurred after the West Virginia coal strike of 1912-1913. On June 7 of the latter year, 19 of the officials of District 17 and the international UMW were indicted for violation of the Sherman Act. The people who labor created a law for their own protection and it was turned upon them by their enemies! And this was neither the first nor the last time that it happened. In this case, litigation drug on for a couple of years, but all defendants were ultimately dismissed.

**Peace in West Virginia**

The furor in the West Virginia coal fields gradually simmered into an uneasy peace. The senatorial investigating committee in the autumn of 1913 concluded its labors, but came to few conclusions. Sen. William S. Kenyon did, however, recommend government ownership of the coal mines: "The basic cause (of the trouble) is the private ownership of great public necessities, such as coal..." thus agreeing with the Socialists, insofar as he went. Kenyon also censured the good Bishop Donahue for saying that the conflict in West Virginia was due to the greed of both coal operator and coal miner.

"It is a little difficult," Kenyon said, "to realize how there can be much human greed on the side of a man who is supporting a family and working day by day in the mines at ordinary living wages, but there is greed on the part of the owners of the property, and there always will be such greed."

But there was no remedial legislation on a national level. Sen. James E. Martine of New Jersey had furnished considerable color and excitement to the investigation in West Virginia, and he was sincere in trying to help the coal miner. In 1914 he made a speech before the U.S. Senate:

> "While I had the honor to serve as a member of a committee or commission, or whatever it might be termed, in West Virginia wherein these armed thugs played an important part. I felt so incensed and so rightly justified that upon my return I drew a bill which was introduced in the Senate and referred to the Committee on Education and Labor, wherein it was provided that every individual corporation or body of men employing armed guards for private purposes should be liable to a fine of at least $5,000 and imprisonment for one year. In the ordinary parliamentary way the bill was referred to the Committee on Education and Labor, and there it seems to sleep the sleep of the unfortunate and the just."

It must have been given a powerful dose of chloroform by the corporation lobbyists, for it still sleeps today.

### District 29 Formed

That the UMW in West Virginia had every intention of continuing its organizational fight is shown by the fact that in 1913 it formed District 29 to cover the New River field. The first president of this district was L.C. Rogers, and his headquarters were in Fayetteville.

Yet the Mountain State situation remained relatively quiet. Other trouble spots involving labor occupied the nation's attention.

On Christmas Eve, 1913, the wives and children of striking copper miners at Calumet, Mich., were having a Christmas party in a schoolhouse. Some 700 children were at the party when a member of an operator group which called itself the "Citizens' Alliance" yelled "Fire!" at the top of his lungs. In the ensuing scramble, 72 women and children were trampled to death. The miners later refused to accept money as recompense, and 150 of the "Citizens" beat up strike leader Charles H. Moyer, then president of the West Virginia Federation of Miners, shot him three times in the back and threw him on a train with a warning not to return to the state of Michigan. A local newspaper told of the incident, and was promptly suppressed.

And then the grim struggle of the coal miners in Colorado jumped into the headlines – West Virginia all over again. "Hell and repeat," that's what the miners called the West Virginia and Colorado strikes. And hell they were. The same Baldwin-Felts thugs who served the coal operators so well in West Virginia were hired by the Colorado mine owners. A steel-armored automobile, fitted with machine guns and rifles, was used in Colorado, just as the "Bull Moose" was used in West Virginia.

## Colorado Strike Grim

The Colorado strike was even more terrible for the miners than the West Virginia battle. During the winter months in that state it gets below zero and stays there for many days. Evicted from their homes, as in West Virginia the miners had been evicted, the strikers had to live in flimsy tents. And the militia and guards were more murderous than in West Virginia. You might say that the West Virginia strike was a sort of "boot camp" in which thugs, detectives, state officials, and coal operators received their training for the Colorado wars.

A telegram to the 1914 UMW convention, sent by International Board Member John R. Lawson and A.W.T. Hickey, secretary-treasurer of the Colorado State Federation of Labor, gives an inkling of what happened in Colorado:

> "Calvary, under the personal command of Adjutant General (John) Chase, with drawn swords, ride down one thousand women and children who were peacefully marching to a protest meeting this afternoon. General Chase, who became so excited that he fell off his horse, issued orders to shoot the women and children and shoot to kill. Woman carrying American flag knocked down with butt of gun and flag torn from her hands by militiamen. Cavalryman slashed another woman with a saber, almost severing an ear from her head. Militiamen jab sabers and bayonets into backs of women with babes in their arms and trample them under the feet of their horses. Mothers with infants thrown into military prison. Feeling is intense. Union officers doing everything to pacify the people"

After receiving such treatment the people, it may be guessed, would certainly be difficult to pacify. And the worst was yet to come.

12/11/52 (Seventeenth)

On April 20, 1914, the miners and families were living in their tents and shacks and Ludlow camp. They had surrendered most of their guns to the state militia under Major Patrick Hemrock and Lieut. E.K. Linderfelt. The militia was camped around Ludlow, heavily armed with rifles and machine guns. Not long after sunrise a battle began between militia and miners. The usual historical cloudiness surrounds the question as to who first shot at whom. But, all partisanship aside, it is not likely that poorly armed miners would deliberately pick a fight with a large number of militiamen armed with machine guns, thus exposing both themselves and their families to the risk of death.

From available evidence, the miners' charge that the militia was guilty of wanton assault and murder at Ludlow is fully justified. Women and children in the strikers' camp were awakened by the murderous cough of machine guns and the ripping canvas and wood as slugs plowed through their temporary homes. They hurriedly ducked into holes which had been dug for their protection.

The miners fired with what guns they had, staying away from the tents in order to keep their families from being killed. All day the machine guns rained lead into Ludlow. The women and children were forced to lie in their holes during that time without food or water.

One 11 year-old boy, little William Snyder, tried to climb out of a hole for water and had his head blown off by an explosive bullet.

One miner's wife, Mrs. Pearls Jolly, acted as nurse, walking through the hail of fire with a large red cross marked on her white dress. She was wounded in the arm.

## Holocaust at Ludlow

Darkness came and still the shooting continued. The women and children crawled out of their holes under cover of darkness and inched along on their bellies to the safety of a freight train. And then the militia swarmed in to Ludlow, set fire to the riddled tents and conducted a kind of war dance while they watched the flames eat into the April night.

The following morning the sun rose on the charred remnants of what had been the "homes" of 1,000 people. And in one of the holes under the tents, "the Black Hole of Ludlow" was 13 bodies. In life, two had been women. The other 11 were children, the youngest a three-month-old baby. Some had been burned to death, others suffocated. One of the dead women was Mrs. Pedelina Costa. Her two children died with her and that same night her husband had been killed by a National Guard bullet. The entire family was wiped out.

Besides Costa, four other striking miners had been killed on April 20. The militia had stolen from the dead and rifled the tents taking $1,500 from one woman. The slaughter at Ludlow will never be forgotten by the coal miners. John D. Rockefeller, Jr., president of the strike-breaking Colorado Fuel & Iron Company, will in future histories be chiefly remembered by this event.

Shortly before Ludlow a grand jury had indicted the Colorado UMW leaders for alleged violation of the Sherman Anti-trust Act, just as in West Virginia, and many miners were sent to jail during the struggle. But not one mine guard, company official or militiaman was ever punished in any way – yet again a parallel to the West Virginia situation.

The grand jury which indicted the UMW leaders made the following interesting comment:

> "The operators appear to have been somewhat remiss in endeavoring to secure and hold the good will of their employees, and the grand jury deduced from testimony that there existed reasonable ground for many of the grievances complained of by the miners."

This writer's ingenuity fails to find words sufficiently explosive to convey his feelings on the above passage. Let it stand without comment.

The murders at Ludlow caused a nation-wide furor. There was something resembling a general call to arms on the part of Labor. Denver Typographical Union No 49 passed a resolution donating $500 as a "first installment" for the purchase of arms and ammunition.

Back in West Virginia, on May 1 an estimated 10,000 miners in District 17 struck, against the advice of the national Union, and asked the national office to call a nation-wide strike to last until the Colorado miners won their fight. Every workingman in the United States was aroused and President Woodrow Wilson sent Federal troops into Colorado with as much haste as he could summon.

But the strike was broken in Colorado, chewed up by machine gun bullets and ripped to shreds by bayonets. John D. Rockefeller, Jr. added further to his list of crimes by inventing the first large "company Union" under what was known as the "Rockefeller Plan." The principal purpose of the Plan was to keep out the UMW, and it succeeded well enough to be copied by many other corporations in the ensuing years. Meanwhile the war in Europe had given a shot in the arm to the economy of the United States, and this, of course, included the coal industry. A Department of Labor had been created in 1913 under the first term of Woodrow Wilson, with William B. Wilson, a former Union official and coal miner, as its first secretary. The United Mine Workers in 1914 boasted a membership of 377,682, and claimed to be, with justice, "the strongest body of organized labor in the world."

## We Go To War

The Socialist Party in the United States reached its zenith in these years before World War I. In 1912 at least a thousand Socialists, under the leadership of dramatic Eugene Victor Debs, held public office in this country, Victor Berger being elected to Congress in that year. In West Virginia a great many miners were Socialists, as were some of the UMW state officials. But it was never true that the UMW in West Virginia was a Socialist organization, as the coal operators charged. The operators were merely indulging in the "red-baiting" of their day.

As time passed the United States stepped closer and closer to the abyss of involvement in the European war. And there was comparative prosperity in the coal fields as American industry stepped up production to meet the appetite of the fire breathing war god. The masses of the people, as always, wanted peace, and Woodrow Wilson was elected to his second term in 1917 under the slogan "He kept us out of war."

But the great world war, like a mighty whirlpool, drew us into its vortex, and Woodrow Wilson did not at all mind seeing Eugene Debs go to jail because of his protest against United States involvement in the bloody struggle. By late 1916 Wall Street had made huge loans to both England and France, our own economy had been tied up with that of the economies of the allies, and the war drums were noisily overwhelming the voices of dissent. Men in the United States Congress who opposed our entry into the war were denounced as traitors. And in we went, the people stampeded by an unprecedented propaganda barrage.

This did not prevent men like Senator George W. Norris from saying: "We are going into war upon the command of gold… I feel that we are about to put a dollar sign on the American flag."

But it did prevent his voice from doing any good. On April 6, 1917 the United States was at war with Germany.

# Chapter Four: World War Wedge

12/12/1952 (Eighteenth)

From Labor's point of view, the First World War did two things of great political and economic importance: It killed the Socialist movement as dead as a fossil trilobite and (2) it dealt American Labor a crippling blow from which it did not begin to recover until 1933.

An external war inevitably creates the need for internal repression in order that at least a semblance of unity may be presented to the foe in battle. The repression of antiwar Socialists in all countries was complete and merciless, before, during and after World War I. Methods of repression of trade Unions were usually not quite so direct as jail and shooting, and took a little longer, but they were just as effective.

Many readers will feel that much of the above has been a far afield excursion for a history devoted to the West Virginia coal miner. But West Virginia was and is a part of a larger whole, and as that large outside world is affected so is West Virginia and its miners. It is bitter truth that after World War I corporation profits were booming, there was unprecedented prosperity, and yet the trade unions were in a very bad way.

For instance, at the high-water mark of so-called "prosperity," just prior to the October, 1929 Wall Street crash, the United Mine Workers of America had become a mere skeleton in the Appalachian area. Regions which had once been Unionized had become nonunion. The 1930 UMW convention reported that District 5,

Western Pennsylvania, had only 293 dues-paying members out of 45,000 men employed in and around the mines.

In West Virginia, District 17 reported 512 UMW members out of a potential 100,000!

The "war to end war" very nearly ended the United Mine Workers of America! But this is getting a little ahead of our story.

## War-Time Negotiations

And this story begins in the UMW operator–U.S. Government joint conference at Washington, D.C. lasting from Sept. 25 to Oct. 6, 1917. The United States had gone to war with Germany on April 6 of that year, and the Lever Act, which created the Federal Fuel Administration, had been passed. Dr. Henry A. Garfield, of Williams College, had been appointed head of the Federal Fuel Administration, and he sat in on the conference.

John P. White, UMW president since 1911, resigned his post to serve as labor adviser to Dr. Garfield. Thus was Frank J. Hayes, then the Union's vice-president, elevated to the UMW presidency. Hayes then appointed "a man of marked ability" to the vice-presidency, one John L. Lewis. Before long this new vice-presidency was actually acting president of the UMW.

This was not, however, at this time true. After the beginning of the World War in Europe and the reaping of unprecedented profits by huge corporations, the

UMW had succeeded in getting some increases for its men. They were certainly deserved increases, paltry in view of the huge blood-profits industry was collecting.

When war finally placed its spiked helmet on the capitol dome at Washington, corporate profits doubled and redoubled. The UMW naturally considered that its miners deserved some of this money, and the Union met in the fall of 1917 at Washington in order to get it.

The miners did get an increase from this "Washington Agreement." It amounted to 10 cents a day for pick men and $1.40 a day to day labor and monthly men, as well as other benefits. But there were jokers in the contract, inserted at the insistence of Dr. Garfield. First, the contract was to last "during the continuation of the war, but not later than March 31, 1920." Secondly, there was in the contract a "penalty" clause which provided for fining the coal miner one dollar for each day he was illegally on strike.

As Garfield would have maintained that any strike during wartime was illegal, this provision had as its purpose the prevention of striking for the duration. And the duration, as the UMW was to discover, was a more flexible concept than appeared at first sight. The miners dug coal with a will during the war years and production in 1918 mounted to a record 346,540,000 tons. In the five-year period of 1913-18, 2,960,938,537 tons of coal were brought above ground. Before 1913, only three times that amount had been produced in the United States in more than 100 years!

## Wilson Refuses Increase

The UMW was successful, after the "Washington Agreement" in getting another advance for the miners in the anthracite fields. And on Oct. 21, 1918 the Union asked Dr. Garfield for a further increase in the soft-coal fields. Dr. Garfield refused. UMW officials met on Oct. 31 at Indianapolis and went over Garfield's head, asking President Woodrow Wilson himself for the increase. Before Wilson replied the war ended. And on Nov. 15, four days after the Armistice, Wilson refused the bituminous increase.

The miners found that their extraordinary production had boomeranged. They had actually hurt themselves by working so hard. Over 100 million tons of surplus coal were above ground. With no war to gobble it, the coal remained unsold and unemployment began.

The 27th convention of the UMW met at Gray's Armory in Cleveland Sept. 9, 1919, with Acting President John L. Lewis presiding. The convention passed resolutions for nationalization of the coal mines, for the organization of a Labor Party, and changed their constitution in order that the members of the "One Big Union," the I.W.W., and the Chamber of Commerce were banned from UMW membership. More important, the convention declared that all contracts in existence "for the duration" would be terminated Nov. 1, 1919, and that if no new contract were signed by that date a national coal strike would occur.

## Wilson Breaks Strike

The miners had served notice that they were no longer bound by a "Washington Agreement" which had been imposed upon them by pleas of patriotism, while coal companies had been making extravagant profits. They asked for a 60% increase in tonnage and yardage rates and a six-hour-five-day week.

The strike order was issued by Acting UMW President John L. Lewis on Oct. 15, 1919, to take effect, as before stated, on the first day of November. United States Attorney General A. Mitchell Palmer wasted little time in taking action to clip the wings of the miners' Union. He petitioned U.S. District Judge A.B. Anderson in Indianapolis for an injunction based on the war-time Lever Act. The Federal Government took the position that the war was still going on, although the Armistice had been signed almost a year before. President Woodrow Wilson said publicly that the proposed strike was "not only unjustifiable but unlawful."

Judge Anderson issued a temporary restraining order on Oct. 31. But the miners walked out on Nov. 1 as per schedule in a unanimous demonstration which left no doubt as to how they felt about their demands. Judge Anderson countered by issuing an injunction on the 8th day of November, ordering the strike to be cancelled by the 11th. After a 48-hour conference of officers and scale-committee members, the UMW complied, under protest, with the injunction.

That is, the UMW officials complied by agreeing that the strike was cancelled. The miners back home did not. They continued to strike, tying up 71% of national coal production. On Dec. 3, 1919, Judge Anderson cited 84 international and district UMW officers for contempt. Every international, district and local Union officer in the state of Indiana was arrested. Martial law was declared in Wyoming, and United States troops were rushed in. It was a rather exciting period.

12/13/1952 (Nineteenth)

The contempt charges against the UMW dragged through the courts for two years, until finally the Lever Act was declared unconstitutional by the U.S. Supreme Court.

On Dec. 6, 1919, UMW officials convened in Washington with A. Mitchell Palmer and Joseph P. Tumulty, Secretary to President Wilson. The federal officials offered a 14 per cent increase to the miners if they returned to work, and promised the appointment of a presidential commission to settle the matter permanently.

This proposal was accepted by the Union officials and ratified on Jan. 5, 1920, by an International Convention of the UMW by a vote of 1,639 to 221. This was a reversal of the Union position in November, when the miners had rejected an identical 14 per cent increase offer by Dr. Henry A. Garfield, an indication that governmental pressure had indeed become heavy.

This decision also showed that the miners expected further concessions from the presidential commission as the price of peace. And they got them. The commission soon announced an award to supplant the original 14 per cent increase. The tonnage men received a 34 per cent increase, but the day men, who then constituted between 27 and 30 per cent of coal mine employees, were awarded only 20 per cent. Disappointed, the miners struck again. An attempt was made at a settlement on the national level, but no agreement could be reached. At length, individual contracts in the various UMW districts were signed which raised the pay of day men to $7.50, the contracts extending until March 31, 1922.

## West Virginia Explodes Again

Comparative peace reigned in the nation's coal fields, with one exception. That exception was West Virginia. The great struggle of 1912-13 was being reenacted all over again. Once again there was a mighty pitched battle between the coal operators of the Mountain State and the men who actually dug the coal.

The root of the trouble at this time was that the counties of Logan, Mingo, McDowell, Wyoming, Mercer and part of Raleigh, all in the southern part of West Virginia, comprised a stronghold of nonunion coal production. All remaining 12 ½ counties in UMW District 17 were strongly organized. When the national strike call came on Nov. 1, 1919, as before detailed, the Union mines in West Virginia closed down solidly, just as they did all over the United States.

But the nonunion mines in the southern part of District 17 continued to operate, and they were exceedingly rich fields. Of the coal produced in the country during the 1919 strike, it is probable that 60 per cent came from the six nonunion West Virginia counties. Just as in 1912 nonunion West Virginia was a "dagger in the heart" of the UMW, so the nonunion section of the state in 1919 remained a serious threat to UMW District 17 and the Union as a whole. Miners saw this coal weakening their strike. The Union sent organizers into Logan and other counties. They found these areas to be armed camps, the county and city governments almost entirely subservient to the operators. The UMW organizers were beaten, jailed and shot. So were all men who talked Union. In the fall of 1919, 12 International UMW officers were arrested and jailed at Williamson on a charge of unlawful assembly, and a number of Union men were badly beaten.

## The Miners Act

In the words of Fred Mooney, then secretary-treasurer of District 17:

> "Some of them had been beaten into insensibility, and they were shot through the head and had different wounds over the body, and they were taken into the Governor's office and were produced to him as what was taking place in Logan County, and they had the stories that men were beaten up, and the public mind became so inflamed at that time that the men got into a state of mind that it was impossible to do anything with them because of that."

The miners evidently tried several times to get help from Gov. John J. Cornwell, but found it not forthcoming. As Cornwell happened to be friendly with the coal operators, and was later to become an attorney for the B. & O. Railway, this was not surprising. The miners evidently decided that if they got no official help they would help themselves. In accord with their marching tradition, they assembled at the mouth of Lens Creek near Marmet, W. Va. They were armed with high-powered rifles and they announced their intention of marching to Logan and cleaning up the situation.

Within a few days 5,000 miners were assembled at Marmet. Governor Cornwell wired UMW District 17 President C.F. Keeney, then in conference with coal operators in northern West Virginia, to hurry back to Charleston. Keeney did so, and the Governor told him to go to Lens Creek and stop the miners from marching. Keeney made an attempt, but returned with a report that the miners wouldn't listen to him. Cornwell then was said to promise that he would conduct an investigation of Logan County if the men would go home. In the Governor's words, in his autobiography: "I lectured him (Keeney) and directed him to go back and carry out my orders." Keeney tried, but found that the men were still determined to march.

## Dante's Inferno

District 17 Secretary-Treasurer Fred Mooney was then sent to nearby Marmet, where he telephoned Cornwell about 9 p.m. on the night of Sept. 4, saying that Keeney wanted the Governor to talk to the men. Cornwell complied, driving to Lens Creek in company with his wife, a secretary and a stenographer. Not too many governors in any state have had such an audience as greeted Cornwell as he spoke from the back of a truck at Lens Creek. One might add that not many governors desire such an audience under such conditions, and Cornwell must have had some uneasy moments – which, because of his refusal to see that the coal miner was treated with respect in Logan County, he richly deserved.

C.F. Keeney described the scene to the federal Kenyon Committee which later investigated: "The moon was shining, and the camp fires were there, and there were in that crowd about 5,000 rifles. It looked more like Dante's Inferno than anything I can think of, with the moonlight shining on the rifles. The Governor got into the machine, and there were several shots fired in the air. That was in the way of a "salute to the Governor.""

Cornwell promised the miners an investigation and asked them to turn back. The Governor in his autobiography indicates that he was very blunt: "I reminded them they had broken the Union's agreement with the coal operators by quitting their jobs without reason when the country was crying for coal." He told the miners that their assemblage was unlawful and that he wouldn't let them go. He was asked how he was going to stop them, but rather discreetly made no answer. It was not likely that he was in any real danger, but it is evident that he thought he was, for he makes this comment:

> "Should I have replied that a regiment of federal soldiers was under arms at the camp at Chillicothe, Ohio, with orders to move when I passed the word they were needed, the crack of a high-

powered rifle might have been the rejoinder, for in the crowd were more than 500 ex-service men in uniform fresh from the bloody battlefields of France."

According to Keeney, one of the miners spoke to the Governor in the following manner:

> "Governor, you have made a good speech, and one that would be alright provided it was carried out. There is a group of men in this audience, who have been overseas fighting to save the world for democracy, but we found the conditions here more hellish then they ever were over there."

12/16/1952 (Twentieth)

The governor did not accomplish much, so he headed back toward Charleston. The next day the miners began to march and about 1,500 had gotten 32 miles to the town of Danville when Cornwell again sent Keeney to stop them. This time the district president succeeded, and the men went home. Not however, without stating that they wanted to pass a resolution allowing the governor a certain number of days to start his promised investigation. Keeney opposed this, the march stopped, and, apparently, Cornwell never did investigate Logan County. If he did, no changes were made.

This 1919 march was an exceedingly bulky straw in the wind as to what was to occur later in the West Virginia struggle.

On March 20, 1920, Woodrow Wilson's three-man commission awarded the 34 per cent increase to the Union tonnage men and the 20 per cent increase to the day men. In the nonunion fields in the West Virginia counties before noted, this increase was not granted. There had been previously a 5 to 10 per cent increase in these fields, but a rise in company store rates had helped to offset it. The miners in the Mingo, Logan and other nonunion fields were quite aware that their wages were not up to the Union scale. In addition, they had many other complaints.

They had no checkweighman, hired by themselves to see that they got credit for all the coal they loaded, despite the fact that West Virginia law required this, as it had in 1912 when coal companies openly flouted this statutory requirement. Not only this, they didn't even have scales in most places. Instead of being paid by weight, they were paid by the coal car. The amount the coal car held varied according to the operator's whim and what he thought he could get by with. Generally it held from two and a half to five tons, and for loading this car the miner was paid from 65 cents to a dollar.

## Operators Flout Law

The state law required these cars be stamped with the number of tons or pounds they held, but this law also was ignored by the coal operator. In many mines the foreman made the miner load the car with a "hump," so that any stamped weight, if it were on the car at all, would be far exceeded. Income, under these conditions, was far from plush. At the nonunion coal comp of

Burnwell, for instance, a miner would draw from $5 to $22 for a two-week period.

The nine-hour day prevailed in the Mingo field, as opposed to eight hours in the Union districts. And the nine hours limit was none too carefully observed, as hours never are under nonunion conditions. For instance, if a man were working on the tipple he had to stay until everything was cleaned up, even when it meant non-paid overtime.

At the mouth of Pond Creek was located the Pond Creek By-Products Company. The company used a coal car which held about three tons. On March 15, 1920, the men were receiving 80 cents for loading this car, on March 16 the wage jumped to 90 cents a car, then on April 1, it went back to 80 cents. Naturally, the men had nothing to say in these fluctuations, they were merely the result of company caprice. Fear of unionization caused this company to raise its pay to $1.25 a car late in June, just before the strike started.

**Contract System Explained**

The "contract system" of mining was prevalent in the unorganized field. This was a system whereby one miner exploited a group of fellow miners who worked for him under contract. This practice probably got its start when docile southern Negroes were imported by coal companies and worked after this fashion, the native white miner being the "boss."

Both white and Negro did contract work in Mingo. A man who was a good boss, that is, one who could get the last ounce of effort out of those under him, would be assigned to a section of the mine with a crew under him. The company would agree to pay the boss, say $2 or more for every loaded coal car delivered to the tipple. The boss would pay the men the prevalent scale, anywhere from 80 cents to $1.25, pay the expenses involved in getting the coal out of his section, and pocket the difference.

A good slave driver could make from $400 to $1,000 a month as a contract boss. But he had ceased to be a wage earner and had become a small businessman, one who was living off the labor of miners. The company liked the system because it generally assured the delivery of more coal to the surface per man involved and in the end reduced operating costs to a minimum. What "kickbacks" were involved in the system, from contract boss to superintendent, are not revealed in the historical record, but the possibilities are obvious. It is not to be doubted that many a coal operator in the old days got his start as a contract boss.

### Operators Employed 'Check-Off'

Docking from the miner's pay for coal company services was thorough and detailed. The miner did not have to pay for the air he breathed on company property – or if he did it was disguised in another form – but his pay statement showed deductions for almost everything else. And no miner in Mingo Count argued about his statement. There were plenty of "deputy sheriffs" hanging around the company store to crack his skull if he did.

For his company house the miner in Mingo in 1920 paid about $2 per room per month. His electricity cost him 40 cents a bulb a month. The doctor fee for a single man was $1 a month, for a married man $2 a month. There was a deduction for the blacksmith as well, whether his services were used or not, and the miner paid for his own blasting powder, dynamite, shotpaper for his powder, and his varied tools.

There was also involved the historic right of the Union miner to his "turn." That is, in Union mines the men were pledged not to compete with one another, no one man hogging everything while another got very little. If a driver hauling cars in a mine (as of 1920, and it was true for years later) finds that one man has not filled his car as fast as the others, he waits till the man does fill it. Or the driver keeps record to see that the man gets an equal number of cars with the others. In the nonunion fields this was not done. The savage jungle-law of the coal operator was brought underground and the men pitted one against the other. The weak, of course, suffered. The strong grew stronger.

Certainly the economic condition of the nonunion miner was deplorable, but his living under constant domination, from work habits to personal habits, was also a bitter source of complaint. The coal operator held the position of the feudal lord, and he kept plenty of armed men in his demesne to enforce his mandates.

12/17/1952 (Twenty-first)

When the miners in Mingo and other unorganized areas began to talk Union the coal operators proved themselves to be the most unimaginative of men, for they used exactly the same tactics which had been practiced by coal operators in West Virginia and elsewhere since before the turn of the century. The "old reliable" Baldwin-Felts Detective Agency, with headquarters in Bluefield, was called into service, with its snooping and beating and shooting. Miners were fired on short notice and then evicted from their homes. And strikebreakers were employed.

There was no difference in the story at all, except that the operators were by this time more brutal, and had learned better than ever how to capture city and county governments and turn them to their use. As before, the state government was also an operator tool.

But let us return to the story of how the UMW began organization in Mingo, Logan and the other non-union counties. The miners in the southern fields were not satisfied for the reasons before given and when they were awarded no increase to compare with the governmental award made to the Union miners the grumbling increased. In point of fact, the terms of the government award were a subject of bitter feeling among all miners throughout the nation.

The feeling can be understood when one remembers the number of millionaires created by World War 1 and knows that living costs in 1920 were 143% above the same costs in 1913!

## Men Ask for Union

C.F. (Frank) Keeney had been elected president of District 17 on Jan. 1, 1917, and was still president in 1920. About May 1 of that year, according to his testimony, a three-man committee from Mingo visited his Summers Street office. The men said that a number of the miners in their county were on strike and they wanted help from the UMW. Keeney advised that it was not in line with the general policy of the organization to take in men on strike, that they should go back and tell the men to return to work. Then he would deal with them. The men did this and returned and Keeney authorized them to swear men into the UMW.

These men quickly formed locals at the towns of Matewan and Sprigg, and by May 16 twenty-five locals had been organized in the Mingo field. By June, Mingo was almost completely organized. And just as fast as the miners "took the obligation" they were fired from their jobs and evicted form their homes. This happened to 2,700 or 2,800 men. In other words, the trouble in Mingo did not start as a strike but as a "lock-out." If you joined the UMW, you were "locked-out" of your job.

At this point it seems logical to give the Union oath in full. Just what terrible things did a miner swear to do, that he should be treated as an undesirable and, with his pitifully few belongings crowded about his ears, thrown unceremoniously into the company street. This is the UMW "obligation," along with a bit of the Union procedure in administering same:

"President: Mr. Doorkeeper, are there any candidates in waiting who have been accepted by this union?

"Doorkeeper: Mr. President, I find Brothers -------- , mine workers, who were elected to become members of this body.

"President: Admit the brothers.

"The doorkeeper will admit the candidates and place them in line opposite the president."

## Obligation of Fidelity

"President: Fellow workmen, the United Mine Workers of America requires perfect freedom of inclination in every candidate for membership to its body. An obligation of fidelity is required: let me assure you that in this obligation there is nothing contrary to your civil or religious duties, with this understanding are you willing to take an obligation which binds you upon your honor as a man to keep the same as long as life remains?

"Each candidate answers: 'I am.'

"President: Raise your right hand.

"I do sincerely promise, of my own free will, to abide by the laws of the union, to bear true allegiance to and keep inviolate the principles of the United Mine Workers of America: never to discriminate against a fellow worker on account of creed or color, or nationality, to defend on all occasions and to the extent of my ability the members of our organization.

"That I will not reveal to any employer or boss the name of anyone a member of our union. (This provision has been eliminated from the present oath.) That I will assist all members of our organization to obtain the highest wages possible for their work: that I will not accept a brother's job who is idle for advancing the interests of the Union or seeking better remuneration for his labor: and, as the mine workers of the entire country are competitors in the labor world, I promise to cease work at any time I am called upon by the organization to do so. And I further promise to help and assist all brothers in adversity, and to have all mine workers join our Union that we may be able to enjoy the fruits of our labor: that I will never knowingly wrong a brother or see him wronged if I can prevent it.

"To all of this I pledge my honor to observe and keep as long as life remains, or until I am absolved by the United Mine Workers of America.

"Answer: I promise.

"President: You are now members of Local Union No. ----- and are entitled to all rights and privileges of the United Mine Workers of America."

## Miners Fired and Evicted

In 1919-20 over 2,700 miners in southern West Virginia took the above oath. They took it in churches, in school buildings, and under the open sky. For so doing they knew that they would be deprived of income, evicted from their homes, oppressed by coal company guards and forced to live in tents. But they took this oath, determined to rid themselves of economic autocracy.

Neill Burkinshaw, attorney for the UMW, graphically described the situation to the Senate Investigating Committee:

"As those men joined the United Mine Workers they were out of a job for taking advantage of their rights as citizens to join any organization they saw fit; they were fired, and not only fired but they were evicted from their homes. These people were driven like cattle from their homes, and their goods were thrown out into the roads, and some lived in tents and railroad stations and temporary shelters and others even without shelter until the United Mine Workers' organization at Charleston sent them tents and to this day (a year later) those people are living in tents. They lived there during the winter. I was down there last November and saw barefoot children, women with a single garment, and men barefooted with nothing but overalls, living in that cold. It is a high mountain country and it's very cold. They suffered tortures that I have never seen before in this or any country."

12/18/1952 (Twenty-second)

The reasons men and women were willing to endure such hardship have been given in this work. Sometimes, as before related they even seized arms and sought to correct that which no one else would correct for them. It is interesting to note the reasons for this assigned by "respectable" people and institutions. The great *New York Times* called it "corn likker and young blood." West Virginia's Ephraim Morgan, who became governor in 1921, said it was "moonshining, pistol-toting and automobiles." *The New Republic* came much closer by blaming the "mine guard system" and Walter Clark, publisher of the *Charleston Daily Mail*, an ultra-reactionary rag, said that it was just one of those hill-billy mountain feuds.                    .

It remained for Fred Mooney, then secretary-treasurer of UMW District 17, to hit the nail on the head: – "The struggle now going on in Mingo County is not a feud, and any insinuation by Mr. Clark to that effect is not true and is subject to proof by anyone investigating the facts that he did not investigate himself, and one that is not biased. For this struggle in Mingo County is an economic one. In fact, it is the continuance of a struggle begun in West Virginia 23 years ago and extending through this period."

Mooney was talking sound sense. The same basic factors at the bottom of the West Virginia organizing drive of the UMW in 1897, and the coal operator resistance thereto were present in 1920. It was still a part of the tussle over the wealth in the West Virginia hills, so little of which came into the hands of the men who actually brought it to the surface.

## Sid Hatfield the Brave

As the men in the nonunion field were evicted from their homes, resentment against the coal companies, and the Baldwin-Felts men who did their dirty work, quite naturally mounted. The Operator's Association of the Williamson field was very busy, with Harry Olmstead as its chairman, in seeing that advertisements were prepared to attract new men to the mines to replace the locked-out miners, and in seeing the judges, law enforcement officers and other key political figures were "friendly."

Olmstead found to his disgust that some few officials in Mingo County were on good terms with the miners. One of these was the Chief of Police at Matewan, in the aforementioned county. This was a young man, 28 years old, by the name of Sid Hatfield. Sid liked the miners and the compliment was returned, though he himself was not a member of the UMW. He saw to it that the Baldwin-Felts detectives toed the legal line when doing eviction work for the coal operators. Evictions were carried out on the basis of opinions of coal operator attorneys that no employee - employer relationship existed between coal miner and coal operator. The relationship, the operators contended, was that of "master and servant," and the short-notice evictions were thus legally justifiable.

It should be emphasized that Sid Hatfield was never the "tough gunman" or "feuding mountaineer," as he was described by a sensation-hunting press. He was simply a man of courage who had grown up with the miners he now saw striking. He was on their side in an industrial battle, and that was all there was to it. Hatfield's personal appearance is given as follows in the May 25, 1921, issue of the *New York Evening World*:

## Hatfield is Described

"The 'Terror of the Tug' does not look the part he has played in the strike disturbances. He is five feet seven or eight inches in height and weighs about 160 pounds. He has firey brown eyes, protruding ears, high cheekbones and a complexion naturally sallow. He wore a cheap, snuff-colored suit, white shirt and collar, and a necktie that looked neater than any other part of his apparel."

Let the memory of this simple, courageous man of the hills be revered by the coal miners. He fought their fight, and gave his life in the struggle.

At 11:47 a.m. on the morning of May 19, 1920, train No. 29 puffed into Matewan with something more than a dozen Baldwin-Felts men as passengers. Their errand was to evict six miners from homes belonging to the Stone Mountain Coal Corporation. The armed thugs were met by Sid Hatfield and Matewan Mayor C.C. Testerman, who inquired if they had legal authority to execute the evictions. According to Hatfield's later testimony the detectives said that they had authority from Circuit Judge James Damron (later an attorney for the Mingo operators). "They said two hours notice was all they wanted." The company hirelings proceeded to evict the miners without resistance, and returned to Matewan about 3:30 in the afternoon.

Mayor Testerman meanwhile had issued warrant for the arrest of the Baldwin men on the grounds that they were violating a town ordinance in carrying weapons. Hatfield proceeded to serve the warrant as soon as the "detectives" returned to the Matewan streets. There were two of the Felts brothers in the group and they informed Hatfield that they had a warrant for HIS arrest, although they refused to show it. Hatfield evidently did not feel inclined to argue with a dozen men who were notoriously trigger-happy, so he obeyed when they stated that he had to go with them to Bluefield. The group, including the Matewan police chief, headed toward the railroad station.

12/19/52 (Twenty-third)

Many eyes, however, had witnessed this scene, and the miners valued Sid Hatfield very highly. Word of his arrest spread quickly, and the miners were in no mood to let the Baldwin men kill Hatfield, as they were convinced was not only possible but probable. Among those who learned of the new development was Mayor Testerman. In the words of Sid Hatfield:

"Someone went and told the mayor that the detectives had me arrested, and the mayor came out to see what the charges were, and he told Felts that he would give bond for me, that he could not afford to let me go to Bluefield. Felts told him that he could not take any bond, and the mayor asked him for the warrant, and he gave the warrant to the mayor, and the mayor read the warrant and said it was bogus, it was not legal, and then he shot the mayor. Then the shooting started in general."

It seems that many of Hatfield's coal miner friends were hanging around, just to see that he wouldn't come up short if any trouble started. He didn't. When the shooting stopped and the smoke cleared, seven Baldwin-Felts men lay dead. Six others escaped. Two Matewan citizens, Tot Tinsley and Robert Mullens, in addition to Mayor Testerman, were also dead. Later, the remaining guards through their coal company lawyers said that their guns were cased and that they were unarmed, so the conclusion must reluctantly be drawn that the mayor and the two other men dropped dead from the excitement. The coal companies also accused Sid Hatfield of killing Testerman so that he could marry his wife, basing this slander upon the fact that the chief of police did very soon marry the mayor's widow.

## Baldwin Men Murderous

This may be safely classified as another coal operator lie. The Baldwin men have too long a record of brutality and deceit for any part of their testimony to receive a place in this work. Lest this seem unduly biased, we shall attempt to prove our point. The utter worthlessness and murderous sadism of these hired strikebreakers was exemplified in their chief, T. L. Felts, two of whose brothers, Albert C. and Lee C. Felts, were killed in the Matewan battle.

The journalist Winthrop Lane, author of *Civil War in West Virginia*, spoke of meeting T. L. Felts in the following words: "Well, the first part of our conversation was in the office of the Pocahontas Coal Operator's Association. During that time there were six or eight men there in the audience in the office to whom Mr. Felts told stories of his various activities in labor disputes, particularly in West Virginia. Then we went to his office and there we spent a half or three-quarters of an hour going through his so-called chamber of horrors in his office there, a room which he has fitted up with the mementos and souvenirs of men whom his men have killed, and some of his men who have been killed – a bloodstained dollar bill taken off the body of a victim, the black hood of a man who was hanged...a great collection of firearms... a necktie framed, which had been worn by a Negro rapist when caught."

These were the knickknacks with which T. L. Felts surrounded himself. We are reminded of the more modern Nazi Beast of Buchenwald who had lampshades fashioned of human skin. The bloody mentality is the same.

### C. E. Lively Career Cited

It will be interesting, we believe, to give a sketch of the career of a Baldwin-Felts detective, for just such vermin still infest Labor today, although they do not have the same name. They are labor spies, paid to snoop and pry and report to bosses, while all the time protesting friendship to Labor. Take the case of Baldwin-Felts employee C. E. Lively.  Lively was born in the Kanawha coal fields of West Virginia about 1888. He began work in the coal mines when he was only 13 years old and joined the UMW in 1902, when he was a mere boy, while working at Blackband, W. Va. About 1912, when he was 24 years old, he was approached by a recruiter for the Baldwin-Felts Detective Agency. He joined the Baldwin men while a member of the UMW Local Union at Gatewood, Fayette County, W. VA.

He attended several Union conventions and in 1913 was a delegate at a convention of the newly-formed UMW District 29. The Baldwin pay at first was $75 a month and expenses. His job for the most part was to report any men who were active in Union organization, and he continued to mine coal and pretend to be a good Union man.

A little later the Colorado strike began and Lively went west. He joined the Western Federation of Miners and became a paid organizer for that Union, at the same time, or course, drawing his pay as a Baldwin detective. He worked in Missouri, Oklahoma, Illinois, Kansas, and Colorado, creating trouble for the miners wherever he went. In the latter state he even became the president of the local Union at La Veta! It seems that he left there after seeing that the secretary of this local was sent to jail on a charge of being an accomplice in a murder.

## McKeller Is Shocked

It is well to interrupt at this point with the observation that Senator McKeller, of the Senate Investigating Committee, was much shocked at this behavior of Lively. But the coal company attorney calmly told him that exactly the same methods had been used by the

United States Government to break up and hang the Molly Maguires. It is not our purpose to speak here of the Molly Maguires (an invented name, by the way, for a group of Irish miners in Pennsylvania), but the attorney for the operators in this case spoke the truth. The Pinkerton Detective Agency was used instead of the Baldwin-Felts.

To return to Lively, all this while he had posed successfully as a simple coal miner, and he came back to West Virginia about the time the miners began to ask for Union organization in Mingo County. Lively had as a boy known Fred Mooney, who in 1920 was secretary-treasurer of UMW District 17, and was also well acquainted with Frank Keeney, the District president, so he had an easy entree into Union affairs. He visited the UMW headquarters frequently and even helped to organize local unions at the coal camps of War Eagle, Glen Alum, and Mohawk. All the while, of course, he was a spy for the coal companies, constantly sending in reports to T. L. Felts at Bluefield.

It happened that Lively at this time had gone to Matewan and had entrenched himself strongly with the Union in that Mingo County town. But on May 19, 1920, when the Baldwin-Felts men were killed in their tangle with Sid Hatfield, he was in Charleston at the UMW District office when the news of the killings arrived. It was natural that the UMW officials shed few tears over the deaths of the Baldwin men – one Charley Batley is supposed to have danced for joy – and the feelings of Lively, if he had any feelings left, can be imagined.

# Chapter Five: Sid Hatfield Indicted

12/20/52 (Twenty-fourth)

Lively was assigned to investigate the killings at Matewan, still, of course, posing as a miner and Union man. He moved to Matewan with his family and actually had the temerity to rent quarters for a restaurant from the Union. That is, the UMW local headquarters was upstairs and Lively, the Baldwin spy, was living just beneath! The restaurant was Lively's blind for operations, and Union men told him of their plans with great freedom. He in turn relayed this information to the coal companies via T.L. Felts. His salary was supposed to be $225 a month.

When a grand jury indicted Sid Hatfield and several others for the killing of the detectives at Matewan, Lively was forced to tip his hand by testifying against Hatfield and other UMW sympathizers.

Anse Hatfield, son of "Devil Anse" of feuding fame and a cousin of Sid's, did likewise and was later shot and killed in front of his hotel at Matewan. But Lively continued in good health, although he was expelled from the UMW for 99 years. The fact that Lively was never injured in any way is evidence that the Union coal miner is not especially vindictive. For if ever a man deserved the hate of the miners, that man was C.E. Lively.

Lively continued his shadowing of Sid Hatfield. He thought he had a real scandal when he discovered that Sid and Mayor Testerman's relict were friendly. On

June 2, 1920, he trailed them to Huntington and triumphantly pounced upon the pair in a room of the Floren-
tine Hotel, where Huntington police arrested them for
vagrancy. But Sid produced a marriage license to the
keen disappointment, no doubt, of Lively.

**Newspapers Splash Story**

The incident was played up by the newspapers
and Lively helped to circulate the story, as has been before related, that Hatfield killed Testerman in order to
marry his wife. That Hatfield would kill the mayor before dozens of witnesses strains to the breaking point
the laws of probability. And who could believe Lively?
It is plain that the coal operators had assigned him the
task of getting rid of Sid Hatfield, a Mingo County official who liked the coal miners.

And that is not all the story. A year went by, and
Lively continued his career as a detective. While he
may have left West Virginia for a time, he was back in
Mingo and McDowell counties in the summer of 1921,
still working on anything which would hurt a Union
miner, or any other decent person, for that matter.

Sid Hatfield, meanwhile, had been indicted on a
charge of taking part in the "shooting up" of the town of
Mohawk. And why was he indicted? On the testimony,
secret of course, of C.E. Lively. It seems that Lively had
been very loud in demands that the miners do something drastic while he who was their pretended friend
owned the restaurant under Union headquarters at
Matewan. On one occasion he encouraged the miners to
arm themselves and shoot up the nonunion tipple at

Mohawk. When the miners arrived at the tipple, they had a reception committee of bloodhounds and deputy sheriffs armed with the machine guns. Lively had been busy on the telephone, and the miners had fallen into his trap.

## Sid Goes to Welch

Sid Hatfield, indicted for the Mohawk shooting, was ordered to appear at the courthouse at Welch, in neighboring McDowell County, in order to stand trial on Aug. 1, 1921. There were probably many who advised Sid not to make the trip, as McDowell, like Mingo, was a stronghold of coal operators who refused to recognize the Union. But Sid, in company with his wife and a friend named Ed Chambers, also accompanied by his wife, nevertheless caught a train from Matewan to Welch about 5:15 a.m. on the morning of Aug. 1. The party was accompanied by a deputy sheriff named James Kirkpatrick, and they had been promised full protection by the McDowell County authorities.

When the train stopped at the McDowell County town of Iaeger, it took on a new passenger. Everyone in the Hatfield group recognized the man at once. It was none other than C.E. Lively. Lively spoke and even sat beside Kirkpatrick and carried on a conversation. Sid Hatfield and the others arrived at Welch between 8 and 9 o'clock and breakfasted in a restaurant. As they sipped their coffee they saw C.E. Lively enter the same restaurant and calmly order something to eat.

## Lively Sticks Close

They then met Charles W. Van Fleet, Sid's law-yer. Van Fleet informed them that he was applying for a change of venue which meant that Sid would be tried in a county somewhat removed from the heated industrial conflict. Back in May, the six Baldwin men who es-caped alive from the Matewan battle in which Sid was involved, had received such a change of venue to Lew-isburg, in Greenbrier County. They had, incidentally, been acquitted of the murders of three men – aside from the seven Baldwin agents – who had been slain on May 19, 1920.

Sid Hatfield took it for granted that his request for change of venue would be granted. Van Fleet per-mitted the Hatfield party to use his hotel room until it was time for Sid to appear in court. The lawyer said that when they heard the whistle of the 10:30 train, which was to bring Hatfield's witnesses to Welch, they were to leave the hotel and come to the Welch courthouse. Van Fleet then left and the party relaxed, Sid stretching out on the bed. Kirkpatrick, the deputy sheriff, happened to look out the window and there, loafing on the court-house lawn, he again saw C.E. Lively. He commented to Sid that the Baldwin man was staying pretty close, and Sid sat up and looked out the window. His remarks, if he made any, have not been recorded.

12/23/1952 (Twenty-fifth)

Both Sid Hatfield and Ed Chambers were armed when they came to Welch. But according to Sally Chambers, wife of Ed, both men removed their guns in the hotel room, and, when they heard the train whistle, went to the Welch courthouse unarmed. The Baldwin men had a different version of course, in later testimony, but they naturally would. That two men would pick a gun battle with a dozen others – unless the two happened to be carrying .50 caliber machine guns, which, certainly, Hatfield and Chambers were not, is a bit far-fetched.

In any case the Hatfield couple, the Chambers couple, and Deputy Sheriff Kirkpatrick approached the courthouse steps. Perhaps one hundred men were gathered on the lawn and around the steps. And among them could be seen their sinister shadow, C.E. Lively.

At the first landing of the steps the Sid Hatfield group paused and Sid threw up his hand and said "Hello, boys." These were his last words. He was answered by a fusillade of shots and rolled back down the steps, dead. Mrs. Hatfield ran into the office of High Sheriff Bill Hatfield, who had promised Sid protection just a few days before. She then attempted to come out of the courthouse but was grabbed by a detective. She was not permitted to see her dead husband until she returned to Matewan.

### Ed Chambers Killed

Ed Chambers, a mere boy of 22, was not to be ignored, for he had been involved in the shooting of the Baldwin men at Matewan. In words of Mrs. Chambers, this is what happened to her young husband. She is replying to questions of Sen. David I. Walsh of the Kenyon Committee. "Lively put his arm across the front of me and shot my husband in the neck: right there in front of me shot.... That was the first time my husband was shot....

"Mr. Walsh: How many times was your husband shot?

"Mrs. Chambers: About 11 or 12 times....

"Mr. Walsh: You say Lively reached around your neck and fired a shot?

"Mrs. Chambers: No: he was up on the step in front of me and kind of on this side, you see, and my husband was on this side of me (indicating), and kind of reached his arm across in front and shot my husband that way, you see, in the neck. My husband, he rolled back down the steps and I looked down this way and I seen him rolling down and blood gushing from his neck, and I just went back down the steps after him, you see, and they kept on shooting him, and when he fell he kind of fell on his side leaving his back up, you know, toward the steps and they were shooting him in the back all the time after he fell.

"Mr. Walsh: how many shots entered his back?

"Mrs. Chambers: All the shots excepting these two: he was shot one time in the neck and the last shot that was fired. C.E. Lively shot him right behind the ear."

## Were Grudge Killings

Thus did C.E. Lively end his "investigation" of the killing of the Baldwin men at Matewan. He started as a spy, became a judge and jury, and finished as executioner! And it is not likely this was his only murder. This is the man that James Damron, erstwhile circuit judge of Mingo County, praised as a fine citizen before the Kenyon investigation committee. If judges in Mingo were like this, what must the "criminal element" have been? Several notches above the judges, without doubt.

All the evidence points to the conclusion that Sid Hatfield and Ed Chambers were lured to Welch, with the connivance of C.E. Lively and the "legal" authorities of at least one county, in order that the Baldwin-Felts detectives might kill them and thus avenge the killing of their brother-rat at Matewan. For Sally Chambers, in wild grief on the courthouse steps at Welch, cried to one of the Baldwin men: "Oh, Mr. Salter, oh, what did you all do this for? We did not come up here for this."

And the coal company gunman replied: "Well, that is all right, we didn't come down to Matewan on the 19th day for this either."

## Lively Still Around

Thus, in a most final manner, was Sid Hatfield denied his change of venue. C.E. Lively was tried for the murder of Ed Chambers. Without a blush, he pled "self-defense." The jury was stacked, the prosecution half-hearted, and Lively, to the surprise of no one in coal operators' West Virginia, was acquitted. No one was ever brought to trial for the murder of Sid Hatfield.

And so we have a picture of the activities of the Baldwin-Felts detectives in West Virginia. The story is incomplete, and the many criminal actions of the organization will never be brought to light. But this portion of the life of C.E. Lively will help form an idea of just what the coal operator tactics were, and also show just why the miners hated the Baldwin men. Lively continued to give evidence against the UMW in later trials, and is reported to now be living in the coal fields around Lochgelly, W. Va. We trust that he continued the good work for the coal companies for a long time after he killed Ed Chambers and Sid Hatfield.

12/24/1952 (Twenty-sixth)

Before leaving the Baldwin-Felts Detective Agency we should like to quote a letter in full, written by Operative 24 of that organization. It is not only good evidence of the thorough spying which the Baldwin men did for the operators, but it gives an excellent description of how the miners organized in Mingo in 1920. The letter is self-explanatory. Oh, yes, it happens that it was taken from the corpse of Albert Felts, when he was killed at Matewan:

"Mr. George Bausewine, Jr.
"Secretary, Operators' Association of Williamson Field (The Williamson field made up of Mingo County, W. Va. and Pike County, Ky.) Williamson, West Virginia

"Dear Sir: I quote you below, report received from Operative 24, dated Matewan, May 14:

"There was a mass meeting of the miners here tonight, which was attended by about 500 men. The speaking was done in the open between the railroad depot and the street. Mother Jones did not arrive, neither were there any district or national men present. Preacher Combs, who is well known and who has been signing up the men, was the first speaker, following (sic) by a Negro preacher named Johnson. The meeting was opened with a song and a prayer, after which Combs made a radical talk, in which he said that the operators bitterly opposed the Union and had managed to keep most of the poor miners in ignorance of the benefits derived from the Union by telling them that the Union was composed of loafers and men who did not want to earn a living by work. He said: 'I am here to say that we do not want to work but we want to earn,' that the operator wanted the miners to load by the ton of 2,000 pounds to the ton. (Op 24 had bad ears in this instance. It was the miner who wanted to load by the ton of 2,000 pounds, not the long ton, and not by the unstamped car, as in nonunion Mingo.) He said that the operators were telling the men that they were now paying them more than the Union scale, and that if this was true, why didn't the operators sign up with the Union and take it off of the men, that the men did not want to take it off the operators; that all they wanted was the Union scale and recognition.

## Operators Use 'Yellow-Dog'

"Combs said the operators accused the miners of criminal acts and that they would burn the tipples and blow up the miners, but that this statement was not true; that there was not a miner in Mingo County who would be guilty of such an act, and that the companies need not nail up the drift mouths and bring in a carload of men to guard the tipples: that the miners only wanted fair treatment and that they were going to have it. He said all business men were organized and that if the laborers did not organize that they would always be in bondage – to do the bidding of the capitalist. He said the superintendents were going to all the members with a paper to be signed, which was an agreement that the miner would sign his birthright away for five years' house rent. Combs said that no man would sign it; that those who did sign it were not as good as a yellow dog.

"He stated that the superintendent or operator who would ask his fellow man to sign such a paper did not have a heart, that he carried a gizzard around in a heart's place. He said he hoped the men would all go home and tell their wives that they had decided to make a change: to tell her that they were going to recognize the miners as human beings, and that they intended to give them their just dues – a part of what they earn. He said the Negroes were once in bondage and

Abraham Lincoln gave them their freedom, and now the miners, both black and white, were in bondage and that the United Mine Workers were going to give them their liberty. He said the sheriff was one man who had lived up to his promises when he was a candidate for office, and that if he continued to do so, he would be elected to any office in the county that he asked for.

## Miners Sign Up

"The Negro speaker was comical and caused much laughter by his speaking. One of his remarks was that if wouldn't be a Union man, he would go home and ask his wife to chain him in the yard with the dog.

"After the speaking, some new miners signed up. I do not know how many, but I saw about 200 go into the hall. I did not hear any expressions from the business men of Matewan and do not know how they feel toward the union. There were some miners at the speaking from Glen Alum. I noticed two Italians and one American man at the speaking, and all left on No. 2 Saturday morning for Glen Alum.

"Judge Evans came to Matewan on Train No. 2 Saturday morning. I was informed that he had been employed by the Union as their attorney. George Allen, a merchant from Thacker, was present at the speaking. After the speaker had finished, he took the soap box and informed the men that he had been a miner 11 years, but was now engaged in the merchandise business in Thacker, and that some of the miners of Thacker mines wanted a place to meet and organize. He said that his place of business was at their disposal and that they could hold their meetings there, and if there wasn't enough room in his place they could get a house on the Kentucky side of the river.

Yours very truly, T.L. Felts."

The killing of Sid Hatfield had an important effect on the coal miners of West Virginia, but this will be taken up in its proper chronological sequence. Let us continue with what was happening in Mingo County in the early summer of 1920.

## Miners Threaten Strike

Some 2,800 miners had been locked out of their jobs and thrown out of their homes. This meant that nearly 10,000 men, women and children were living in tents and shacks while the coal companies attempted to starve them into submission. The principal tent colonies in Mingo were near Holan and Hermit and Lick Creek and Sprig. Every week the UMW international organizers dispensed relief, as was at that time required by the UMW constitution. The operators attempted to stop this by arresting the international man. They succeeded only temporarily.

In keeping with historical precedent, the coal operators brought in strike-breakers. And, as in previous strikes, the Union men shamed many of them into going back home. During one week in the Mingo County town of Williamson, 200 strike-breakers were sent back home by the UMW, the Union paying their transportation. The state police had been formed just a short time before under Governor Cornwell, who was still in office at this time. The legislation creating the state police was bitterly opposed by the miners for they knew the record of such officers in the neighboring state of Pennsylvania. They feared similar use of the state men in West Virginia.

These police were present in some numbers in Mingo, in addition to the Baldwin-Felts detectives. And the miners found their fears to be true. The state police, to put it mildly, were not friendly. The miners at the time called them "Cossacks."

The situation in Mingo was still in the lock-out stage, and District 17 President C.F. Keeney was making efforts to meet with the operators of the Williamson Field. But the operators answered with a scurrilous letter, which Keeney read from the courthouse steps in a speech at Williamson. On June 22, 1920, a convention of miners at Williamson asked that one more effort be made to affect a meeting with the operators; that if the operators again refused to negotiate a strike would be called.

12/26/1952 (Twenty-seventh)

On June 26 Keeney sent a wire to 71 coal companies:

"Dear Sir: In compliance with the instructions of the delegate convention of sub-district

No. 2 of District 17 of the United Mine Workers of America, recently held in the city of Williamson, W. Va., representing all of the organized miners of Mingo County, W. Va., and that part of Pike County, Ky. bordering on Tug River, I desire to request that you meet the representatives of our organization in an effort to negotiate a wage agreement for this section, and to arrive at an amicable settlement of all matters in difference between the miners and their respective employers.

"There is certainly no valid reason why the same harmony and good will that prevails in other large organized industries should be absent in such an important industry as that of coal mining, and it is with this feeling that we solicit your cooperation and make this request.

"Trusting that we may have an early reply indicating your willingness to cooperate with us in promoting harmony in this industry. I am pleased to remain,
        Yours very truly,
        C.F. Keeney."

Most of the coal companies replied by letter in no uncertain terms. One sent a telegram which will give an idea as to the general tone of all:

"Your wire twenty-sixth. We have no organization in this section: our men working every day making big wages, and most kindly relations and perfect understanding exist between our employees and the company. Our men bitterly opposed to your irresponsible organization, and we respectfully but emphatically decline to meet you or your representatives.

"G.C. Woods,

"Gen. Mgr. Tierney Mining Co."

## Operators Are Unbending

However, three tipple mines and 19 tiny "wagon" mines in Mingo did sign contracts with the UMW effective July 30, 1920 and extending through March 31, 1922. This, however, had no effect on the main situation in bloody Mingo. The attitude of the operators is again given quite frankly in a statement they prepared for the Senators who investigated the strike which was attracting nationwide notice:

"Under no circumstances whatever will the operators of the Mingo field recognize the United Mine Workers of America or any of its officials or representatives: we will not establish any business relations with them, because we have now all the men we can possibly use, and in many instances we are under contract to keep them as long as their work is satisfactory.

"First. They propose and defiantly proclaim that they will take our property from us and appropriate it to their own use without paying us one cent of consideration therefore.

"Second. They will not respect their contracts with their employers, but break them at will and stop work whenever required so to do by their national officers, although they have no complaints or grievance against their employer.

"Third. They look upon and treat as their deadly enemy every executive, administrative, and legislative official who seeks to preserve law and order.

"Fourth. They endeavor to deprive us and our employees of our lawful and constitutional rights to contract with each other, and peaceably pursue our occupations.

## Call UMW Conspiracy

"Fifth. The organization itself is a conspiracy to commit robbery by force and arms, resulting in the assassination and murder of innocent men, women and children.

"Sixth. The courts have found that it is an unlawful conspiracy per se: and is engaged in an attempt to destroy the coal mining industry of West Virginia.

"Seventh. To deal with them in any form necessarily means the recognition of their organization and its right to prescribe terms and conditions of employment.

"With such a band of men as this, with their avowed purpose and object, we will have no business relations under any consideration.

"Operators' Association of the Williamson Field."

It may easily be seen that the coal operators of Mingo were in no conciliatory mood.

Perhaps we might look still further into the "most kindly relations and perfect understanding," to repeat the words of Mr. Woods of the Tierney Mining Co., which existed between employer and employee in Mingo County. A fine example may be found in the case of Frank Ingham, a Negro who had, in 1921, mined coal for 30 years, 14 of those years in Mingo County. His story is rather long, but it will be given fully, as it is in many ways typical of the experiences of hundreds of miners who were blessed with the kindliness and understanding of the coal operators. Frank speaks:

**Blessing of the Blacklist**

"When I joined the Union I was discharged, and notice was served on me by the constable, William Blair, of Mingo County, to vacate the company's premises, and the notice said five days from date, and that was given to me on Friday, and it was two days that had passed, and I only had three days in which to vacate the premises, including Sunday.... I went to McVeigh, Ky., about 11 miles from Williamson, and went to work for the Pond Creek Coal Co. I worked there for two weeks, when Mr. Hogan, the manager, came to the mine and says, 'Frank, I have had a telephone message from the manager of the mine that you left, and he says that you belonged to the union, and he advised us to get rid of you.'

"I says, 'All right, Mr. Hogan.' and I left there then and came to Alfex, and I only worked there five days before Mr. Lecky discharged me for the same thing.

"I came back to West Virginia and went to L.G. Brady, and I said, 'I have been blacklisted by the operators after serving about 30 years in the mines, and I would like to get some work to do to make an honest living.' He says, 'All right, Frank.' I went there and went to work and my wife was teaching school at the place I was discharged from at the time I joined the Union, and (she) told me that I had better not come out in that district any more, not even to the school house, because if I did it would not be good for me. I went to the superintendent of the Lee District Board of Education and asked him to transfer my wife to some other place to teach and I explained the conditions surrounding the case to him, and he said no, that he could not transfer her...."

12/27/52 (Twenty-eight)

Ingham then relates that the operator who had fired him and had him blacklisted asked him to come back to work, which Ingram did. But he is again discharged after about six weeks.

"The reason that he gave for discharging me the last time was that all of the white men that had joined the union, he had discharged them, and he said that he was going to put all of the colored fellows back to work and put the colored fellows in the place of all these white fellows, and I told him that I did not think that would be a very safe thing to do, from the fact that it would terminate in a race riot, and I would not like to see my people in anything like that because they were outnumbered so far in Mingo County. He said that he was going to discharge them, and he called them by very abusive names, and put colored fellows in their places, and I – I told the colored people in justice to themselves, that they cannot afford to take those peoples places.

"My motive for advising the people was, I am the pioneer colored man in that part of the country. I worked for two years in the mines before any more colored people went to work on that creek. Before that they had been denied the privilege of working in those mines, and since they have got well established in there, many of them had found employment there. I did not want them to make enemies of the white race by taking their places that they had been discharged from, and when I intervened in the interests of myself and my people he told me my tongue was too long, with an oath, and to get out and stay out."

Thus did Ingham incur the enmity of the coal operators in Mingo County. He was a Union man and a leader of the Negro people in his area. Such a man, according to coal operator psychology, had to be "taught a lesson." Frank Ingham describes his higher education as follows:

## Majesty of the Law

"On the morning of August 8, 1920, my wife and I left Williamson, W.Va., (McDowell County), to visit my sister who lived there. We made the trip safely, and after reaching Anawalt my wife decided to spend a while with a sister.

"I left Anawalt on August 10, 1920, for Williamson, W.Va. I had to change trains at Welch, W. Va., from the Tug Fork branch. This I did about 3:30p.m.

"Just as train No. 1 came into the station I was arrested by a Mr. Collins, a prohibition officer, who searched me in front of the station, marched me to the station where he was joined by Ed Johnson, a deputy sheriff, and a Mr. Crider, a deputy sheriff and a prohibition officer. These men said, "We should not put this d------ in jail, but should riddle his body with bullets here on the street." Whereupon I asked, 'Gentlemen, what is you charge against me?' Their reply was, 'Move on, open your mouth and we will blow your brains out.' They marched me on to the jail, stopping in the jail office, they searched me and my belongings, which consisted of my clothing, traveling bag and other papers. I was then taken down on the lower floor of Welch jail where there was no other prisoner. About 30 minutes later the high sheriff, S.A. Daniels, came down, and I asked, 'Sheriff, could I see Lawyer Joe Crockett? He knows me and may be able to tell me why I am detained.' Daniels replied, with an oath, that he would not let me see anyone. Then I asked if I could get a message back to Anawalt to my wife that she may know that I am detained at Welch. The sheriff replied, 'The only message that you can get out of here to anyone will be to God and unless you hurry you will fail in that.' Then others came down and all held a whispered conversation, and went out.

## Smuggles Word Outside

"I then called to the prisoners above, and said to them. 'I believe they are planning to mob me.' These prisoners did not share my opinion, saying, 'They have had other Union men in here and did not let them talk to anyone or see anyone but kept them a while and turned them out.' I then told them that I did not believe the officers would treat me that way, adding that about midnight I thought they would take me out and mob me, but if I could get word out, that someone would come to my relief. The prisoners said that if I had a dollar they would smuggle a letter to the post office for me. I told them I had no paper or envelopes, after which they reached down a writing tablet, envelopes and pencil. I then wrote a letter to Mr. C.H. Workman, Williamson. W. Va., telling him that I was in Welch jail, McDowell County, and that the authorities there would not allow me to see a lawyer or anyone, and to please come or send someone to my rescue. I handed this letter up to the prisoner, and he called a lady, and asked her if she would mail it, and after she went out he called to me saying 'Your letter is gone to the post office.' I paid this prisoner one dollar.

"At midnight the sheriff, S.A. Daniels, came down and said, 'Get up and come up in the office, there is some men that want to talk with you.' I did so and found seven men in the office, and two automobiles standing outside in front of the office.

"The officers pointed to the front car and said to me, 'Get in that car, some men down the road wanted me to make a statement.' I said to them, 'Gentlemen, this is an unusual hour to take a prisoner out of jail and carry him down the road to make a statement, whatever this statement is. I would prefer to make it here.' Whereupon Officer Crider struck me on the head with an iron club and drew a pair of suspenders from his coat pocket and twisted them around my wrists. Then the officers picked me up and shoved me into the automobile, three of them getting in the auto with me and four in the rear car. They then drove off westward to about a mile and one-half between Welch and Hemphill. Here they stopped in a strip of woods and pulled me out of the car and dragged me about one hundred yards from the road into the woods. Then they began beating me over the head and back with clubs. This they continued to do so long as they thought there was life in me. Then they drew away from me and stood talking for a while among themselves. Then Edward Johnson, a deputy sheriff under S.A. Daniels, came back to me and kicked me in the face and took from my pockets my purse containing twenty-five dollars and seven cents, a receipt from R.H. Campbell and one from Dentist Amburgy. Then he left me and joined the six men, all going out to the road, got in their cars and drove back toward Welch.

## Gets No Redress

"When the noise of the cars was out of my hearing I raised my head from the ground, and saw my blood in pools on the ground where I had lain. I sat there for about three minutes, struggled to my feet and staggered out to the railroad, as my hands were still tied and I was weak and very sore. I walked to a coaling station which was a very short distance away, finding there an engineer and fireman who saw my condition and asked me what the trouble was. I told them I had been in the hands of a mob. They wished to know what the mob had me for. I told them I was a member of the United Mine Workers of America. They said that this is a shame, and asked me where I was going. I told them I wanted to go to

Williamson. They said you cannot catch a train
going that way and for me to wait there until we
back up to Wilcoe and get our train and we will
pick you up as we come down and take you to
Williamson. This they did, I arrived in Williamson on the morning of August the 11$^{th}$, 1920,
about eight o'clock and left on train No. 15 the
same day for Charleston, W. Va., to see Governor Cornwell, who promised to investigate. A
week later I received a letter from the Governor,
saying, 'That each county in the state had its own
local government, and the law only made it possible for the Governor to cooperate with the
county authorities in preserving law and order
and there were many things that he would do different from what he was then doing if the law
made it possible for him to act.'

"To this date I've never gotten any redress."

12/30/1952 (Twenty-ninth)

The date Frank Ingham is referring to is 1921,
but it is just as true that he has yet received no redress in
the waning days of the year 1952. Somehow the legal
flunkies of the coal operators in Mingo and McDowell
Counties seemed immune to legal action. This may well
have been because there were legal flunkies higher up
in the governmental scale in West Virginia.

Which brings us to a consideration of John J.
Cornwell, who was governor of the Mountain State in
1920, and is now publisher of the weekly newspaper,

*The Hampshire Review.* This will be brief, as Cornwell's anti-union bias has already been shown earlier in this work in reference to a miners' march in 1919. Evidence that he has not changed has been seen in his cooperation in publicity matters with J.G. Bradley, president of the Elk River Coal & Lumber Company at Widen, an operation currently (December, 1952) on strike. Bradley is importing strikebreakers and hiring armed mine guards and "deputy sheriffs" in the traditional West Virginia manner. Cornwell is abetting him editorially. When Cornwell left the governorship he became an attorney for the B. & O. Railroad, and in 1923 and 1924 aided the presidential candidacy of notorious union-hater John W. Davis, once of Clarksburg, W. Va., Davis at this time is arguing before the United States Supreme Court to maintain Negro segregation in the nation's schools.

Perhaps two incidents of Cornwell's career as 15th governor of West Virginia will bear repeating. He tells of them in his autobiography, *A Mountain Trail*, published in 1939. There was a rumor, according to Cornwell that the miners were going to march again, and that they were getting guns from a New York dealer for $1 apiece.

## Cornwell Hires Detective

So the governor hired a detective to watch the trains coming from the East. The man reported that guns were going to the secretary of a UMW local Union in Boone County. So Cornwell prepared a warrant, citing the Red Man Act, ordering seizure of the guns as evidence. Deputy Sheriff Given of Kanawha County served the warrant and returned to Charleston with a boy and two truckloads of guns and ammunition. This boy, Cornwell says, is the only person ever arrested in West Virginia on a Governor's Warrant, and the former chief executive seems rather proud of his distinguished "first." However, it developed that the boy was the wrong person, and he was released.

The other incident bearing on Union affairs involved an election, probably about 1919, of the president of UMW District 17. C.F. Keeney was running for reelection. About 11 p.m. one night, Governor Cornwell received a telephone call from a man who said he wanted to see him at the rear of the gubernatorial mansion. With what might seem a lack of caution the Governor agreed to meet this perfect stranger, and so did. The man explained that he was opposing Keeney for the District 17 presidency and feared that he would be shot. So he wanted a permit to carry a gun. He had come to the Governor because the statute required a notice in the newspapers. The man wished to have the statutory requirement waived; that is, he wanted a pistol right that minute. Cornwell said that he couldn't do that, but, "if you do carry a gun and use it only in self-defense, and you should be convicted, I could and would pardon you." The unidentified aspirant to Union office, who would certainly have been a willing operator tool, judging by this evidence, then demonstrated that he considered his friendship with the Governor to have reached a really fraternal basis: He asked for $45 with which to buy a gun!

Cornwell apparently did not feel that their friendship had reached this stage, for he refused the money. But by a happy coincidence there was a pistol concealed behind a picture above the mantel on which his visitor was leaning. The Governor agreed to lend him this weapon. The man then glanced to see that it was loaded, stuck it into his pocked and let him out through the back door....

> "The only explanation of this indiscreet performance of mine," says Cornwell, "is that I thought the man was honest and square."

Whatever the explanation the above is as Cornwell gives it in his book, and it must be pronounced as most unusual behavior for the Chief Executive of a state – or at least as most unusual RECORDED behavior. Nothing further concerning Cornwell need be mentioned except that he employed a "work-or-fight" law before the federal draft of civilians went into effect in 1917, using as a pretext a "shortage of labor." Under the provisions of this act a census form was prepared which, in the words of the Governor, "was a thing of beauty, for there was no part of a man's life neglected in it." These census forms were given to mayors of all towns who then gave them to police who had the job of tracking down men not gainfully employed. The idea apparently was to force into the Army all men not then employed!

**Same Old Team**

How this law could be used in a strike situation is obvious. That it was so used is not at this time known.

The federal draft started in July and very soon there was a real labor shortage as men were swallowed up into the AEF. It should be noted that Cornwell's draft officer was Col. George S. Wallace, who was the military equivalent of prosecuting attorney of the Paint Creek secret military trials of coal miners during the 1912-13 strike.

Likewise to be recorded is the fact that his adjutant general was Maj. Tom Davis. It will be recalled that Davis had also formerly served the coal operators on Cabin and Paint creeks by being, in effect, a strikebreaker. He was the man who arrested the editor of the labor paper at Huntington, wrecking his print shop in the process. And, in this Mingo strike, Tom Davis was again a military aide of the coal operators.

As has been related, the miners of Mingo County, in late June, 1920, made a final attempt to face the coal operators over the bargaining table. Their approach was rejected, and, as scheduled, a strike was declared effective on July 1. This made little or no difference in the actual situation, as coal production, except for that of imported "transportation men" had already ceased in Mingo County.

# Chapter Six: Coal Operators Defy U.S.

The Federal Government interceded in July by sending two mediators from the Labor Department to West Virginia. These men met C.F. Keeney at the Virginia Hotel in Williamson, but the Mingo operators refused to consult with the federal officials. The following proposition was submitted to the mine owners through the Department of Labor.

"THE WILLIAMSON OPERATORS' ASSOCIATION

"GENTLEMEN: During the last few weeks trouble has existed between the operators and the miners of the district which has reached a stage wherein certain coal mines have been closed down by a strike of the miners: efforts were made to adjust the difficulties, but neither side would waive from their original stand in order that the matter might be settled in a fair and equitable manner and in the interest of the public.

"The government had data and information that serious trouble is probable, constant agitation is on which might result in further loss of life and possible damage to property. The coal situation is such that the government demands immediate settlement of this controversy in order to allow production to continue. The government, desiring to always deal justly with problems of this character, has given this matter fair consideration from the standpoint of both employer and employee, therefore, as representatives of the government, we submit to you the following proposition:

"1 – The government is in favor of the policy of collective bargaining and advises that the policy be put in effect. There are two types of collective bargaining as thus defined: one in which the employees act as a group through the trade union. The other in which a group of employees are represented by committees to confer with employers regarding conditions of employment.

"2 – There shall be no discrimination against employees in the exercise of their constitutional right to belong to any organization.

"3 – All employees evicted from homes shall be restored immediately and no discrimination whatsoever as to eligibility to employment shall be made against any one of said workmen on account of said strike or their participation therein.

"4 – We recommend the removal of the private agencies now employed and that the regular constituted authority of county and state being invoked in the preservation of law and order in this district, provided such becomes necessary.

"Subscribed and agreed to this ---- day of July, 1920."

The coal operators of Mingo County did not, of course, agree to any such thing, and the strike continued. The Labor Department men went back to Washington and nothing was done by the coal operators to implement the expressed wishes of the United States Government. The government rather pointedly refrained from taking action to enforce its demands upon the operators, and on July 31, 1920, President Woodrow Wilson wrote the UMW that

"It is with a feeling of profound regret and horror that I have learned that many of the members of your organization, particularly in the State of Illinois, have engaged in a strike in violation of the terms of the award of the Bituminous Coal Commission and your agreement with the government that the findings of the commission would be accepted by you as final and binding."

The truth was that the last Wilson administration, despite the reputation of the President in some liberal circles, was a very long distance from being sympathetic with the aims of Labor. This has been demonstrated in the account of the breaking of the national coal strike of 1919 through a forced interpretation of the applicability of the unconstitutional Lever Act.

This was also the time of the great steel strike, when nearly 400,000 steel workers walked off their jobs only to be beaten in early 1920. The post World War I era, it may readily be seen, was a time of great social unrest. In Russia there had been a revolution, and many were the large industrialists who feared that the same thing would occur here. They took steps to see that it did not. A great "Red Scare" was started, with the aid of the press and legislative business sycophants. The bearded Bolshevik with his bomb was a familiar cartoon subject. Attorney General A. Mitchell Palmer, before mentioned in his connection with breaking the 1919 coal strike, was making raids on all sides.

Eugene Victor Debs was still in jail, and Wilson refused to release him. On Jan. 2, 1920 the Department of Justice arrested 2,758 men and women and held 556 aliens for deportation. By the beginning of February more than 10,000 persons had been arrested because of their real or supposed radicalism. The country seemed to have gone mad over the "Red Menace," and federal and state governments ignored constitutional guarantees while private vigilantes committed acts of terror.

## Miners Called 'Bolsheviks'

Such was the atmosphere in which the miners of Mingo were conducting their strike. It may well be believed that they were the targets of many accusations of Bolshevik sympathies. These accusations the miners shrugged off, as they saw that they came from the camp of the enemy. For some years the Union miners in West Virginia who were on strike had worn red bandanas around their necks in order to be able to distinguish friend from foe. From this habit the Union men had come to be called "Rednecks," and they accepted the title rather proudly. But there was not necessarily any political implication in the term. A strong Union man was a Redneck, no matter what his politics.

The struggle in Mingo and the other nonunion counties in W. Va. was an economic, trade Union battle, not a political one. The political attitudes of the miners of West Virginia in 1920 should, however, be discussed. The coal operators had been red-baiting the UMW and the miners since at least 1912, as has been noted briefly in our discussion of the 1912-13 strike. The mine owners complained that the UMW was a socialist organization which had in mind the utter confiscation of their property. This they used as an excuse for their inexcusable unwillingness to participate in collective bargaining.

It may have been that some of the miners in West Virginia, as well as some of their leaders, did in 1920 have some sympathy for the new-born Soviet Union, but this was not a factor in their strike. Certain it is that Mother Jones did, as in her autobiography she tells of a speech she made before the Pan-American Federation of Labor in 1921, when she was 91 years old. "Soviet Russia, I said, had dared to challenge the old order, had handed the earth over to those who toiled upon it, and the capitalists of the world were quaking in their scab-made shoes." But Mother Jones was never a Communist, nor even a Socialist, though many of her remarks have a Marxist flavor.

1/2/1953 (Thirty-first)

But the general rule was that the leadership in the UMW, both nationally and on a state level, was more conservative politically than the membership. The coal operators based their "socialism" charges against the UMW on a change, made in 1912, in the preamble to the UMW national constitution. This was the year in which American Social Democracy, or Socialism, probably reached its zenith. Mighty Socialist orators, headed by Gene Debs, spread the new gospel of the workingman through opera houses and chautauguas; mighty Socialist writers, headed by the famous Jack London did likewise. No man who toiled for a living had not heard of Socialism in 1912. The miners of West Virginia had most emphatically heard of it, and many of them had seen the great Debs in person as he helped them in their strike struggles.

It was natural that many should embrace the economic philosophy of a government owned and controlled by workingmen. It was all too painfully obvious that the miners were getting very little from a state government owned and controlled by the coal operators.

But the Socialists in the UMW were a tiny minority, even in the peak year of 1912. The movement, however, was of such vigor that it came up for discussion in the UMW's 23$^{rd}$ Annual Convention which assembled in that year. For some little time prior to 1912 there had been dissatisfaction in the ranks of Labor with the treatment given the worker by the Democratic and Republican parties. There were many indications that Labor wished to form its own political party.

**Resolution Introduced**

It was, therefore, very logical that the following resolution be introduced at the UMW Convention: "To the officers and delegates of the Twenty-third Annual Convention:

"Whereas we believe that the emancipation of the workers can only be accompanied through the action of the workers as a class; and

"Whereas in the class struggle between the capitalist class and the working class, the workers should avail themselves of every weapon at their command; and

"Whereas the ballot is one of the most powerful weapons in the hands of the working class; and,

"Whereas the workers should work in Union and harmony on both the industrial and political fields; and,

"Whereas the Socialist Party has always and everywhere proved itself the champion of the working class; Therefore be it.

"RESOLVED. That we, the mine workers of the entire country, adopt and indorse the Socialist Party as the political party of the working class, and urge all workers to rally under the banner of universal brotherhood. And be it further

"RESOLVED. That we request the officers and delegates of said convention of the United Mine Workers of America to adopt these or similar resolution,

"David McKee, Secretary Local 1771
"Anton Trotter.
"S.A. Woodbury."

**A Delegate Speaks**

It seems that most of the support for the resolution came from the Illinois delegation. A delegate from UMW District 12 had this to say:

> "I am in favor of an industrial organization for the purpose of educating the workers politically. It is the only school the workers of this country have got. The workers of this country have got to organize politically if we ever expect to get out of the old rut we are in. If we have been making a mistake for all these years, for heaven's sake, let's get wise. If we have not got a remedy, let's get one, and if the Socialist Party is the remedy – and I believe it is – let's get into it and vote right."

As stated, the resolution to endorse the Socialist Party was not adopted, but the Socialists did succeed in getting the other UMW members to insert a bit of Socialist phraseology into the preamble to the Union constitution. It did not amount to much. Prior to 1912 the preamble asserted that the miners were entitled to "an equitable share of the fruits of their labor." For this phrase the Convention substituted "the full social value of our product."

The West Virginia coal operators were still wailing about this in 1920, giving this change in the preamble, which meant not a thing in actual practice despite the theoretical implications, as the reason for refusing to negotiate with the UMW. They pointed to the alleged fact that District 17 President C.F. Keeney and Secretary-Treasurer Fred Mooney, as well as Sub-district No. 2 President William Blizzard and UMW attorney Harold Houston, were or had been Socialists, hoping in this way to vindicate their own obduracy.

## Strike Economic Issue

That the West Virginia Union leaders in 1920 might once have been Socialists had no bearing on the strike then in progress. The fact was that the Socialist Party had been a casualty of World War I, for all practical purposes, and there was no organization in West Virginia. Again and again and again, the 1920-21 strike in West Virginia was an economic, trade union battle, not a political demonstration. The coal miners were treated as less than citizens of a free republic, they had no redress from any governmental body, and, like brave men, they preferred armed revolt to abject slavery. That is the story in a nutshell. With the death of the Socialist Party the miners had, as a group, no special political direction in West Virginia in 1920. The same is true today.

To revert to what was happening in Mingo County in the summer of 1920: No coal was being mined. State police were everywhere in evidence. The coal operators had, besides employing the Baldwin-Felts detectives, hired a great number of "volunteer" policemen. Many were members of the American Legion, who were given a gun and told to "preserve law and order." As they were paid by the coal operators, their definition of law and order might have been subject to some bias. At one time there were 780 of these "volunteers" hired in the Williamson Field.

This practice happened to be illegal, as a West Virginia statute forbade the hiring of mine guards except by a county court through public funds. Harry Olmstead, coal operator spokesman in Mingo explained the hiring of a few of these men as follows: "By agreement with the circuit judge and the governor and the county court of Mingo County, we paid about $1,800 for these deputy sheriffs, with the understanding with the county court that that money would be returned when they had it available to pay back." In other words, a law which inconvenienced the operators was ignored, with the calm agreement of the officials who were supposed to enforce same!

1/3/1953 (Thirty-second)

The operators had also seen to it that they had good "public relations" in Mingo County, although one might have thought they would have been satisfied with the coverage they were receiving from the regular West Virginia press. It seems well established that they bought the *Williamson Daily News* and hired a George Booten as its editor. We quote from one editorial in order to give the reader an idea as to its general tone. Events alluded to will be explained later:

"A few weeks ago we had C.F. Keeney issuing pronunciamentos and announcements with respect to what he would do to help restore order and reestablish the supremacy of the law in West Virginia, and the conditions under which he would do it.

"Then came John L. Lewis to tell both President Harding and Governor Morgan what he was willing to do to help out the State and National Governments, and the conditions under which he would do it.

"Now we have Harold W. Houston denouncing Governor Morgan and instructing the public in regard to what had failed to be done and what should be done with respect to the recent insurrection in this State and the present pervading unrest.

"This is impudence run mad.

"Each of these men aided, abetted, and encouraged the insurrectionists in their mad march from the heart of Kanawha County to the edge of Logan, and each is liable to indictment for murder and larceny, if not for treason. Instead of being given newspaper space in which to publish their insolent outpouring they should each be given jail space until the juries of Logan and Boone counties can have opportunity to send them to the penitentiary or to the gallows."

Such was the calm journalism of the coal operators of the Williamson Field.

## Army Moves to Mingo

Meanwhile a grand jury had indicted Sid Hatfield and others for the killing of the Baldwin-Felts guards at Matewan. Anse Hatfield, a cousin of Sid's had testified against his relation and in August was shot dead by an unknown assailant on the front porch of his hotel in the same Mingo County town. Governor Cornwell evidently used this incident as a reason for calling for federal troops. He maintained that his state police were not sufficient to keep order, and that a great number of threatening letters had been received by a number of people, including the deceased Anse Hatfield.

On August 29, 1920 a battalion of infantry, consisting of about 500 men, arrived in Mingo County, where they camped on Sycamore Creek, near Williamson. They were equipped with rifles, machine guns, trucks, motorcycles and a one-pound cannon. After a conference between their commander, Col. Samuel Burkhart, Jr., and acting Adjutant Gen. Thomas B. Davis, the soldiers were scattered in groups of ten or more at mining camps along a 35-mile range of territory.

With the strikers facing federal bayonets they could do little but stare helplessly as imported strikebreakers took their jobs. However, it appears that bringing in the soldiers the first time was a bluff on the part of Governor Cornwell, in the hope that the miners would be frightened into submission. For the troops stayed only a few days, leaving on Nov. 4. Cornwell took the opportunity to warn the miners, when the soldiers decamped, that if it became necessary to call them back "They will be vested with full power to suppress lawlessness and preserve order."

A free translation of this official language (and the miners understood the language well) might run as follows: "Unless you striking miners sit idly by and let the coal operators break your strike the militia will be called in with orders to shoot to kill."

## Miners Use Guns

Striking West Virginia coal miners, however, were and are exceedingly hard to bluff. They were miserable in their tents and not eating too well and watching other men deprive them of their livelihoods. And they had rifles concealed in the woods. It can not be denied that they used them, although a vast amount of shooting was done more in order to shatter the morale of the scabs than to shoot to kill. The coal operators replied with guard-mounted machine guns. This incessant nightly gunfire had the desired effect, apparently, on the nerves of the strikebreakers, many of whom were only too glad to say farewell to the beautiful scenery of West Virginia. And it made the recruiting of the other scabs quite difficult. In fact, there was a grave danger that the miners were going to win their strike in Mingo.

This had to be prevented. On Nov. 27, 1920, Governor Cornwell proclaimed a state of insurrection in that county, and asked President Woodrow Wilson for a declaration of martial law. Wilson refused, but for the second time he consented to send federal troops to the Tug River area. A portion of the 19th Infantry Regiment under Col. Herman Hall established headquarters in the courthouse at Williamson. Governor Edwin P. Morrow of Kentucky honored Cornwell's request to permit troops to patrol the Bluegrass side of the Tug River.

The soldiers settled down to their occupation tasks, the strikers were again frustrated, the influx of scabs mounted, and the coal operators sat behind their machine guns and wondered how long their former employees could hold out.

Winter in the tent colonies of the strikers at Lick Creek and Blackberry City and elsewhere was a numbing, bitter enemy. The snow was a menace and the cold rain a mud-producing curse. The striking miners, with their wives and children, huddled around their little iron stoves and cursed the fact of their compelled inaction. It was a weary day-to-day struggle and Christmas brought little cheer. But the miners held fast, hoping for the withdrawal of the federal troops who were breaking their strike.

The coal operators, however, were grimly content with the situation. They used every maneuver to retain the soldiers in the coal fields while they put ads for "transportation men" in all the large eastern newspapers. But as the new year of 1921 rolled around it became apparent that they could not persuade the Federal Government to use troops as strikebreakers for an indefinite period. Not unless some violent incident could be manufactured. The miners were peaceful under U.S. Army occupation.

1/6/1953 (Thirty-third)

The testimony before the Senate investigating committee of R.H. Kirkpatrick, who had been fired from a job as mine foreman for the Burnwell Coal & Coke Company, gives an idea as to the tactics the operators employed in at least one case in order to keep the soldiers around. The mine had been shut down by the strike when Kirkpatrick took the job on Dec. 15, 1920. He took a small crew and repaired timbers and put the mine back into shape and on Jan. 18, 1921 a large group of scabs were imported by train.

The scabs were escorted by two men who represented themselves to be U.S. Marshals. About ten o'clock that night the two Marshals and the superintendent hatched up a scheme in which Kirkpatrick was an accomplice. There were at that time about 400 federal troops in Mingo County, but none in the coal camp of Burnwell, where this mine was located. And it was rumored that the soldiers were about to go back to Ohio at any time. The superintendent at Burnwell wanted to keep the soldiers to guard his scabs, and get them to come to Burnwell if possible. And so, as stated, a scheme was hatched. Kirkpatrick listened and did as he was told.

He took a group of the scabs up to the mouth of the mine. Some of them were curious for the simple reason that they had never before seen a coal mine. As had been planned, a U.S. Marshal, or deputy, had gone on ahead and was waiting on the hill above. The Marshal opened fire, blazing away right merrily. Kirkpatrick with great bravery stood his ground and returned the fire with a heavy-barking .45 pistol. Not content with this exhibit of intrepidity under fire he seized a rifle and did battle with his imaginary enemy by shooting about 18 times.

## Power of Suggestion

The mine superintendent and the other U.S. Marshal, meanwhile were back at the club house in Burnwell with the excited stories of the mine being shot up by strikers. A little girl, the daughter of a scab, had been so excited by the shooting that she said she had seen six men run as the fearless Kirkpatrick poured hot lead in their direction. This information, with ad lib embellishment, was telephoned to the proper military authorities.

It worked. The federal troops were in Burnwell that very night.

There had been an election in November, 1920, of both state and national officials. Warren G. Harding swept into the White House on the crest of a Republican landslide. In West Virginia, the new governor was Republican Ephraim F. Morgan of coal producing Marion County. Both he and the Republican-dominated legislature had promised the miners relief from the mine guards. How well they redeemed that promise will be seen. There had been an unusual feature in the state elections in that Labor had a gubernatorial candidate in the field. This was Sam Montgomery, who had been a friend of the coal miners for many years. He had at first entered the primaries as a Republican. Defeated there, he had run in the general election on a Labor platform.

On paper, Montgomery was defeated, but many old-timers to this day contend that he actually won. The corruption of West Virginia elections was incredible beyond belief, and Montgomery's supporters declared angrily that Republicans and Democrats had combined to steal the election from their man.

This, needless to say, is not impossible to believe. The coal operators must have received quite a fright from Montgomery's strong showing, for by this date they have seen to it that the entry of any third political party on the scene is almost blocked by varied legal impediments. There is no justification for this at all. It is simply a method used by the machine politicians, to keep a tight rein on the will of the people. And behind the machine politicians, of course, stand the coal operators and other financial interests.

## Morgan and J.G. Bradley

So the coal miners in 1920 got themselves another coal operator servant for a governor. The strikers in Mingo could not look to the state machine for redress, for there had been no real change at the statehouse in Charleston. The coal operators were just as firmly entrenched as ever. The June 8, 1923 issue of the *Unionist*, a trade-union publication, makes the charge that "Ephraim F. Morgan was dragged from the obscurity of the State Public Service Commission by (J.G.) Bradley and elected chief executive for $250,000."

J.G. Bradley was and is the millionaire owner of the Elk River Coal and Lumber Company at Widen, West Virginia, one of the most powerful and viciously anti-union coal operators in the State of West Virginia. Bradley was the head of the West Virginia Coal Operator's Association. This gentleman is still alive, and still owns a sizable segment of Clay County, W. Va., where he runs the only large coal operation in the Mountain State which is nonunion.

Just at this time (Jan., 1953) he is having a little trouble, as most of his miners went on strike in September, 1952, and are still picketing his mines. He has hired a number of mine guards equipped with high-powered rifles, and has imported strikebreakers in the time-honored tradition.

It is a bit aside from our main narrative, but we should like to point up the obvious and tremendous political influence of Bradley. It is impossible to prove just how much money this coal operator has avoided paying in taxes because of his alleged control of the Clay County Board of Equalization and Review. This board sets tax rates, and it is charged that Bradley has always seen that his assessment was comfortably low. In 1923 this feudal king listed the sum of $1,021,111 as the taxable assets of the Elk River Coal and Lumber Company. But there were many in Clay County who confidently placed the real worth at $15,000,000.

1/7/1953 (Thirty-fourth)

The miners in Mingo continued to shiver in their tents and rude shacks and few had confidence in the demagogic promises of Morgan that he would get rid of the mine guards. What the miners could expect from Morgan was very soon demonstrated.

The federal troops finally, on Feb. 16, 1921, left Mingo County. This was evidently over the protests of the coal operators, which is easily understood. After all, it is much cheaper to get the Army to do your strike-breaking. Mine guards cost money, sometimes almost $1,000 a month.

But the federal troops did leave, and the coal operators had to solve their gunman problem in some other way. This they did, as has been before related, by getting American Legion members, small business men and professionals, as well as clerks and other white-collar men dependent upon the coal companies, to serve as policemen. Such "volunteers" were supposed to have been authorized by an extraordinary session of the Legislature in 1919. Who urged the passage of such legislation may be guessed.

Lists of men available for "volunteer" duty were submitted by the coal companies to a committee composed of a Methodist minister, a wealthy jeweler, a coal operator attorney and others for approval. Once approved the men were given guns and put under the command of Captain J.R. Brockus, who headed both the regular state police and the "volunteers." Brockus was a retired Army man the operators presumed had the right degree of toughness, and it was charged by the miners that he had been appointed state police chief before he had resided in West Virginia long enough to become officially a resident!

## No Federal Troops

One reason the bright idea of arming local company men was conceived and acted upon was a War Department ruling that the local officials had to show the federal government that everything possible had been done before they would send troops. The operators were anxious to prove they had worked hard at "law enforcement," because the bringing back of soldiers to patrol the coal camps was an end devoutly to be wished. Just who paid this army of private gunmen is not clear, for they were under the jurisdiction of the state and as such should have been paid by the state. It is likely, we submit, that those for whom they performed the service of strike-breaking saw that they did not go hungry. The "volunteer" dodge was without doubt a legal cover up for the hiring of privately-paid gunmen.

It was resorted to because Governor Morgan had asked for the return of Federal troops not long after he succeeded John J. Cornwell on March 4, 1921. The new President of the United States was Warren G. Harding, much more of an easygoing politician than the rather moralistic Wilson, and he refused Morgan's request, evidently feeling that if the State of West Virginia wanted a strike broken it had to do it itself.

The miners, in the absence of federal coercion, had hunted up their concealed rifles and once again the scabs got very little sleep at night. State police and armed guards did battle with the miners, but were no match for the men who had spent a bitter winter in tents in the West Virginia hills. It seems that on May 12, 13, and 14, 1921, as nearly as it can be placed, a number of battles took place between the striking miners and guards armed with machine guns. It should not be understood that these battles consisted of attacks by strikers and defense by stalwart defenders of the law and order. Ample evidence will be given to show that this was far from the case. On at least one occasion the state police were ordered by their leaders, headed by Major Thomas B. Davis of prior union-busting fame, to "clean out" the tent colonies of strikers.

## Morgan's Martial Law

Who the attackers were in the battles culminating in the three-day war spoken of above is not known. But the battles took place for the most part at or near the strikers' tent colonies. The miners' colony at Blackberry City was shot to pieces, but the attackers did not fare as well as those who burned Ludlow, Colorado to the ground. It will never be known how many men were killed in Mingo District 17. President C.F. Keeney said they "carried men out of the woods for days." Other battles took place around the mining camps of Merrimac, Springg, and McCarr. Captain Brockus claimed that four of his men were killed.

It was at this time that Governor Morgan asked President Harding for federal troops and martial law and was notified of Harding's refusal on May 17, 1921. The next few days were exceedingly full of activity. Coal operator "volunteers" were inducted into the state police. District 17 officials went to Washington to ask for a federal investigation of Mingo County, and C.F. Keeney issued a call to all nonunion miners in Mingo to strike, and he would promise Union benefits and care.

And, on May 19, Governor Morgan issued a proclamation of martial law.

This proclamation will be given rather fully as it is a most amazing document. The miners of Mingo were rather bitter toward the man who just a few months before had campaigned on this platform:

> "We deplore the abuses that have grown up under the so-called private guard or Detective System in this State, and we pledge a Republican Legislature to enact laws that will correct these abuses..."

No such laws had been enforced. Instead, in his martial law proclamation the Governor gave the miners of Mingo more bitter regimentation than they had ever before experienced. After stating that a state of war and insurrection existed in Mingo County, Governor Morgan set up the following rules for the miners to live by:

1/8/1953 (Thirty-fifth)

(Yesterday's installment told of Governor Morgan's proclamation of martial law in Mingo County in 1921. The following were Morgan's directives.)

> "1. No person or persons shall compose or take part in, or encourage, aid, abet or assist any riot, rout, tumult, mob or lawless combination or assemblage, or violate, or encourage, abet or assist in the violation of any of the civil laws of the state of West Virginia.

> "2. No public assemblages or meetings will be permitted in city, town or village, or in any enclosure or open air place within the county, except by special authority.

"3. All processions and parades, except by special authority, are prohibited, as well as demonstrations against the authorities and officers.

"4. No persons, except the constituted municipal, state and federal authorities, militia, troops, police, and other officers of the law, are permitted to carry or have arms or weapons of any character or description or equipment, explosives, ammunition or munitions of war in their possession or at any place, except at their own homes or places of business.

"5. All military and other officers shall have the right of way in any street of highway through which they may pass.

"6. Any person or persons entering or remaining in said Mingo County for the purposes of interfering in any manner whatever with the rights of citizens or property of said Mingo County shall be arrested, detained and imprisoned.

"7. All persons are admonished to observe and carefully and rigidly comply with the civil laws of the state of West Virginia and with the letter and spirit of this proclamation and these rules and orders; and any person or persons violating the same in said Mingo County shall be arrested, disarmed, detained and imprisoned.

"8. Any person or persons, except the constituted municipal state and federal authorities, militia, troops, police, and other officers of the law, carrying or in possession of arms or weapons of any character or description, or equipment, explosives, ammunition or munitions of war, at any place other than at their own homes or places of business, shall be arrested, disarmed, detained and imprisoned.

## Suppression of Press

"9. No publications, either newspaper, pamphlet, hand bill or otherwise, reflecting in any way upon the United States or the state of West Virginia, or their officers, or tending to influence the public mind against the United States or the state of West Virginia, or their officers, may be published, distributed, displayed or circulated in said Mingo County, and the publication, distribution, displaying or circulation of such publication above specified is prohibited, and any person or persons violating this paragraph shall be arrested, detained and imprisoned."

Major Thomas B. Davis was appointed the director who was to enforce the Governor's ukase. On the same day UMW President John L. Lewis told the country: "Peace will not be attained in Mingo County until the operators recognize the fundamental and recognized right of the miner to belong to a Union and to meet in peaceful assembly to discuss the problems and to bargain collectively."

And the Buffalo, N.Y. *Commercial*, like many another newspaper, editorialized.

"The West Virginia miners have no doubt been easy prey for the Bolshevik propaganda of the labor demagogues. It should not be long before even the men lying in ambush in the hills realize that they are merely playing a dangerous game for enemies to their country."

Attorneys for the UMW were quick to point out that the only military "force" in West Virginia was the Adjutant General. For the National Guard had been incorporated into the armed services during part of the regular Army. And the lawyers asserted that the martial law proclamation was invalid without a military force. The State Supreme Court considered the problem, and meanwhile the dictatorship in Mingo County continued. Morgan's first proclamation was evidently not invalidated, but on June 27th the Governor issued another proclamation which fortified the first by creating a "West Virginia Enrolled Militia." This, simply stated, was a draft of enough men to police Mingo County.

Specifically, Morgan's second martial law proclamation authorized the drafting of 130 men in Mingo County, to be made into two military companies of 65 men each. Martial law continued, and under provision No. 9 of Morgan's pronunciamento, the whole of which had the effect of suspending the state and federal constitutions in the affected area, miners were arrested for reading or being caught with copies of the *United Mine Workers' Journal* or the *Federationist*, a labor publication from Charleston.

Shortly after the first in Mingo, Senator Johnson of Colorado introduced a resolution in Congress asking for an investigation of the Tug River area. Johnson evidently took this action at the request of the District 17 officials and attorneys who traveled to Washington for the purpose of securing such an inquiry. It will be noted that it was not the operators who asked that the real facts be brought to light. They were well content with the picture the outside world was receiving via the money-press whose owners were in sympathy with the coal barons.

Senator Johnson's resolution was adopted on May 26, 1921, and a subcommittee of the Senate Education and Labor Committee was designated to visit West Virginia the following week. The Committee actually began hearings on July 14th, and this history could not have been written without a close study of the evidence it procured.

# PHOTOS

The following images are rightly viewed as William C. Blizzard's family album. The Blizzards – Ma, Timothy, Rae, Bill, and no few number of their kin and friends – did the heavy lifting for the United Mine Workers in West Virginia for nearly a half century. Without "young" William C. Blizzard who died in 2008 at the age of 92, they would be forgotten. Yet these hard working ordinary folks rose to the challenge to end the ruthless exploitation of the miners. They provide a critical beacon to future generations that leaders grow from the grass roots and are rarely, if ever, imposed from above.

Each of the following photos is from the William C. Blizzard Collection archived at Appalachian Community Services, unless individually noted.

*Timothy and Rebecca Blizzard*

## Timothy and Rebecca Blizzard

Timothy worked in the mines of Cabin Creek for several years with his son Bill, only later to spend years suffering from black lung (also called "miner's asthma"). Sarah Rebecca was known to join other women in tearing up railway track during the Cabin Creek/Paint Creek struggles in order to prevent coal operator's gunmen from attacking their men folk from handcars. As a result, the women were penned up in a military confinement area.

Years later, to survive during the hard times of the '20's and '30's, she ran a roadside restaurant known as "Ma Blizzard's". Back then hot dogs could be purchased at two for a nickel, including chili and slaw. Granddaughter Margie would visit during her early teens and was instructed on how to pour the beer with lots of foam. This arrangement came to an abrupt halt as soon as father Bill Blizzard learned of his daughter's new "skill."

Timothy Blizzard ( right) with brother Reese.

**Bill Blizzard at about age 17 on Cabin Creek**
Already active in UMW affairs, young Bill was also "trapping" and performing other mine operations.

Lava Rae Cruikshank
circa 1914

Future wife of
Bill Blizzard

Young Bill and Rae
out for a stroll

1921

The Blizzard Family in the early 1920's

Bill and Rae enjoying
each other's company

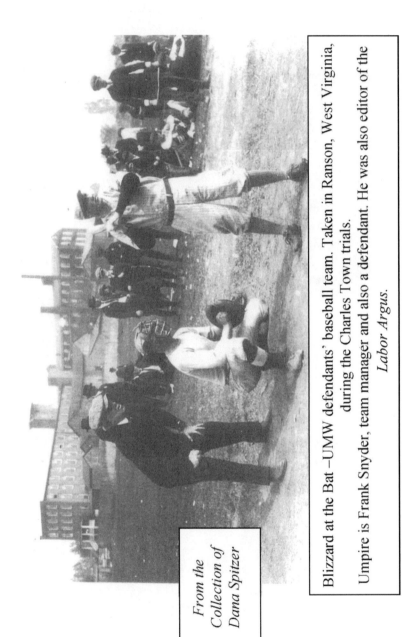

*From the Collection of Dana Spitzer*

Blizzard at the Bat –UMW defendants' baseball team. Taken in Ranson, West Virginia, during the Charles Town trials.
Umpire is Frank Snyder, team manager and also a defendant. He was also editor of the *Labor Argus*.

EX-CIRCUIT JUDGE
EX-U S. ATTORNEY
CORPORATION PRACTICE A SPECIALTY.

*Reese Blizzard*
LAWYER
*Parkersburg, W. Va.*

June 19th, 1923.

William Blizzard, Esq.

Lewisburg, West Virginia,

Dear Nephew,

I wish you would write me, now and then, and tell me
how your trial is getting on, and what you think of things.

You know if there is any thing I can do for you how I
feel about it. I always have an abiding confidence in the
right prevailing. Therefore I have no doubt about your
acquittal.

Please give your counsel my warmest regards, and tell
them that if they know of any thing I can do, to let me
know.

Very sincerely yours,

RB/GL

5. UMW officials, with attorney Harold Houston, at Ronceverte, Greenbrier County, railway depot, before getting aboard to go to Lewisburg, where Blizzard was tried on murder charges in June, 1923, with a "hung jury." Other officials shown here, with exception of Keeney, had charges dropped. Keeney (C. Frank Keeney, District 17 President at that time) was acquitted of murder charges in March, 1924.

Shown here are, left to right: WilliamBlizzard, C. Frank Keeney (still alive) Harold Houston, defense attorney,(Bill) Petry, Dist. 17; V. P., who shot Don Chafin in Charleston, Fred Mooney, Dist. 17 Sec.-Treas., and Andy Porter, U.of A field representative.

Original typewritten notes for photo on previous page

Pictured left to right: Raymond Lewis, Charley "Tuck" Payne and Bill Blizzard.

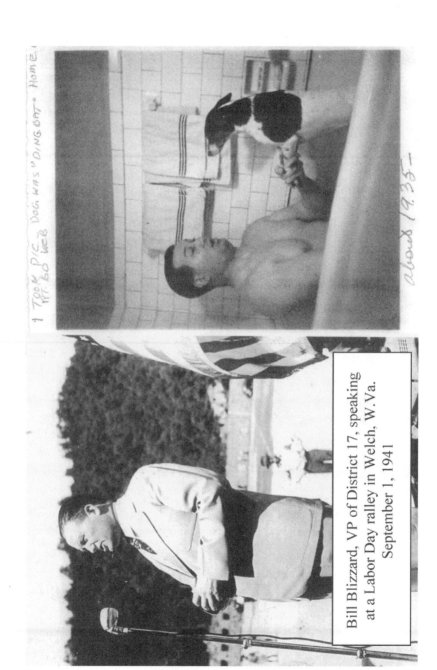

I TOOK PIC. DOG WAS "DING BAT" HOME.
PIT. BD WCB

about 1935 —

Bill Blizzard, VP of District 17, speaking
at a Labor Day ralley in Welch, W.Va.
September 1, 1941

Blizzard breaks ground for a new Union hospital.

Bill Blizzard and other UMW officials as they leave
Charleston, W.Va. to visit hospitals in the coalfields.

Bill Blizzard pictured above 4th from left with Union colleagues

Bill and Rae Blizzard, Feb. 1, 1941, on the day they became grandparents. Photo by William C. Blizzard.

August 15, 1958     *United Mine Wo*

# William Blizzard, 65

*William Blizzard,* retired former President of *UMWA District 17* with headquarters in Charleston, W. Va., died July 31 in Memorial Hospital, Charleston. He was 65.

He had been a patient in the hospital for five weeks. His death ended a two-year fight against cancer.

*William Blizzard*

The International officers, *President John L. Lewis, Vice President Thomas Kennedy* and *Secretary-Treasurer John Owens,* sent the following message of condolence to Mrs. Blizzard:

"We are saddened to learn of the tragic passing of your distinguished husband and appreciate the burden of grief that it brings upon you and the members of your breaved family. He gave a lifetime of service to the United Mine Workers of America and helped in the great work of perpetuating it as an enduring institution that has brought great rewards to countless numbers of the men engaged in the mining industry. The severance of the ties of a lifetime are hard to bear, but we hope that the grief of you and your family may be lightened to some degree by the knowledge that your husband's friends and associates grieve with you."

Born in Kanawha County on September 19, 1892, Mr. Blizzard went to work in the coal mines of the Mountain State when he was only ten years old. *The Charleston Gazette,* in a front page story on Mr. Blizzard's death, referred to those early days as "a time when operators of many coal companies treated their employes as chattels."

### 'A Tough And Articulate Spokesman'

Mr. Blizzard became active in UMWA affairs when he was still a teen-ager. When he was still in his 20s he had taken his place

"As a coal miner, and as a union official, he was, as a newspaper described him, 'a tough, articulate spokesman of workers' demands'. As parent and as friend, he was gentle, kindly of temperament and generous. In the promotion of the fundamental rights of labor he exhibited the spirit of a warrior; and the achieved and recognized rights of the laboring man and his Union in West Virginia will ever stand as a monument to his integrity, courage and tenacity of purpose and objective.

"A poet once aptly stated that:

'To sit in silence when we should protest
Makes cowards out of men. The human race
Has climbed on protest. Had no voice been raised
Against injustice, ignorance and lust,
The Inquisition yet would serve the law
And guillotines decide our least disputes.
The few who dare must speak and speak again
To right the wrongs of many . . .'

William Blizzard was one of those who dared to

'. . . . speak and speak again
To right the wrongs of many.' "

Above are the closing paragraphs of the glowing full page tribute to beloved Bill Blizzard, clipped from the August 15, 1958 issue of the *United Mine Workers Journal*.

Portrait by Connie West.

John Hilt was a great folk musician who had been a coal miner and active in building the Union when gun thugs invaded the mountains.

*Away with pious references*
*To patriotism and prayer,*
*As the naked child is born*
*Let the truth lie warm and bare!*

*If there is a thing to tell*
*Make it brief and write it plain.*
*Words were meant to shed a light,*
*Not to cover up again!*

by Don West

Don and Connie West were longtime friends of author William C. Blizzard.

Bill Blizzard

Rae Blizzard

"Yes sir, that old Bull Moose would parade up and down and shoot up the woods, where the miners were, so me and three other women decided one night to put an end to that. We slipped out after dark, took crowbars, and pried up the rails and rolled them down the hillside. The next morning, when the Bull Moose came along, it didn't go on to Leewood like it was supposed to. The men inside the train cussed and fumed and we stood on the side laughing at them."

*Ma Blizzard*

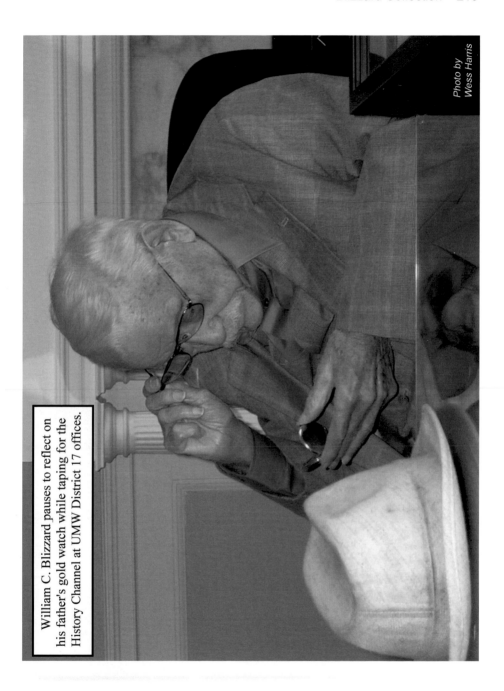

William C. Blizzard pauses to reflect on his father's gold watch while taping for the History Channel at UMW District 17 offices.

Photo by Wess Harris

Gold watch presented to Bill Blizzard.

Photos by Tom Rhule

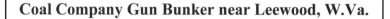

**Coal Company Gun Bunker near Leewood, W.Va.**
Tommy Phillips of UMWA Local 8843 visits
historic machine gun placement off Cabin Creek Road·
Photo by Tammy Phillips, January 14, 2005.

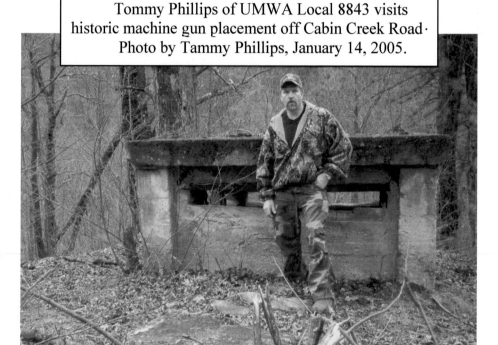

The '03 Springfield was the miner's weapon of choice.
Photo by Tom Rhule.

This vintage artillery piece has been restored through support from the UMWA, UMWA Local 1440 (Matewan), Appalachian Community Services, and the Union families of West Virginia. James W. Sheets II has kindly made the weapon available to the When Miners March Traveling Museum.

While the gun is no longer used to kill Union miners living unprotected in tents near Matewan, it is not retired. The gun sees action regularly as it speaks the Truth to those who would deny future generations knowledge of their hard-earned Union heritage.

Revisionist historians can be found (bought) who will argue that "most company stores offered necessities at affordable prices", and others note benignly that "Between paydays, companies issued workers scrip as a line of credit."

Kneeling before the altar of Big Coal, revisionists will preach that, "the public thought union members were violent militants who wanted to overthrow the government." They will not hesitate to label Bill Blizzard an "ardent Socialist", despite the reality that he was a Republican for most of his life. Such falsehoods are readily exposed when confronted by the Red Neck Army's Field Artillery!

*Above quotations are from the West Virginia State Museum, 2010*

# Chapter Seven: Liberty Will Yet Arise

1/9/1953 (Thirty-sixth)

The reaction of the coal miners to the unilateral action of Governor Morgan can be shown no better than by quoting fully from a letter signed by Fred Mooney, Secretary-Treasurer of the UMW District 17. According to the information this writer has received Mooney later developed into a "bad actor" and died a suicide. Nevertheless, this letter, written in early June, 1921, exemplifies perfectly the fighting attitude of the miners, as well as being informative in many other ways:

"TO THE LOCAL UNIONS OF DISTRICT NUMBER 17:

"Greetings:

"We take this method of keeping you informed concerning the recent development in Mingo County.

"Following the declaration of military dictatorship set up by Governor Morgan at the instigation and behest of a few coal operators, wholesale arrests and imprisonment of miners followed. Today the Mingo County jail is filled and eight or ten have been transferred to Huntington jail.

"A.D. Lavender and seven other miners have been taken to Welch in McDowell County. This is the same jail from which Frank Ingham was taken at midnight by Baldwin thugs in the guise of deputy sheriffs, beaten into insensibility and left for dead.

## Cites Miners' Enemies

"Every charge made against the politician prostitutes now misgoverning the state has been substantiated and in addition thereto, more atrocities are being committed than anyone ever predicted. Governor Morgan in a speech to the Rotary Club of Charleston sometime ago said that the uniformed body of Private Kackley who was killed in a drunken brawl in Mingo County, 'was worth more than all the agitators in Mingo County.' This was insinuating that the lives of four thousand Union men were worthless compared to the life of one man because he wore the uniform of the state.

"No one regrets that Private Kackley met death in the manner he did, more than we, but we disagree with the gentleman who had kicked the Constitution and Bill of Rights into discard. One miner is worth a thousand men in uniform because a miner produces and the man in uniform does not.

"In this struggle, the political prostitutes have the advantage of the workers because they have their publications through which they obtain publicity for their rabidly biased and corporation controlled opinions. These publications are closed to the workers. No expression of your side of the controversy will be admitted to the columns of the daily press. In addition to the support of the daily press, the pawns of coal and steel now ravishing the state are supported by the Chamber of Commerce, the Rotary Clubs, the American Legion, the Y.M.C.A., the Kiwanis Club, the Steel Combine, and in many instances, self-styled ministers of the gospel ally themselves with the open shoppers as some did in Williamson. One minister declared in the law and order meeting that he did not know much about a rifle, but he knew he could use one like a baseball bat.

## Daily Mail Attacked

"The editor of the *Charleston Daily Mail* spouted at length in his 'At This Hour' column on May the 25th, concerning labor leaders and the decency of his paper. This editor of Alaskan effigy fame (Mooney here refers to the late *Charleston Daily Mail* owner Walter Eli Clark, who was Governor of Alaska from 1909 to 1913. It was asserted by many that Clark had left Alaska in something of a hurry, and that irate citizens of the Territory had burned him in effigy after his departure – -Ed.) should look up the word 'decency' in the dictionary and learn its meaning before he attempts to criticize even the physically deaf, mentally dumb, or morally blind, and he should tell the people that he was run out of Alaska between two suns for participation in graft. Now he is here in the state of West Virginia assuming the role of a dictator. Let him clear up his own record before he assumes to criticize people whom he knows nothing about. Let the miners hold their forces intact whatever happens and remember that sham battles do not make good soldiers and a point fought for and gained is worth everything in the world (rather than) if it be handed down to us on a silver platter, and even though the strikers of Mingo County are shot down in cold blood by the hirelings of the Coal Operators and the Steel Trust as they were at Stanaford Mountain in 1902, Holly Grove in 1912-1913, Ludlow, Colorado, in 1913, and even though these corporation hirelings and murderers are supported, protected and defended by pawns of the interests in state government, we will win. The spirit of the strikers in Mingo County cannot be broken by military dictatorships set up by corporation hirelings. Expect anything! For if they think they can get by with it, these ravishers of liberty will commit the same atrocities in Mingo County that were committed at Stanaford Mountain in 1902, Holly Grove and Ludlow in 1912-1913, and no one is responsible but the workers. These corporation dupes only do what you empower them to do with your ballot, and every injustice heaped upon the workers as a class is brought about by themselves. Every abuse of power by men who are supposed to administer the law in an impartial manner is attributable to the negligence of the working class.

"President Keeney, Secretary Mooney, Board Member Workman, Sid Hatfield, and many others will face the federal court in

Charleston on June 21<sup>st</sup> for the alleged violation of an injunction.

"Let this be as it may, Liberty will yet arise from the depths of degradation and despair, and when an outraged citizenship asserts itself and demands justice, they will be met with the organized opposition of invisible government within the state. Anonymous letters are received at this office every few days embodying all kinds of threats, but none of the low, cringing curs have yet the guts or gall to sign their names.

"Study, educate, agitate and work to enlighten your fellows in order that you can function when you are called upon to do so."

1/10/53 (Thirty-seventh)

As can be seen, the miners were filled with a sense of outrage. And on June 14, just about the time Mooney's letter was written, an incident occurred in Mingo County which fanned the miners' anger to an even hotter flame.

This was the Lick Creek affair. There were two strikers' tent colonies on Lick Creek, about one mile south of the southern limits of Williamson, where lived about 300 men, women and children. One tent colony was in the river bottom and the other on the hillside. The testimony of Captain J. R. Brockus of the State Police was that the incident started when someone fired on a car. He and Major Tom Davis, Sheriff A. C. Pinson and three other men went out to arrest the culprit responsible for the firing. Brockus maintained that their party stopped and they were fired upon, though no one was hit. They answered with a submachine gun, but decided to look into the situation no further. They went back to Williamson for reinforcements. All of the above shooting is supposed to have taken place in the vicinity of the Lick Creek tent colonies.

Back at Williamson Major Davis, the acting Adjutant General of West Virginia, demonstrated that he was somewhat irritated by this defiance of law and order. He had the fire station whistle give four blasts three times in succession. This, it seems, was a prearranged signal for the vigilantes, otherwise known as "volunteer" State Police, to assemble at police headquarters. Some hundreds did so and were supplied with rifles and plenty of ammunition. They piled into cars and headed for Lick Creek with instructions from Major Davis to "clean out" the hills and the tent colonies in order to investigate the shootings. Major Davis himself remained in Williamson, presumably to take care of any supply problems which might arise in the rear.

### Alex Breedlove's Murder

Arriving at a little distance from the scene of the crime, the vigilantes and State Police unloaded and Captain Brockus deployed his men. Some formed a unit in order to cut off escape by the strikers. With his remaining men Brockus formed a line about a mile long, and, with his intrepid band of strikebreakers, advanced with rifles and submachine guns at the ready. They marched right through the tent colonies, where one of the police and a miner were killed, and rounded up 57 men, who were marched to Williamson and put in jail.

There they were kept for three days and grilled, but they would tell the good Major Davis nothing, except that there might have been a shotgun or two in the tents.

This was the version of the Lick Creek affair given by the police. The striking miners tell it a little differently. Here is an affidavit concerning the killing of the Union man, whose name was Alex Breedlove, and the State Policeman.

"James Williams, being duly sworn upon his oath, says that he is a resident of the Lick Creek tent colony and that he was there on the 14th day of June, 1921, when the same was raided by State Police and their confederates and deputy sheriffs, and when Alex Breedlove was murdered; that he was about 30 feet from Breedlove when he was shot and saw James Bowles, State Policeman, shoot him; Bowles was about six or seven feet from Breedlove, and Breedlove had his hands up above his head at the time he was shot; Bowles said to Breedlove, 'Hold up your hands, God damn you, and if you have got anything to say, say it fast,' and Breedlove said, 'Lord, have mercy,' and instantly the gun fired and Breedlove fell. They were standing facing each other and Breedlove just above him on the hill.

**Brave Killer Faints**

"At the same time Victor Blackburn, a special State Police, was shooting at Garfield Moore, who was behind a tree, the same tree that

Breedlove had just been behind, and after Bowles had called Breedlove to come out from behind the tree and put up his hands and come to him and he had done so and then was shot, Bowles immediately turned his gun on Garfield Moore, but did not have time to fire until he was shot in the back by another State Police who was lying flat down on the ground straight down the hill below Policeman Bowles; at the crack of his rifle a half dozen or more women who were there screamed out, 'Look out, man, you are shooting your own men,' and asked him to get away from there, that he would get them all killed.

"Affiant, thereupon said to the man who had shot Bowles, 'Yes, you done shot this man up here now,' and at that he said to Affiant, 'You are a damn liar, you damn black --------, you get away from there.' And thereupon the said Police who had shot Police Bowles fainted and was carried off the ground by Willie Ball carried under a bridge across Lick Creek. He remained under this bridge 30 or 40 minutes with a lot of Union miners who had taken shelter under said bridge."

The above is substantiated by other witnesses. If the killing of Policeman Bowles seems farfetched, remember that most of these raiders were clerks and businessmen who handled guns very little. The same sort of men invade our woods during deer season, and excited with the novelty of their surroundings, they yearly shoot one another with gusto in the mistaken notion that they are slaying game.

So much for the actual shooting at Lick Creek, except to note that from one to four thousand people attended the funeral of Alex Breedlove. Union men mourn a fallen brother, and something of a fighting unionist lives after him in the hearts of his fellows. It is unnecessary to relate that no one was punished for his murder. Now let us refer to what followed the shootings, as described in another affidavit signed by one William H. Ball, the Union miner referred to in the statement of James Williams:

## Law and Order at Work

"...Brockus gave orders to take the miners out from under the bridge (where they had huddled for protection. – Ed.) and line them up in county road, and all the miners and the women and all were ordered out and required to come out from under the bridge and line up together, and then orders were given by Brockus to break into the tents and to break locks if necessary, and go in and search the tents, and thereupon his orders were carried out. They broke into tents where they had doors and were locked and where no doors existed they cut their way in. They then proceeded to cut the tents all to pieces; break up the furniture; break up dishes, trunks, rifle drawers and destroy food and clothing. They rounded up 56 of us, and after they had destroyed everything we had they drove us at the point of their rifles down through the City of Williamson and put us in the city lockup. This was a room about 20 by 40 feet with a concrete floor, without chairs or beds, and only one open window not more than 28 by 32 inches in size, and one door which opens from the hall. The sink was stopped up and running over; there were five commodes, and four of these were stopped up and standing full of human excrement; the floor was covered with water about half shoe-sole deep and all kinds of filth lying around on the floor in this water. Fifty-six of us were put in this place and a guard placed at the door and were denied the privilege of speaking to our attorney or any other person, and held in this room from about 3:30 Tuesday evening until about 9 o'clock Thursday night, when we were taken out and taken to the jury room in the courthouse and there detained until Saturday evening, and all released except Garfield Moore, Richard Combs, Sam Muney, and Floyd Chaney, none of whom are guilty of any crime any more than the rest of us were, which was not guilty, at all."

1/13/1953 (Thirty-eighth)

(Today's installment continues the affidavit of miner William H. Ball concerning the Lick Creek raid in Mingo County in 1921.)

"Affiant further says that he served 18 months in France in the World War and possessed a Victory medal and an American Legion badge and a Moose button and a regulation uniform in his tent; that they entered his tent and cut his tent all to pieces; cut up his uniform and a $65 suit was missing, and no trace of it could be found except a stack of ashes in the stove, which indicated that they had been put into the stove and burned; the Victory medal was never found and the American Legion badge was never found, Moose receipts gone and a $12 set of knives and forks gone; coal oil was poured into my flour, and groceries thrown away; all the dishes broken, trunk torn all to pieces, and all the damage done that could be done.

"I also heard Capt. Brockus and Bill St. Clair, the deputy mine inspector who was a volunteer state police, say that all the "God damn --- ----- ought all be burned"; that the women ought to all be piled up and the tents put on top of them and burned. I also heard Dr. Lawson, a volunteer state police, say to a woman "he would knock a kid out of her big enough to walk," and used such language toward others, and all of this was done in the presence of Capt. Brockus."

None of these miners were ever charged with anything, and there were no warrants for their arrest issued or shown. Martial law in the West Virginia coal fields in 1921, as in 1913, was justification for any abuse.

Miners all over West Virginia, already indignant because of the Mingo situation, were now furious. A UMW attorney named Thomas West took a Judge Bailey, an assistant prosecuting attorney named Breese, and a photographer to Lick Creek in order to verify the damage to the tent colonies. While they were on the spot a car drove by, occupied by two armed state police.

West and his part were mistaken for miners and the police yelled: "If you damn rednecks haven't got enough we will give you some more of it."

## Operators Starve Miners

This excess of patriotic zeal was reported back to Captain Brockus, but nothing, evidently, was done about it, and these true-blue Americans continued in the employ of the State of West Virginia.

The rumblings of discontent in the Union coal fields of West Virginia to the north of Mingo County were growing louder by the day. The miners wrote letters to state officials, passed stirring resolutions and assembled in mass meetings in protest over the treatment of their fellow miners in Mingo, but the state machinery of West Virginia was deaf to the miners' complaints and demands.

And the coal operators in Mingo struck yet another blow. The striking miners were being fed by the UMW, the relief being dispensed by International Representatives in conformity with the Union constitution. It was unlawful, under martial law, for two or more strikers or UMW members to congregate together. If they did so they were subject to arrest.

It happened that there were FIVE of these International Representatives who were responsible for distribution of food, clothing and medical supplies and attention to the thousands of men, women and children in tents in the Tug River area. They were stationed in Williamson. As these five men had to get together in order to make reports as to relief distribution they were, ipso facto, in violation of Governor Morgan's edict. At least that is the way Generalissimo Tom Davis interpreted the matter, and he had Capt. Brockus arrest the five UMW representatives on a charge of unlawful assembly!

They were housed in Williamson jail that night and then rushed to the Welch jail in neighboring McDowell County. One of them named John Brown (a very brave, intelligent man, incidentally, who had fought unbelievable battles for the miners for many years,) was not even given time to put on his coat by the arresting gendarmes. The thought of having five UMW men meet together was intolerable to the freedom-hating West Virginia authorities. Unless, of course, it happened to be in a jail cell.

This maneuver of the coal operators was designed to cut off all food, clothing and medicine from the striking miner, and their women and children. And it did, of course accomplish this purpose for a time.

## Hard Times for Union

The UMW instituted habeas corpus proceedings in order to get its members out of jail, and the Union stated its case before the West Virginia Supreme Court on Thursday and Friday, July 14 and 15, 1921. The Supreme Court remanded the miners to jail, declared that a state of insurrection and riot existed in Mingo County, and decided that Governor Morgan's proclamation of martial law was not only legal but necessary.

The rumble of miner protest became more ominous. The smoky air of West Virginia was heavy with the foreboding of a coming storm.

And still the coal operators continued to act as if their employees were docile sheep, to be herded this way and that by gunmen shepherds. It is an odd fact that the civil courts in Mingo County continued to function insofar as the trials of bootleggers and thieves were concerned. They had their rights as citizens. But striking coal miners had no rights. They were subject to the military. It was a SELECTIVE martial law, which applied only to one class of people: strikers and their representatives. The close tie between the coal operators and the state, county and municipal governments was now a naked thing, unclothed by democratic platitudes.

District 17 was reeling from these blows. The following letter to the president of UMW Sub-district No. 2, which took in Mingo County, is self-explanatory:

"June the twenty-eighth,1921
"Mr. Wm. Blizzard,
"Box 600,
"St. Albans, W.Va.,

"Dear Sir and Brother:

"I am writing you concerning action taken by the District Executive Board on date of June 28, 1921, which was as follows: That all resident officers, District Board Members, Field Workers, Organizers and Auditors accept half salaries during the depression and until the District Organization is in financial condition to assume its full responsibilities.

"You being the head of the Sub-district, I was instructed to communicate with you and request that the Sub-district officers comply with this same ruling and accept half salaries with their legitimate expenses.

"Fraternally yours,

"Fred Mooney, Sec. – Treas.
"District No. 17."

UMW International Vice-President Philip Murray hurried to Charleston, West Virginia, in order to look into the relief situation in Mingo County. For the strikers simply had to have food and medical care. Murray visited Governor Morgan on July 18, protested the arrest of the relief men and asked for reinstatement of the relief system in Mingo County. Governor Morgan passed the buck by saying that Major Davis was the man to see, that he, the Governor, could not change a decision of Major Davis.

1/14/1953 (Thirty-ninth)

Murray saw Davis and got a promise that the strikers' relief would be started again; that UMW representatives would be protected in the martial law area, and even extended courtesy. These were sweet words, but let Phil Murray tell of what happened when he personally visited Mingo County:

"Upon my arrival in Williamson – just got off the train – a member of the State Police accosted me at the station. I never met the man before or since, and do not know who he was, except that he was a member of the State Police. He insulted me in very insulting language; told me that the presence of a mine worker representative in Mingo County was positively repulsive and that I could not expect to be permitted to remain within the confines of that county more than forty-eight hours. Of course, I appreciated the circumstances that surrounded me, and I did not utter to him the faintest murmur of protest, fearing the possible consequences, I journeyed on to the Shumate Hotel, registered, and got a room. was hounded to my room by a member of the State Militia or State Police. They came to the room, looked in the door, and hollered vile language at me.

"I left my room and went to the restaurant to have lunch and he followed me to the restaurant and stayed outside of the restaurant while I was eating lunch. He followed me around everywhere I went all day, and that night when I retired, on going to my room, they came and knocked on my door about one o'clock in the morning. They did not want in at all, but just simply to annoy me. The following morning I got out of the hotel and went to Major Davis and protested. I said, 'Major, this situation here is very bad. I do not know that you know of its existence, but I tell you frankly and candidly the experience I have underwent since coming to Williamson leads me to believe the stories that come to us about the members of the State Police and the State Militia in Mingo County, and I will urge you not only for the United Mine Workers of America but for the sake of the country as a whole that you lend whatever assistance that you can to put an end to any such practices.'

## Miners' Terrible Anger

"Major Davis promised to have the matter investigated; he said a lot of these things happened that he could not be held responsible for. I went back to the Shumate Hotel. I was followed back to the hotel; I was followed to my room; then I checked out of the hotel and went to a rooming house, feeling that I could occupy the privacy of my own room without the necessity of being disturbed constantly by outsiders. I stayed in Williamson from Monday, the 18th, until Wednesday, the 20th, the 18th, 19th, and 20th. I never visited anywhere in the city of Williamson that I was not followed, hounded and cussed at by members of the State military."

The amount of confidence which could be placed in the words of Governor Morgan and Major Davis are thus demonstrated. There seems no doubt that the labor career of Phil Murray was in danger of being closed in the hills of West Virginia in the year 1921. For it was only 12 days after Murray's visit, on August 1, that C.E. Lively and the other Baldwin men killed Sid Hatfield and Ed Chambers on the courthouse steps at Welch.

This incident has been treated earlier in this work in some detail. At that time it was mentioned that these killings had an important effect on the coal miners of the state. They did. The news went out to every hamlet and coal camp and miners already furious could contain themselves no longer. The air rang with curses upon the heads of every coal company flunky in public office, from Governor Morgan down to the lowliest justice of the peace. Angry words of condemnation of the State Police, impromptu militia, Baldwin men and their coal operator employers thundered and shook the walls of hundreds of Union halls.

## Early Resolution Cited

The esteem in which Sid Hatfield was held by the miners, as well as their anger at his murder, may be deduced from the following resolution. It was written almost a year before Sid was killed, and it refers to his trial for the Baldwin killings at Matewan. If the miners were in the mood indicated by this resolution in 1920, their feelings a year later, when they learned of Hatfield's cold-blooded murder, may well be imagined:

"Ward, W. Va., Sept. 13, 1920

"Whereas, Justice is denied the workers in the courts of this great commonwealth, by and through a lot of red tape and expense, and,

"Whereas, Our governor has always taken a stand against the workers and for the exploiting class, and the time has come when we as workers know there is no longer Justice to be had in the courts of this state, therefore be it.

"Resolved. That we go on record as demanding that our District Officials prepare a referendum vote of our membership for the purpose of a general strike in this state as a protest to our legislators and governor against the passing of any laws to assist in railroading workers to the penitentiary or gallows at the behest of the capitalist-controlled governor, and be it further

"Resolved. That Local Union No. 2681, in special meeting assembled, go on record as demanding for Sid Hatfield a fair and impartial trial, by his peers. And be it further

"Resolved. That we pledge our moral and financial support, (and physical support if necessary); and we also ask all local unions in this state to take similar action, in order that Justice be not denied. And be it further

"Resolved. That we send a copy of these resolutions to the governor, to our District Officials, to Sid Hatfield and to the press.

"LOCAL UNION NO. 2681, U.M.W. of A.
"E.G. Kay,
"Rec. – Secty.
"(Seal)"
"E.G. Kay,
"G.E. Tucker,
"Will Gray"
"Resolutions Committee."

1/15/1953 (Fortieth)

In short, the miners, after the Aug. 1, 1921 killing of Sid Hatfield, were incensed past all alleviation by usual methods. Reports were circulated, later proved false, that UMW representatives A.D. Levender and Charley Wordman had also been killed in Mingo County. The miners began to reach for their rifles, as they could see no possibility of help from any official source.

But an armed uprising is a serious matter and evidence points to the fact that a decision was made to appeal once more to Governor Morgan. There apparently was formed by the miners what was called a "Constitutional League," headed by UMW officials and other interested citizens, with the avowed purpose of ending martial law in Mingo County and thus reinstituting the West Virginia and United States Constitutions. Word was passed to all local unions, including those in Mingo, that a great mass meeting was to be held on the capitol grounds at Charleston on Sunday, August 7. At this meeting the Governor would once more be asked to intercede on behalf of the miners.

The response to the call for the mass meeting was impressive. A great crowd of miners thronged the capitol grounds, where a series of speakers reviewed the long list of grievances which had led to the present situation. Frank Keeney and Fred Mooney spoke, as did a number of lesser District 17 officials. Frank Ingham, the Negro who had been beaten and left for dead in McDowell County, retold his bloody story to an angry and attentive audience. Mother Jones added her own special brand of speaking to the swelling tide of accusing voices.

Beautiful Sally Chambers, young widow of Ed Chambers, described how her husband and Sid Hatfield were murdered before her eyes just a week before, and how she had pluckily struck C.E. Lively with her umbrella. And many were the anonymous miners who rose to give their own stories of brutal coal company oppression.

Thus regaled with tales of their own woes – and that they were very real and outlandish woes no reader can doubt – the anger of the miners reached fever pitch. They submitted to the Governor a series of resolutions wherein were reiterated the demands submitted to the coal operators of Mingo by C.F. Keeney on July 11, 1921. One might think, from the violent opposition of the operators, that the miners were asking for the immediate delivery of the coal industry into UMW hands.

## The Miners' Demands

For this reason the miners' demands are set forth, just as they were presented on August 7, 1921. Resolved:

"1 –That the coal operators involved agree that all employees return to work without discrimination against any employee belonging to a labor Union as provided in state law.

"2 –That establishment of an eight-hour day as applied to all classes of labor in and around the mines as provided in contract in contractual relations between employer and employee.

"3 –That miners get the semi-monthly payday.

"4 –That the employees have the right to trade where he (sic) pleases and without molestation and duress.

"5 –That employees shall have the right to elect checkweighmen, as provided in the mining laws; and that two thousand pounds shall constitute a ton as provided in the weights and measures law.

"6 –Where the coal is not weighed over a standard scale, and the miner is paid by the car or by measure, the weight of each car shall be stamped thereon in plain numerals as provided by law.

"7 –There shall be appointed a joint commission consisting of three representatives from each side for the purpose of adjusting wages of all workmen and miners working in and around the mines; to determine the mining rates, yardage, etc., and to endeavor to reach an equitable basis whereby parties in interest can meet any competition: to adopt rules and methods for the adjustment of any disputes which may arise between parties to this agreement.

"To avoid any failure to agree, a Board of Arbitration consisting of three members shall be created, one to be chosen by the operators, one by the employees, and these two to select the third man who shall be a non-resident of the state.

"Whenever the commission of six members shall fail to agree, the Board of Arbitration shall sit with the commission and decide the question in dispute which decision shall be final and binding on the contracting parties. The findings of the commission shall date from the time work is resumed, and shall continue until April 1, 1922."

These were the proposals of the UMW. They seem rather mild demands to be answered by jail sentences, starvation and gunmen. The coal operators were absolutely unwilling to talk with the miners on any terms whatever.

## The Operators' Attitude

Let us quote Z.T. Vinson, a coal company lawyer in 1921. He is speaking to the investigating subcommittee on Education and Labor:

"It is understood, or rather it ought to be understood – and I think the Committee does understand it – what our position is, and it is absolutely unchangeable, that we will have no dealings whatever with the United Mine Workers of America. They are not in our employ; we have no connection with them and will not under any circumstances meet them in consultation about the difficulties down there. Now, with that absolute policy, I see no reason to go on and keep on insisting that we shall recognize their Union when we have so positively stated that under no circumstances will we do it, either through this honorable committee, through the president of the United States, or any other tribunal."

A workingman talking to a Federal investigation committee in this manner might have been thrown into jail for contempt for so long that he would never again see the light of day. But the coal operators got by with it. Some reasons why this was so will be developed later.

The miners on the lawn of the statehouse presented their resolutions to Governor Morgan, asking that he request a meeting of operators and miners on the above terms, and if either refused to agree to call a special session of the Legislator to carry out campaign promises that the mine guard system would be abolished by law.

Governor Morgan answered the miners by letter on Aug. 17, 1921. Though the letter was quite polite, and took up the miners' demands point by point, it nevertheless said quite plainly; "Go to Hell!" If this seems to put the matter bluntly, we shall illustrate.

As regarded the request that strikers be not discriminated against, Morgan replied that he had no "authority to say to the coal operators of Mingo County or any other county, whom they shall employ in their coal mines...." This was quite true. The coal operators had seen to it that there was no legal coercion possible insofar as they were concerned, for they made the laws of West Virginia. And they also saw to it that Governor Morgan DID have the authority to invoke martial law in order that strikers might be beaten and starved into submission. The attempt to dictate to the coal companies, Morgan said, would be "unjustifiable usurpation of authority by the executive."

The same Governor wrote this who also wrote the proclamation under which men were arrested for reading the *United Mine Worker's Journal,* and five Union men peaceably sitting together were thrown into jail for unlawful assembly!

1/16/1953 (Forty-first)

As to the eight-hour day, Morgan said that this was already in effect in Mingo County, so there was no point in discussing the matter. The obvious answer was that the men worked eight hours if the company felt like letting them work eight hours, and then only because of outside Union pressure. Governor Morgan very well knew this. He did not mention it.

Governor Morgan solemnly stated that he had "been advised" that there was no company pressure in Mingo County for men to trade in the company stores, and that twice-a-month paydays were general rule. Governor Morgan does not name his advisers, but they were certainly not strikers.

Checkweighmen, Morgan noted, were called for in state law, and a coal company should be prosecuted for violation of the law. He therefore urged that the matter be taken up with the courts of Mingo County. This was written with Morgan's absolute knowledge that the Mingo Courts were in the hands of the coal operators, who are not noted for masochistic tendencies.

As to the proposal that a joint commission of operators and miners be established in order to begin negotiations, and the appointment of a board of arbitration if this method failed, Governor Morgan pointed out that this would involve recognition of the UMW by the operators, and that the Mingo coal owners had said they would have nothing to do with this union.

For Morgan, this ended the matter, for he pointed out that "the operator has a constitutional right to not recognize the Union if he so likes." The Governor then went on to cite the infamous U.S. Supreme Court Decision in the Hitchman Case in 1917. This case originated in West Virginia, and was finally decided when the Supreme Court upheld the validity of the "yellow-dog contract." In part, the decision was as follows: "An employer is acting within his lawful rights in making non-membership in a Union a condition of employment, and no explanation or justification for such a course is needed."

This anti-union decision was used as an authoritative legal reference for many years, until at last the passage in 1932 of the Norris-La Guardia Act alleviated its harsh ruling.

## Morgan's Refusal Last Straw

"The proposal of the UMW that a special session of the Legislature be called in order to implement Republican campaign promises to end the mineguard system is not an issue in the strike in Mingo County, as I am advised by the county official that its deputy sheriffs are paid out of the county treasury."

The reader will recall elsewhere in the history testimony of a Mingo County coal operator that the guards or deputies were really hired by the coal companies, with the understanding with the county court that it would pay the operators back when the county had the money.

This was the flimsiest kind of evasion. The coal operators in Mingo were the county court and vice versa, so that in effect the operators would have been paying themselves back if they had really gone through with this announced scheme. There is no evidence that they ever did. On the contrary, there is real reason to believe that this was a story manufactured, as the old-time orators used to say, from the whole cloth. Morgan must have known this fact. His absolute refusal to act on any of the suggestions submitted by the miners on August 7 surely makes him in great measure responsible for the events which followed his complete exposure as a coal company governor.

The events which followed, we repeat, are in part to be attributed to Morgan's deafness to the plight of the miners of nonunion West Virginia. But he can not, of course, be held wholly responsible. The miners had throughout their history in West Virginia been victims of exploitation, cruelty, bad working conditions, miserable pay, and murderous treatment if they dared to protest. This they knew. And they were well aware of the role which many governors before Morgan had played in aiding the coal companies to dominate their lives. They had seen their employers grasp control of all governing bodies in West Virginia, from the statehouse to the county court.

They had for many years appealed to their elected representatives for some sort of justice. And they had seen these same representatives give aid and comfort to their enemies after the most demagogic of pre-election promises. The miners of West Virginia, after these years of neglect and oppression, had lost faith in the ability or willingness of any governing body to aid them in their fight for a decent life. Governor Morgan's refusal of aid was merely the final act which they could no longer bear. The weight of official indifference and hostility became suddenly too much to bear. In miners' language, Morgan's act was the "straw that broke the camel's back."

## Miners Reply With Action

It seems quite apparent that the miners decided that they could rely only upon themselves. Morgan's refusal of aid was dated August 17, 1921. By August 19 every Union miner in Kanawha, Boone and other counties had been informed of his reply. They grimly decided to reply to Morgan – in their own way. On August 20 the miners, armed with rifles, began to congregate at the mouth of Lens Creek, a point about 12 miles from Charleston. They arrived by the hundreds. It began to be evident that the miners traditional form of struggle in West Virginia, practiced since 1897, was about to be used again. This was the mass march of workers from coal camp to coal camp. But this time the atmosphere was grimmer.

Grimmer even than in 1919, when some thousands of outraged miners had before assembled at Lens Creek, bearing rifles. For two years of bloody industrial warfare had gone by, the miners had been toughened by the conflict.

Just why the coal diggers chose Lens Creek as a congregating spot will be obvious when a glance is taken at a map of the area, and the purpose of the assembled group is made clear. Lens Creek is the beginning of a sort of natural pass through the hills from Kanawha County into neighboring Boone, which was also strong UMW territory. Boone County borders Logan County, and through Logan it is a comparatively short march into Mingo. At this date a modern highway, U.S. Route No. 119, has been built, and is one of the more convenient methods of getting to the towns of Logan and Williamson when traveling from the Charleston area. There was no hard surfaced road in 1921, but this route was nevertheless a convenient and logical choice for men who wished to march first to Logan, and then "on to Mingo."

# Chapter Eight: Call for Federal Troops

1/17/1953 (Forty-second)

The miners at the mouth of Lens Creek did not escape observation, nor, at this stage of the affair, did they make any efforts to conceal the unconcealable fact that huge numbers of men were camping at the base of the hills. It seems that they did, however, put out sentries in a roughly military manner in order to keep enemies from a close-range look. A *Charleston Gazette* reporter was supposed to have been informed that he was not welcome, which may well be believed, for neither the *Gazette* nor the *Charleston Daily Mail* had demonstrated sympathy for the miners' cause.

Someone, possibly another news hawk, had the bright idea of taking photographs from the air. Rifle shots encouraged the plane to return to Charleston. By the last week in August some 8,000 miners were at Lens Creek, most of them armed. We quote from the following letter, partly in order to show the attitude of the Kanawha County authorities toward the miners and partly in order to demonstrate the seriousness of the situation:

"Aug. 23, 1921.
"HONERABLE E.F. MORGAN
"GOVERNOR OF WEST VIRGINIA,
"CHARLESTON, WEST VIRGINIA.

"Dear Sir:

"For more than four days a large body of armed men have (sic) been congregated in Kanawha County, about 12 miles from Charleston, near the town of Marmet, using this place as a camp from which they have been threatening to march into and through other counties of the state.

"This afternoon, an aeroplane, on a peaceful mission, flying over the camp, was fired into and the driver narrowly escaped death. Patrols have occupied the county roads running close to and through this camp and have held up private citizens and officers of the law and prevented their uninterrupted passage through the territory. This afternoon, this body of men started on their march up Lens Creek and actually proceeded several miles.

"The situation has reached a point where the county authorities are unable to cope with it, and we feel compelled to request that you obtain, if possible, the aid of Federal Troops in order that law and order may be restored in this county.

"We have wanted, and now desire, to reach no hasty conclusion, but in order that bloodshed may be avoided, we respectfully ask that you call to the aid of the people of this county (Miners were evidently not considered people by the authors of this letter. –Ed.) such forces as may be able to restore to them the right to go about their business without interruption.

"There have not been for several years any labor strikes within the border of Kanawha County. No cause, so far as we have been able to ascertain, has been given this body to interrupt the citizens of the community in the peaceable and uninterrupted pursuit of attending to their own business....

"We hope that you can bring the forces of the Federal Government to our assistance so that some action can be taken which can punish those guilty of breaking the laws of the state and menacing the lives and property of the citizens of Kanawha County, and that the preservation of law and order may once more obtain.

"Respectfully submitted,

"HENRY A. WALKER
"Sheriff, Kanawha County,
"West Virginia.

"FRANK C. BURDETTE,
"Prosecuting Attorney,
"Kanawha County, West Virginia.

"S.E. CHILDRESS,
"President, County Court of
"Kanawha County, West Virginia.

"H.K. Black.
"Judge of the Intermediate Court,
"Kanawha County, West Virginia."

The last paragraph of the above letter should be reread. It will be noted that it sounds the usual cry for "law and order," which in itself is no bad thing. However, nothing exists in itself, but only in relation to the concrete circumstances surrounding a given situation. We hope that we have shown that the miners of West Virginia had by this time exhausted every possible avenue of "law and order" in their appeals to the governor, to the legislature, to county officials and to federal investigators.

Such conscientious appeals through usual legal channels had brought the miners a period of unemployment of more than a year's duration; they had seen their wives and children shiver with cold in inadequate garments; they and their families had been deprived of food through the arbitrary action of military dictator Tom Davis acting in the name of Governor Morgan; they had been beaten, jailed, shot and murdered.

## Operators Real Culprits

Such were the blessings of the observance of law and order, by the coal miners in the State of West Virginia. For coal company law and coal company order were not made for the benefit of coal miners, and such was the harsh legal situation in the Mountain State.

We accuse the coal operators of West Virginia of being the real violators of law and order. For therein lies the truth. Such statutes as those requiring the hiring of checkweighmen and prohibiting the employment of gunmen mine guards had been openly and contemptuously flouted. Murder had been committed by men hired by the coal operators, and the murderers had gone unpunished. Fundamental rights of speech and assembly as guaranteed in both state and federal constitutions had been denied the coal miners through the institution of martial law by a servile state administration.

We hope that we have documented the above statements sufficiently to allow of no doubt as to their accuracy. By late August, 1921, the miners had exhausted every legal means of redress. They were now faced with a choice of two alternatives: the meek acceptance of slavery or action which was in violation of coal company "law and order." The inevitability of the latter course is obvious to anyone familiar with the traditions of the miners.

Before we continue to follow the progress of the Union miners who had become so incensed over the fate of their brothers in Mingo and Logan counties that they had seized arms to redress their wrongs, we wish to discuss two other matters. One is a further analysis of the economic forces at work in West Virginia. The other is a discussion of Logan County, which has not yet received treatment in this work. We hope that we have furnished enough evidence to prove the coal company autocracy in Mingo County. The reader may not believe this, but the situation in Logan County was even worse.

## Story of a Giant

We shall speak further of Logan after we give brief mention to a giant which lived and still lives, in the United States. Its name is the United States Steel Corporation. It is a powerful giant before which rulers bow and governments tremble. It has a peculiarity in that it is hard to see, even though it may be present everywhere. This is because it has learned very well how to hide itself through the tutelage of erudite gentlemen called corporation lawyers. Teaching a giant how to disguise itself so that it does not seem present is a neat legal trick, and corporation lawyers are sometimes rewarded by being appointed either as Federal, District or Supreme Court judges.

By 1921 this giant named U.S. Steel had at least one scaly foot in West Virginia. It was exceedingly powerful, although, as before noted, mostly invisible. And it must be reported, in 1953, that its power has not decreased with the years.

Although it was never visible in the forefront of the battle, it should be emphasized that U.S. Steel in 1920 was the most powerful enemy of the coal miners of West Virginia. Elsewhere in this work we have pointed out that the Norfolk & Western Railroad became the owner of 300,000 acres of coal lands in the Pocahontas field in 1901. U.S. Steel bought the land and simply turned it over to the railroad. That this was not an act of charity may be deduced from the fact that the Norfolk & Western was a subsidiary of the Pennsylvania Railroad, which had a close tie with the Girard Trust Company, which was in turn dominated by the banking house of J.P. Morgan. And the financial control of U.S. Steel centered in the House of Morgan, which meant that the steel company was all this while doing business with itself.

After it gave, or "sold" the properly to the Norfolk & Western, the steel corporation then leased 50,000 acres of this same coal property for its own exclusive use. It continued this same method of self-dealing and, with further financial pressures of a time-honored nature, it apparently became the actual ruling head of the whole coal network in the southern part of West Virginia. The explanation of all of this maneuvering would be so complex, even if it were all known, as to preclude presentation in these pages. But we shall amplify a little further.

1/20/1953 (Forty-third)

The following quotation will not be especially easy reading. It is full of facts and figures. But it is clear and it presents a complicated picture in as simple a manner as possible. It gives something of the ramifications of U.S. Steel in West Virginia, and for this reason is valuable. The document from which this was taken was submitted in 1921 to the investigation Subcommittee of the Committee on Education of Labor.

It begins by citing a Report to Congress by the Interstate Commerce Commission on Discrimination and Monopolies in Coal and Oil, made Jan. 25, 1907:

> " 'As to the Norfolk & Western Railway Co., we desire to report that prior to the year 1901 there were 300,000 acres more or less of coal lands in what is known as the Pocahontas Flat Top Coal Field, in the states of Virginia and West Virginia which were owned  by the Flat Top Coal Land Association.
>
> 'In the year 1901 the Flat Top Coal Land Association gave an option thereon to certain persons, to wit: Messrs. E.H. Gary, William

Edenborn, and Isaac T. Mann, known as syndicate managers.... So at present the situation is that the Pocahontas Coal & Coke Co. owns the fee simple title or mineral rights upon about 300,000 acres of Pocahontas coal in the states of Virginia and West Virginia....

'The Norfolk & Western Railway Co. purchased the entire stock of the Pocahontas Coal & Coke Co., and thus acquired control of the coal lands aforesaid, with the idea that the acquisition of these coal lands by any other person or corporation than itself would be detrimental to the interests of that company, and in the sale of the coal fields aforesaid to the Pocahontas Coal & Coke Co. it was arranged, through Mr. E.H. Gary, one of the syndicate managers who was connected with the United Steel Corporation, that said corporation should have a lease upon 50,000 acres of said land for the purpose of furnishing it with a fuel supply.

'The lease for the benefit of the United States Steel Corporation is operated under the name of the United States Coal & Coke Co., which is a subsidiary company of the Steel Corporation..."'

## Interlocking Directorates

The Pocahontas Coal & Coke Co. is closely allied to the Pocahontas Railroad, both through the Norfolk & Western Railway Co. and through their several directorates. Three directors and one vice-president of the Pennsylvania Railroad are directors of the Norfolk & Western Railway, and three of the same men are directors of the coal company. The Norfolk & Western Railway Co., is closely allied with the Pennsylvania Railroad and The Pennsylvania Co., having four directors in common. The Girard Trust Co. of Philadelphia – one of the Morgan & Co. group of banks – (and) the Pennsylvania Railroad Co. have five directors in common. Both the United States Steel Corporation and the Pennsylvania Railroad Co. are dominated by Morgan & Co. interests.

"The Norfolk & Western Railway, while already owning the large Pocahontas Coal & Coke Co. tract in the Pocahontas Field, as previously described, in 1917 extended its interests into Mingo County and Pike County, Ky., as shown by the following extract from its annual report of Dec. 31, 1917.

" 'Owing to the high prices of fuel coal, your company decided to acquire leasehold interests in coal mining properties in order to mine a substantial portion of its supply. Accordingly leasehold interests in mines in Mingo County, W. Va., and Pike County, Ky., known as the Howard and Vulcan operations, have been acquired. These operations include about 3,800 acres, and it is estimated that they will furnish one-sixth of your company's present fuel coal requirements.'

"The Steel Corporation's subsidiary company in the Pocahontas field, the United States Coal & Coke Co., is the largest producer in the

State of West Virginia, putting out in 1918 nearly 5,000,000 tons, or more than one-fourth of the aggregate of the seven companies producing above a million tons per annum. (Annual Report Director of Mines, West Virginia, 1918.) This company in 1918 operated 11 plants at different places in McDowell County and employed 3,888 men, or nearly twice as many as the next largest company in that field.

"The second largest producer in the Pocahontas field is the Pocahontas Fuel Co., producing in 1918 nearly 3,000,000 tons and employing over 2,000 men. The president of this company is Mr. Isaac T. Mann, who was associated with Messrs. Gary and Edenborn of the United States Steel Corporation in the syndicate purchase in 1901 of the larger portion of the Pocahontas field to which we have previously referred.

## Absentee Owners Get Rich

"Since that transaction Mr. Mann has become the head of a coterie of men living in and near Bramwell, W. Va., who control a group of banks and operating coal companies, which, including the Pocahontas Fuel Co., employed in 1918 nearly 7,000 men and produced almost 5,500,000 tons of coal. Included among these companies is the Red Jacket Consolidated Coal & Coke Co., of which, according to the Pujo report of 1913 on the money trust, Mr. E.T. Stotesbury is a member of the firm of Morgan & Co. Mr. Stotesbury also was director of the Girard

Trust Co., and of the Penn Mutual Life Insurance Co., of Philadelphia, and at that time each of these companies held $100,000 of the bonds of the Red Jacket Co.

"The third largest producer in the Pocahontas Field is the New River and Pocahontas Consolidated Coal Co., producing in 1918 over a million and a half tons and employing about 600 men in McDowell County. The controlling director and president of this company is Mr. E.J. Berwind. Mr. Berwind is a director of more than 40 industrial and financial corporations. He is a director of the Girard Trust Co., of Philadelphia, and of the Guaranty Trust Co., of New York, both of these institutions belonging to the recognized Morgan group. In 1905 Mr. Berwind was one of the large shareholders of a syndicate formed to acquire the property of the Tennessee Coal, Iron & Railroad Co. to be turned over to the United States Steel Corporation. This property included over 240,000 acres of coal land located in the Birmingham district...

"The Cleveland-Cliffs Iron Co. operates mines in Logan County, whose output in 1913 was nearly 300,000 tons and employed about 300 men. One of the directors of this company is a director of the United States Steel Corporation."

We hope that the above documentation is enough to show the domination of the West Virginia scene in 1921 by United States Steel – that is, by absentee ownership, which simply means that the wealth of the larg-

est bituminous coal producing area in the world was si-
phoned away, leaving West Virginia a comparatively
poor, backward "hillbilly" state, without the fine roads
and schools which its miners had so richly earned.

1/21/1953 (Forty-fourth)

We shall linger with a discussion of the United
States Steel Corporation for just a little longer. For fear
that there may be someone in 1953 who does not yet
know the anti-union attitude of this financial giant we
quote the missive conveyed to all subsidiaries of the
corporation by its executive committee six weeks after
it was organized in 1901.

> "That we are unalterably opposed to an ex-
> tension of Union labor and advise subsidiary
> companies to take firm position when these ques-
> tions come up and say that they are not going to
> recognize it; that is, any extension of unions in
> mills where they do not now exist; that great care
> should be used to prevent trouble, and they
> promptly report and confer with this corpora-
> tion."

The West Virginia coal companies in Logan and
Mingo demonstrated in 1920-21 that the order "to take
firm position" was not ignored. The chain of command
was like this: coal company, then railroad, then U.S.
Steel, then Girard Trust Co. of Philadelphia, then Morgan & Co. of New York. It is not too strong a statement
to aver that the State of West Virginia in 1921 was a
sponge in the hands of J.P. Morgan, to be squeezed dry
of wealth, and woe to him who opposed that squeeze!

Samuel Untermyer, a nationally known lawyer and industrialist of liberal tendencies, did not hesitate to point out the role of U.S. Steel on the West Virginia scene. In reply to a coal operator testifying before the Kenyon subcommittee he retorted: "I would like to say in reply, with all due respect, that when you have seen as much of the subterranean operations of the company as I have, and the agencies through which it deals, and know as much as I do about the effect of its interlocking directorates and its indirect control of industries, you understand, you will change your mind as to whether or not the United States Steel Co. under cover has anything to do with the labor situation in West Virginia. Its fingerprints, in my judgment, are all over."

## An Analogous Case

Untermyer brings out an interesting illustration of the power of the steel company which had an almost exact parallel recently in President Truman's decision to change a government action against an oil cartel from a criminal to a civil suit. The reasons given were that such a criminal suit would endanger our national security.

The same thing came about in regard to U.S. Steel. Under the Sherman Act, President Theodore Roosevelt brought a civil suit in the first place, however, against the huge corporation, rather than instituting a criminal action. The case was postponed for a long time until finally we found ourselves involved in World War I, with the case still pending before the Supreme Court. The court, needless to say, did not dissolve United States Steel when it finally made a decision. Untermyer explains the matter thusly:

"And then after it had postponed the case, finally the situation was acute along at that time and they granted a reargument and I presume – I am not criticizing the court, because we were in a terrible situation and the Steel Co., with its power, had grown more and more, and it was supplying the Allies and supplying us, and we were in a terrible condition, under financial stress, and if the court had enforced what I believe to be the law against the Steel Co., it would have brought on a financial cataclysm.

"The thing had been allowed to grow and grow until it had gotten so big that it was bigger than the law; that it was bigger than the nation, until it had such a monopoly that they did not dare to touch it."

The recent governmental tenderness with the oil cartel is an analogous situation.

So much for the tremendous financial forces which were opposing the miners in their organizational drive. The enemy, it must be conceded, was sufficiently powerful to give any man or group of men pause; but the miners of Mingo held on grimly. And the miners of the Kanawha field mobilized with their rifles at the mouth of Lens Creek.

Most of this account has been concerned, understandably, with Mingo County, for this was the strike field in 1920-21. We have stated, however, that neighboring Logan County was even worse than Mingo, insofar as coal company autocracy was concerned. This is true. Miners in Mingo County had managed to organize UMW local unions and had set up sufficient organization to maintain a strike for longer than a year. In Logan County this was not possible.

Most everyone had heard of a company town. Logan County in 1921 was a company county, manned by coal company police, governed by coal company authorities, and taught by coal company teachers. A coal company doctor brought you into the world and a coal company undertaker – especially if you mistakenly talked like a Union man – ushered you out of it. The undertaker, perhaps, was given much of his business by one or another of the many "deputy sheriffs" of High Sheriff Don Chafin.

Chafin was first elected sheriff of Logan County in 1912. He was the son of an ex-sheriff from whom he was supposed to have inherited about $15,000 and a small business. But he was a long distance from being a wealthy man before he found profit in becoming the head of the armed forces who kept a good-sized chunk of southern West Virginia a police-patrolled private domain. He let his brother-in-law, Frank P. Hearst, have the sheriff's job in 1916, but Chafin was once again a mighty champion of "law and order" in January 1921.

Being sheriff of Logan County was lucrative, although the salary was only $3,500 a year at that time. Chafin, as a matter of fact, paid only a little less than that in taxes, exclusive of income taxes, every year. He had been presented with stock in coal companies worth from fifty thousand to sixty thousand dollars.

Chafin was commander of the deputy sheriffs in Logan, and he fixed the amount of money which each received. The county of Logan did not pretend to pay these men in the usual way, as is stated by the Kenyan subcommittee: "The operators of that county (Logan) contributed in 1920 $46,630 to the payment of deputy sheriffs. The year 1921 it was $61,517.... We have the astounding situation of deputy sheriffs performing duties of deputy sheriffs in the county, and not merely defending property of their employers, paid by contributions from the operators. It is amazing that anyone would seek to defend such a condition."

That Chafin had many ways of making money known only to corrupt politicians is demonstrated by the fact that in 1924 he was convicted of violation of the national prohibition law, fined $10,000 and sentenced to two years in the penitentiary. The system of government in Logan is also shown by the fact that he, Circuit Court Judge Robert Bland, and Prosecuting Attorney John Chafin, the sheriff's cousin, were afterward indicted in federal court at Charleston for beating up or having beaten up the principal witness in the whiskey trial.

1/22/1953 (Forty-fifth)

This writer has in his possession a large number of sworn affidavits or copies of same attesting to the treatment received by persons unfortunate enough to have business in Logan County in these years. As early as 1919 the UMW had attempted to send organizers into Logan. Some few did get into the county long enough to find the jail, but nearly all received the treatment outlined below:

"This day, Samuel Arthur personally appeared before me, B.S. Hastings, a Justice of said county and being by me first duly sworn, says that... in the year of 1919, he was commissioned (along with others –Ed.)... by the United Mine Workers of America, as an organizer for the purpose of organizing Logan County, and they went to Huntington, West Virginia, and purchased railroad tickets over the Chesapeake & Ohio railroad for a station on the Guyan Valley in Logan County called Mann, (named for one of the U.S. Steel syndicate men of 1901 –Ed.) and Logan, county seat of Logan County, there were a bunch of gunmen or Deputy Sheriffs got on (the) train and asked them where they were going and what their business was, and he and other organizers told them they were going to a station called Mann, and that the United Mine Workers of America had leased a piece of land at this place where they were going to erect a tent and organize Logan County and the gunmen told them they would advise them to not set their feet on the ground of Logan County as they would be killed and that the United Mine Workers did not have a lease on a damn thing in Logan County and that the coal companies owned all the land and at every station there would be a bunch of gunmen or Deputy Sheriffs get on (the) train until they reached Mann, and when they got to Mann, there were two machine-guns trained on the train they were on, and he and the others decided that they would not get off at Mann, as they thought they would have trouble or be killed outright...."

## Machine-Gun Persuasion

The affiant continues by relating that the organizers simply remained on the train and went back to Huntington and "every station they passed, there were a number of gunmen and that there was an armored train followed them from end of line to Barboursville and there was also a box car on rear of the train they were in and it had a machinegun in the car." Such were the powerful means of persuasion the coal operators of Logan County used in order to keep out the UMW. The UMW men were able to do nothing but ride the train for approximately 16 hours.

Don Chafin's deputies did not find it necessary to know that you were a UMW organizer, in order to have an excuse to beat you mercilessly. Mere suspicion of Union sympathies was enough for these thugs. Witness the affidavit of one Sam Copley, a UMW member:

"...Upon mere suspicion on the part of any of the said deputies that a man is a member of the United Mine Workers of America or any other labor union, the said deputies either order him from the county or set upon him and beat him or kill him.

"Affiant says that upon two occasions he has been set upon and beaten by said deputies while in said county for the sole and only reason that he was and is a member of the United Mine Workers of America, and that he has seen many other persons beaten for the same reason; that in the month of May or June, 1921, while at Ethel in said Logan County, he was assaulted and beaten by John C. Gore and eight or ten other deputies, who used pistols and blackjacks upon affiant until spit blood for over two weeks thereafter, that upon said occasion affiant was merely passing through said county from Mingo in Coal River when the said deputies learned of his going through and followed him in automobiles, and, after passing him on the road, turned about and, without any warning of any kind, beat affiant almost to insensibility; and that then the said deputies warned him never to pass that way again under penalty of instant death...." It should be noted before continuing that the abovementioned John C. Gore was evidently one of Chafin's principal underlings, and that he later met with a bad end on top of Blair Mountain in the county he so zealously guarded. But this will be covered in some detail a little further on in this history. Let us continue with the affidavit of Sam Copley.

## The Logan Way of Life

"Affiant further says that, in common with many hundred others, he was indicted in Logan County in connection with the armed industrial disturbance occurring in August and September, 1921, and, on the 13th day of April 1922, having been required to go to the county seat of said county for the purpose of entering into a new bond for his appearance, he was again set upon by several of the said deputies at the said town of

Ethel as he was getting off the train on his way home, and was struck with a pistol, knocked under the train and bruised until he was scarcely able to reach home; that the said deputies again warned affiant never to pass that way again under penalty of being killed. Affiant further says that shortly after his said indictment he was arrested by members of the Department of Public Safety and lodged in the Logan County jail and was confined therein fourteen days; that during said confinement he contracted smallpox, and was fed mostly on rocks and beans, and affiant believers he would have almost starved had it not been for some food he was able to get from the outside; that upon the slightest protest being made as to the food, the jailer, a man by the name of White, would beat and abuse the complaining prisoner; that upon one occasion, when a prisoner made a complaint about his treatment and asked for a broom with which to sweep out his cell, the said jailer White beat him with a large jail key until he was very bloody about the head and face and was almost insensible.

"Affiant further says that the blanket which was given him while in said jail was stiff with human blood, and that the mattress was covered with blood, and affiant was then advised by other prisoners in said jail that a prisoner had been killed in the bed given affiant. Affiant says that the ceiling and walls of his cell, which was about eight by twelve feet in size, were spotted with blood, the said cell being commonly referred to by prisoners as the 'Bull Pen' and, at the time herein referred to, contained twelve prisoners."

Such was the admirable state of things in Logan County that at no time was the governor required to declare martial law as was his habit in Mingo. This was because, as can be seen, there was REALLY law and order in Logan!

We shall labor this point a bit further, as it was not necessary that you be a Union organizer, a Union member, or anything else but a plain decent citizen who happened to offend Don Chafin in order to get beaten or shot in Logan County.

The pastor of the First Baptist Church of Stone Branch, in this most blessed section of the United States, happened to be in Logan town, the county seat, eating a bit, when asked this question by Chafin: "You belong to the God Damn Union, don't you?' The pastor replied that he did not, whereupon

> "...Sheriff Chafin assaulted affiant and punched him in each side and said get up God Damn you, he (affiant) arose and the sheriff smacked him on the side of the head with a pistol, then he ordered his gunmen to go through this affiant, who then and there searched affiant's grip and person, and took affiant's credentials from his vest pocket, examined and returned same to him and said, 'Be God Damn sure you do nothing here but preach," then they rushed affiant out the door."

Another gentleman named D.E. Gunther was a stock and mine salesman in Logan County who had prudently gotten a letter from Chafin which said he was all right. When Gunther was stopped by a deputy sheriff, which happened at least 25 times in his travels, the letter from Mr. Big was all the pass needed in order to go on his way, sometimes with a friendly automobile lift from the deputy.

But the favor of tyrants, as Gunther discovered, is a transient thing. He was staying one night at a Logan town hotel, and was awakened by loud singing and later by some noise in the room next to his. This happened to be a bathroom, the door of which was locked. Turning on the light to investigate the noise, Gunther discovered that it was 3:58 a.m., and that someone was trying to enter his room by kicking at the locked bathroom door. Gunther told the kicker that it wasn't his room and not to come in. The kicker, however, had a mind of his own, and declared with adequate swearing that he intended to enter.

Gunther phoned the hotel clerk and asked for peace and quiet, and the clerk told him to repeat what he had said, which Gunther did, as the noise next door stopped. The hotel clerk said he would be right up. Let Mr. Gunther continue:

> "I sat on the edge of the bed, and in about as long as it would take for a person to come to the third floor someone rapped on my door. I asked what was wanted, and the reply was 'Open

the door.' Thinking it was the clerk, I opened the door and was confronted with Sheriff Chafin, who had a gun in his hand against me. I asked, 'What is the matter, Mr. Chafin?' and he replied, 'You dirty ------, what is the matter.' and struck me on the chin, knocking me partly across the room. As I went backward, I turned a chair over and fell, my head striking something, and before I could recover from the blow and fall, Chafin was over me and kicked me in my right side and back over my kidney. He then jerked me to my feet and knocked me down again.

"I begged him to stop, for I knew I was not guilty of anything wrong. Chafin then told me to dress and get out of there, to leave the hotel, town, the county and state...."

### 'Law and Order' in Logan

Gunther tried to dress and Chafin left the room. Then the sheriff returned and "started swearing at me, still covering me with his gun. He then knocked me down three times and kicked me twice. I was yelling for help, but no one came. (The proprietor's room was just opposite to my room on the same floor. He told me the next morning that his wife became hysterical as a result of the racket and yelling, but he never made any effort to come to my assistance.)"

The hotel clerk also told Gunther that "it would have been just like committing suicide to have even put his head out the door." So we see that sometimes the hotel accommodations in Logan in 1921 were all that might have been expected of a cell in the Nazi Buchenwald. Gunther was comparatively lucky, for he did collect $2,500 damages from Chafin in an out-of-court settlement, something which no coal miner ever got.

The truth of Senator Kenyon's statement that "there is complete industrial harmony in Logan County" should by the above be documented sufficiently to satisfy most readers. Certainly the coal miners in 1921 had been convinced in a brutal and bloody manner, and part of their resolve as they gathered at Lens Creek seems to have been to capture the county and take it out of the hands of Don Chafin.

Let it be most solemnly and emphatically stated, lest there possibly be any doubt remaining at this point, that the thousands of miners assembled for their now-famous march to Blair Mountain were no armed hoodlums intent on plunder, murder and assorted villainy. These were men of the same stamp as those who opposed the Stump Act, who fought Royal Governor William Berkeley under Nathaniel Bacon, who suffered with Washington at Valley Forge. They were men who wished to make a reality of their mocking state motto which proclaimed that Mountaineers Are Always Free.

A great many, perhaps most, of these miners were familiar with Jack London's famous novel, *The Iron Heel*, a fictional representation of an iron-shod dictatorship. But to them this was no fanciful world but a reality which existed in their own state. And they, like brave men, preferred to risk their lives rather than exist under such a regime. The coal operators prepared long lists of the names of miners who participated in the

March of 1921 in order that they might be jailed and prosecuted or hounded out of the State of West Virginia. The operators did not realize that in so doing they were preparing something else, and that something is a Roll of Honor.

## Democratic League Is Formed

Reference has been made to the fact that on Aug. 1, 1921, the date of the murder of Sid Hatfield and Ed Chambers, the miners attempted to establish what they called a Constitutional League. The nomenclature is perhaps unfortunate, as it may be confused with an operator organization named the American Constitution Association, a pro-Fascist group formed before the term "Fascism" was coined in its present-day significance. We shall pay our respects to this latter association and its principal spokesmen a little later. Just now we want to quote from the original invitation that such a Constitutional League be formed, as this shows the real nature of the demands of the marching miners.

And it also indicates that many citizens other than miners were sympathetic with the Union cause and angry at the dictatorial methods used against Union organization. Though the league itself never became effective, due to later developments, the proclamation of purpose is interesting and revealing. It begins thus:

"TO LABOR, ORGANIZED AND UNORGANIZED, AND ALL GOOD CITIZENS OF ANY PROFESSION OR CALLING WHO BELIEVE IN THE MAINTENANCE AND PERPETUATION OF

THE CONSTITUTION OF THESE UNITED STATES AND THE BILL OF RIGHTS OF THE STATE OF WEST VIRGINIA, GREETINGS:

"In view of recent developments in Mingo County and elsewhere, and because of the admissions made by Captain J.R. Brockus of the state police in his testimony before the Senate Committee appointed to investigate conditions in Mingo County, we here and now call upon you to take cognizance of the fact that all civil liberty and constitutional rights are fragments of past history insofar as West Virginia is concerned.... Pioneers inscribed upon the emblem of this great state that 'Mountaineers are always free men.' The freedom signified by that emblem has ceased to exist..."

1/24/1953 (Forty-seventh)

"THE MEN IN CHARGE OF THE SO-CALLED MILITARY OCCUPATION OF MINGO COUNTY AT THIS TIME ARE THE SAME MEN WHO BROUGHT THE STATE INTO NATIONAL DISREPUTE IN 1912.

"Do you not think the time for action has arrived? Do you not think some organization should be formed that would protect the Constitutional Rights of even the most humble citizen? Do you not think that a Constitutional League should be organized for the purpose of publicity and to secure political action in the interest of the majority of the people instead of a few corporations who are absentee land owners, paying no taxes to the state, contributing nothing to its up-keep and only interested in the state of West Virginia for the dividends they are permitted to clip by exploiting its natural resources? Why not call mass meetings in every locality and get an expression from the citizens and write the Secretary of the West Virginia State Federation of Labor as to whether they are in favor of organizing a Constitutional League or not, and if so, the proper literature will be furnished with which to complete each branch of the league. Ask the doctors, lawyers and all professional men to join you in the resurrection of civil government in Mingo and other counties of West Virginia....

"Resolutions and protests are not heeded by the political office-holders of today. They adhere to nothing but action and if you expect your activities to count for anything, you must perfect an organization that will effectively combat political aspirants who are owned and controlled by Big Business.

"THINK OF THESE MATTERS AND ACT AT ONCE."

The above signed by C.F. Keeney, then President of UMW District 17, James Riley, President W. Va. State Federation of Labor, H.L. Franklin, Sec.-Treas. W. Va. State Federation of Labor, and Fred Mooney, Sec.-Treas. of District 17.

## Hatfield Murder Gives Impetus

The decision to form a Constitutional League and the printing of the above occurred before the authors had learned of the murders of Hatfield and Chambers. This outrage, combined with the refusal of Governor Morgan to intercede when appealed to on August 7, pushed the pace of events to blinding speed. The miners of the Kanawha field would not be stopped in their desire to liberate their brothers in Mingo and Logan.

The sub-district system was then in effect in the organizational setup of District 17. William Blizzard, who had entered the mines on Cabin Creek at an age when children in nearby Charleston were entering school, was president of Sub-district No. 2, which encompassed the Mingo and Logan territory. He was credited by the coal operators with being the field-general of the army of marching miners, although he was still in his twenties.

From the written notes and diaries of coal company spies and coal operators it is evident that there was considerable "unrest" in the whole Kanawha field from the time of the killing of Hatfield and Chambers on August 1 until the culmination of the miners' anger in the Armed March. It is significant to observe that these records reveal that standard equipment of every coal company in these peaceful, organized localities seemed to be a large supply of high-powered rifles and an occasional machine gun. Just why they kept such arsenals is not clear, but it was certainly not to hunt the squirrels that abounded in the surrounding hills.

The miners knew of the arsenals and simply appropriated them; in many cases, however, promising their return at a later date. There is every reason to believe that the coal miners, after learning of the refusal of Governor Morgan to listen to their requests of August 7, met in their local unions and made decisions as to their willingness to participate in an Armed March into Logan and Mingo, the assembly point to be at Marmet.

## War Veterans Among Miners

World War I veterans among the miners helped to give the group an appearance of military discipline. Mention is made of one man being shot as a spy near Marmet, and this is not difficult to give credence to, as many other lives were at stake. There was a password for getting into and out of Lens Creek (some testimony asserts that it was "redbird" at one time), and the official "uniform" was a pair of overalls and a red bandana handkerchief around the neck. It was a citizens' army which assembled at Marmet, crudely organized, but well armed and serious, with great unity of purpose.

During late August the miners drove toward Marmet in wagons, in old Fords and Reo Speed Wagons; some came on foot, others on the family horse or mule. If they had guns they brought them, if not they came without, evidently believing that they would be supplied by arms from coal company caches. By August 23, the whole valley below Marmet was teeming with armed miners and their varied vehicles. Their District 17 leaders and others, including Mother Jones, were obviously in contact with the miners, and made frequent speeches. At this point the story becomes even cloudier and more contradictory than is usual at a time of social crisis. We shall not attempt to assess the role of Keeney, Blizzard and Mooney as regards their attitude and action in the 1921 march. All were later tried on murder charges and acquitted of same. Blizzard had the additional honor of being tried for treason against the State of West Virginia at the scene of the John Brown trials in Charles Town, West Virginia. He was acquitted and is at present president of District 17 of the UMW. From his office window on a clear day he can almost see the old encampment site near Marmet.

**Intentions Not Clear**

If the District 17 and sub-district UMW officials were actively supporting the armed gathering of miners it is not clear as to whether they had in mind only a public demonstration which would draw national attention to the plight of the miners or whether they expected to win their fight by the last resort of armed force. This writer inclines toward the latter opinion.

It seems, however, that Mother Jones had different ideas. The fighting old champion of the miners had been a leader in West Virginia coal fields since before the turn of the century. By this time she was 91 years old, but definitely with a mind of her own and a tongue to back it up. It is almost certain that Mother was in touch with federal officials in Washington, and was using the gathering of the miners near Marmet as a lever in order to get strong governmental action to aid the miners in feudal West Virginia. At a speech at Lens Creek on August 23 Mother intimated that she would soon have good news for "her boys." This could only mean that she anticipated friendly treatment from President Warren G. Harding or his associates.

The young District 17 leadership had been to a man something like the pupils of Mother Jones. They had grown to manhood under her tutelage, but now believed her to be an old woman who was not as alert-minded as in former years. They put no faith in President Harding or any other political office-holder, for they had been too many times promised everything and given nothing. They evidently trusted only their own strength. In this it must be said that the students had outstripped the master, and this led to an interesting conflict between Mother Jones and the young UMW leaders.

# Chapter Nine: Mother Makes Mistake

1/27/1953 (Forty-eighth)

The extent of the involvement of the District 17 officials in the organization of the Armed March of 1921, if there was such involvement, will never be known. And the initial part played by Mother Jones will also remain dark, for even today men do not chatter freely about what was literally a life-and-death matter. This writer is also the author of a short work on the life of Mother Jones and is as a result rather familiar with her methods of work over a number of years. Considering the hostile press of her time (which is certainly no less hostile today), Mother was a fine agitator, who knew how to use events for maximum publicity effect.

Whatever her part in the organization of the march, it is clear that she was intent on using it in late August as a means of focusing attention on West Virginia and procuring federal intervention in the miners' behalf. It is also clear that she was horrified by her discovery that the miners had every intent of actually going across the hills by foot, car, horse and even commandeered freight train, and that their attitude toward Don Chafin and the Baldwin-Felts guards was just this: An eye for an eye and a tooth for a tooth.

Knowing Mother's history and her real devotion to the miners, this writer can not think that Mother, in her whole life, ever sold them out. She simply felt that the Armed March was a mistake, that it would accomplish no good end, and would play into the hands of the coal operators by giving them grounds for wholesale legal reprisals. There is evidence that some operators in the unionized fields felt the same way and gave money and arms and encouraged the marchers in their armed protest. For in this way they could hurt their competitors a little, and, much more important, have a weapon with which to fight the hated UMW.

It is also true, however, that Mother Jones was 91 years old, and in all those years was entitled to a few mistakes. In seeking federal intervention in 1921, as she had gotten it in 1912, she was pursuing a policy which had worked before. But it is not easy to see just what she hoped to accomplish in this case. In 1912 her work procured an investigation committee which did much to help the miners win their later contractual victory. But in late 1921 another federal investigating committee was already in West Virginia, and had been for months. Aid from the Harding administration was possible of course, but not likely. The men who helped to make an American historical landmark of the Teapot Dome scandals were not apt to be overflowing with ardor to help coal miners.

And it is a fact that Mother Jones thought a great deal more of Governor Ephraim Morgan of West Virginia than an active partisan of the coal miners should, a circumstance which the District 17 leadership pointed out with much acerbity. Mother, herself, in her autobiography, says this:

> "For myself I always found Governor Morgan most approachable. The human appeal always reached him. I remember a poor woman coming to see me one day. Her husband had been

blacklisted in the mines and he dared not return to his home. The woman was weak from lack of food, too weak to work. I took her to the Governor. He gave her 20 dollars. He arranged for her husband to return, promised his executive protection.

"I was with the Governor's secretary one day when a committee called to see the Governor. The committee was composed of lickspittles of the mine owners. They requested that the Governor put *The Federationist,* a labor weekly, out of business. The Governor said, 'Gentlemen, the Constitution guarantees the right of free speech and free press. I shall not go on record as interfering with either as long as the Constitution lives.'

"The committee slunk out of the office.

"I think that Governor Morgan is the only governor in the 23 years I was in West Virginia who refused to comply with the requests of the dominant money interests. To a man of that type I wish to pay my respect."

## Mother and Keeney Clash

The young leadership of District 17 did not at all agree with this estimate of Governor Morgan, and this writer must side with them as opposed to Mother Jones. This is written in no carping, or "debunking" manner. Mother Jones was great and selfless champion of the miners, with few peers. But even the great may err, as we feel that in this case she did. Morgan was as much on the side of the coal companies as any other governor of West Virginia, as we think we have already shown. And we will have more to say.

In any case the District 17 leadership and Mother Jones disagreed on a number of points. People who know the labor movement will not have to be told that those who lead labor generally possess positive opinions. It is not an unusual thing for equally positive opinions to clash in internecine labor battle. The men who led the UMW in West Virginia were perhaps a little jealous of Mother's great prestige, and this may have been a complicating factor, plus the undoubted fact that Mother Jones was a rugged individualist who took no orders from anyone and frequently did not advise other UMW organizers or the District organization of her plans until they were confronted with a fait accompli.

On the night of Aug. 23, 1921, Mother made a speech before the assembled miners on Lens Creek in which she promised that she should soon have good news from Washington in the form of a telegram or communication from President Harding. According to District 17 Secretary-Treasurer Fred Mooney, some Union committeemen visited him the following morning in Charleston and wanted to know what Mother meant. They wanted to know why President Harding would wire Mother Jones instead of the District organization.

Mooney and Keeney were just as curious as the men were, and they went to Lens Creek to see what Mother was going to say. They arrived as the old woman was concluding her talk, the main burden of which was that the men should go home and give up the idea of an Armed March to Logan. She held in the air what was purportedly a telegram from President Harding advising them to do the same. C. Frank Keeney, District 17 head, asked Mother if he might look at the telegram – there is some testimony that he tried to snatch it from her hand – but she refused the request. Mooney also asked Mother for a look and was likewise refused.

1/28/1953 (Forty-ninth)

It is almost certain that both Mooney and Keeney then told the assembled miners that the telegram did not exist, that the piece of paper in Mother's hand was a fake. It is absolutely certain that they said this later, for Mooney went back to Charleston and telephoned George B. Christian, Secretary to President Harding. Christian advised that the President had sent no such telegram. The miners were immediately notified of this fact. Mooney explained later that he released this information because Mother Jones had told the *Charleston Daily Mail* that he and Keeney urged the miners to go right on to Logan and pay no attention to Mother. Mooney said this was not so, that he and Keeney had on the contrary told the miners to return to their homes. Who is here bending the truth a bit is not known. It is known that the coal operators later used this story in the *Charleston Daily Mail* in their attempt to convict of murder and hang Mooney, Keeney, and Blizzard.

There is a nice lesson here for Labor: If you are going to have family fights don't publicize them in anti-union newspapers, for this can lead to a severe pain in the neck.

The coal operators in later court battles tried to prove that the majority of the miners on the march were coerced into going by a minority "radical" element. That there were leaders in the affair, and that leaders are by the nature of things in a minority can not be denied. But it is obvious that the majority of miners were boiling mad and ready for anything. Individual coercion of the fainthearted exists in any struggle involving personal danger. That it existed on a large scale in the "Armed March" of 1921 is not borne out by the records.

**The Miners March**

Secretary-Treasurer Mooney testified later that Mother made her speech before only about 600 of the miners on Lens Creek and that "the main column had gone on up the creek, further over the creek toward Racine." Attempting to determine exactly what happened by consulting files of Charleston newspapers is a hopeless task. As Mooney pointed out: "I have written an article myself and sent it in and they have twisted it so you would not recognize it – both papers."

This speech of Mother Jones' and the consequent argument occurred August 24, and that day and night the armed miners left their encampment near Marmet in great numbers, pouring up Lens Creek and over the hills toward Boone County. Through the town of Racine they traveled, up Drawdy and Rock Creek into Danville and Madison. A few reports aver that they were sometimes accompanied by miners' wives and daughters wearing nurses' caps with the letters "U.M.W. of A." sewn neatly to the brims.

The "uniform" of the angry miners, for those who observed such regulations, were blue denim overalls and red handkerchiefs around the neck, in accordance with their traditions. Some sang as they went. Reliable sources allege that one of the tunes was "John Brown's Body" and that the improvised words announced that "they would hang Don Chafin to a sour apple tree." Don Chafin, it will be recalled was the autocratic sheriff who ruled Logan County for the coal operators.

As has been told before, the miners had a sort of military organization for the march, with sentries posted, patrols organized, and passwords for the identification of enemies and friends. At first it seems that the password in reply to a challenge was "I come creeping." It was later changed so that the challenge was "Where to" and the reply from a Union man was "Mingo" or "to Mingo." If you challenged a party of men by waving your hat up and down they were supposed to reply, if friendly, with the word "Selma," according to some evidence.

## The Army Lands

Miners were supposed to have commandeered freight cars which bore numbers of men and such titles as "Blue Steel Special" and "Smith & Wesson Special."

The general movement of the miners was toward Blair Mountain, a high ridge over near the town of

Logan, where centered the demesne of Sheriff Don Chafin. A fiction writer might well use Blair Mountain in some symbolic manner, as it was the dividing line between the Union forces and the nonunion fields. A small portion of Logan County on one side of Blair Mountain was unionized. On the other side, to the south, was a howling wilderness, so far as Union men were concerned.

This concerted march of thousands of armed miners, needless to say, was brought to the attention of the state and federal governments. Governor Morgan, through Major Tom Davis, dispatched Capt. James R. Brockus from martial-law-ruled Mingo County to the aid of Don Chafin. With him Brockus took 71 regular state police and about 15 of the "volunteers" before mentioned in this history. This turned out to be an important action, historically, as we shall show later, but these police did not arrive in Logan until about 6 a.m. on the morning of August 27. The Federal Government had meanwhile intervened.

This was at the request of Governor Morgan, who evidently had men reporting to him who were in close touch with the situation. Gen. Harry H. Bandholtz of the United States Army arrived in Charleston at 3:05 a.m., August 26th, and proceeded to the temporary "pasteboard" capitol which had been erected to replace the stone building destroyed by fire on Jan. 3, 1921. Here he met Governor Morgan and they summoned Keeney, Mooney, and UMW Attorney Harold Houston. The sleepy-eyed Union officials found Morgan and Bandholtz in a room crowded with policemen, state officials of varied ranks, and the military staff of Band-holtz. They were ordered to proceed at once to turn back the marching miners.

District 17 President Keeney explained that he might well get shot if he attempted such a thing without something to show that the United States Government had given him orders. Keeney asked General Bandholtz for a letter, signed by the General, ordering him to turn back the marchers. Bandholtz at first refused, but later consented to this arrangement, according to Keeney himself when interviewed recently.

1/29/1953 (Fiftieth)

Keeney and Mooney then took off toward Boone County, where most of the miners had by this time congregated, in order to talk with the marchers. The Union leaders telephoned later in the day (August 26) telling General Bandholtz that they were having success in inducing the men to withdraw.

On August 27 General Bandholtz, with two other military officials, got in an automobile at Charleston at 11:15 a.m. with William Blizzard, then President of UMW Sub-district No. 2, and followed in the path of the marching miners over a "very difficult road" to the Boone County town of Racine. In view of later events, part of the courtroom testimony of Bandholtz should be given verbatim:

"Q. Why did you make that trip that morning, General?

"A. To satisfy myself that the miners were re-turning as reported. In addition to that, I had sent Major Thompson further up the river for a like purpose.

"Q. Did you satisfy yourself that they were re-turning home?

"A. I did.

"Q. Did you receive any report from Major Thompson on that occasion, as to what he found?

"A. I did – confirmatory of my own."

After satisfying himself, as he relates above, that the march of the miners had ended, General Bandholtz returned to Charleston and took the 6:40 train back to Washington, D.C. This was on the 27th day of August, 1921. It is clear that the General was correct in his esti-mate – the miners were returning to their homes, al-though none too willingly. But a very little match can cause a mighty conflagration in such an explosive situa-tion.

**The Sharples Incident**

And on the same night that General Bandholtz and his retinue left West Virginia the coal operators through Don Chafin and a contingent of state police which Governor Morgan and Major Tom Davis had sent from Mingo to Logan County, furnished that match. This was the Sharples incident.

There is reason to infer, both from this action near Sharples, Logan County, and the seeming fact that some of the operators in the Union fields aided the marchers with arms and food and encouragement, that in the Armed March the coal operators saw an excellent club with which to break the back of the United Mine Workers of America; with the coal operators superior firepower, if not numerical superiority, and the backing of the United States and West Virginia governments, they had nothing to lose by provoking the armed miners into revolt. They had, in fact, much to gain, for with the Government of West Virginia their docile tool they would not themselves be subject to prosecution in the courts. And they stood an excellent chance of obtaining severe legal penalties against the UMW.

But this would not have been easy if the miners had merely returned peacefully to their homes after having been warned by representatives of the Federal Government. So, if the inference is correct, something had to be done by the coal operators to again rouse the miners to hot-blooded anger; an incident had to be manufactured which would again set the miner on the march. Such an incident was manufactured, if the theory of this writer coincides with the facts.

It will be recalled that Mingo County was still under martial law, with Major Tom Davis, a veteran of such labor-quelling measures, in charge. About 2:30 a.m., Aug. 27, Davis ordered State Police Captain James R. Brockus, of Lick Creek fame, to proceed to the aid of Don Chafin in Logan County. Brockus, with about 85 or 86 other regular state police and "volunteers" did as he was told. The Captain did not go into Logan just to help Chafin in a general way, but for a specific purpose. This was to lead a group of men across Blair Mountain and serve warrants on Union coal miners. This Brockus proceeded to do, augmenting his armed force by adding a number of Chafin's deputies thereto.

Let us look at this move more closely. Major Davis ordered Brockus to Logan on orders from Governor Morgan. This request to Governor Morgan for men to serve warrants could have come only from Don Chafin. Chafin of course knew exactly what was going on as regarded the armed march of the miners. And Governor Morgan knew that the miners were returning home, and that General Bandholtz was going back to Washington that same day. Just why did Morgan rouse police in Mingo County out of bed at 2:30 a.m. in order to be able to serve warrants in Logan County that same day? ESPECIALLY IN VIEW OF THE FACT THAT DON CHAFIN HAD THE WARRANTS IN HIS POSSESSION FOR SOME DAYS PRIOR TO AUG. 27?

## March Starts Again

Why, in other words, did the warrants have to be served by state police in such a hurry? It seems apparent that Morgan wished to cause an "incident" which would encourage the miners to resume their march on Logan County, thereby forcing the armed intervention of the Federal Government, and giving the coal operators more opportunities to file charges of murder, insurrection, and even treason against the miners and their leaders. If he waited until all the miners had gone home, it might be too late. The iron was, on the night of the 27$^{th}$ day of August, 1921, still hot, and Governor Morgan struck with haste.

Brockus left Mingo County with his armed force about six o'clock on the morning of the 27$^{th}$ and met Don Chafin, who gave the Captain warrants for the arrest of 30 or 40 miners who lived on Little Coal River in Union territory. Brockus picked up some deputies from Chafin, swelling his forces to about 130 men, and they crossed Blair Mountain about dusk in regular military formation. That is, there was an advance guard of 15 men and two guides about 200 yards in advance of the main body of police.

Just on the other side of Blair Mountain they were met by five Union men who challenged them but surrendered without resistance. These men were arrested, evidently without warrants, and placed at the head of the column. This was a thoughtful measure, for the miners were advised to tell anyone who challenged not to fire, and it was also a protection or shield for the police. This same process was repeated several times, with the number of prisoner-shields increasing, until Brockus and his force reached the town of Sharples, where they found another detachment of five miners. Brockus of course maintains that these men fired upon his group of 130 men after he had asked what they were doing there at that time of night. (It could not have been later than eight o'clock.) Whoever fired first, two of the miners were killed and the other three fell, wounded. Shooting then became general, according to Brockus, with miners firing from houses in Sharples and the police shooting back.

However it was, it is a fact that not one of the 130 police and deputies was scratched, while houses in Sharples were pierced by bullets and the challenging patrol of miners lay dead and wounded. News of this shooting at Sharples, done by what had all the appearances of an advance guard of a much larger force, spread through the coal camps of Boone and Kanawha counties. "Don Chafin's thugs are invading the Union fields, and they have already murdered our men!" was the alarm that struck the ears of the Union miners.

Miners returning home from their intended march to Logan simply turned on their heels, and with angry faces declared that once again they had been doubled-crossed. No leader could have stopped the movement then, not with the tongue of Demosthenes. The Armed March began again.

1/30/1953 (Fifty-first)

That Governor Morgan had ample intelligence reports from the vicinity of Sharples is indicated by his evident close relationship with William M. Wiley, the Vice-President of the Boone County Coal Corporation, and also an operator at Sharples. For both he and Morgan were directors of the reactionary and operator-bossed American Constitutional Association, which we have already mentioned and will treat more fully a little later. Wiley, a South Carolinian by birth, also belonged to the equally reactionary National Association for Constitutional Government and the National Security

League, with headquarters in New York. All of these organizations are evidently precursors of the Committee for Constitutional Government, a group which, with John T. Flynn as one of its leading spokesmen, furnishes a warm nest for every reactionary idea ever spawned in America.

Wiley's Corporation was capitalized at $7 million and was composed as he said, of 32,000 acres of the "best coal land in the United States." In addition to bossing the above, Wiley also taught Sunday School, and considered himself something of an intellectual. "The doctrines of Karl Marx," Wiley solemnly told the Senatorial Investigating Committee" have been taught to these people until they have accepted them as a religion instead of the teachings of their mothers." What their mothers taught Wiley does not indicate, and the exaggeration in his statement has been treated in previous chapters.

### Marchers Go to Sharples

Wiley very well understood his own interests, and was evidently exceptionally shrewd in his dealings with the union, enough so that he bowed to the inevitable without outward manifestations of his inner hate. He was without doubt interested in seeing the UMW driven from every coal field in the nation and it pleased him not one bit that his nonunion competitors might also be unionized. This is his revealing remark on the subject: "I met Blizzard on the street the other day – the president of the subdistrict in which my operation is – and he told me that soon the nonunion fields would be unionized and men in my position would be relieved from that competition, and he expected me to join with him in the joy he was anticipating." What reaction Blizzard really expected from Wiley is not known. What he got later is matter of record – a legal barrage with extermination as its object.

Wiley was at Sharples on Saturday night, August 27 – when Captain Brockus and his men descended on the town. He admits to the Kenyon Committee that he had been informed by telephone that the police were coming, but he says he didn't believe it. Be that as it may, he certainly told none of his miners. And he confirms the fact that it was not till after this shooting that the miners poured into Sharples from every direction, more or less taking control of the railroad above Sproal, where Little Coal River goes over toward Logan, and the Big Coal River valley extends to Whitesville, and leads through a railroad tunnel into Cabin Creek, Paint Creek and other fields, Wiley says:

> "These men (the miners –Ed.) came in on the trains, and some of them marched into our clubhouse where our officers lived and at the point of a gun demanded that food be cooked for them at most unusual hours. Colored people were not supposed to go into the dining room, and they took them as they pleased and they refused to pay for what they got."

From part of the above statement it seems that the gentlemen from South Carolina did not support certain sections of our Constitution pertaining to race, creed and color, despite his affiliation with organizations carrying the name of that document in their title.

## Solons Blame Chafin

Further confirmation that the specific instigation of the latter and more serious part of the Armed March must be placed at the door of the coal operators is found in the report of the investigating Kenyon Committee.

"The cause of this turning back was without doubt the ill-timed service by Captain Brockus, of the state constabulary, acting under the direction and with some of the deputies of Sheriff Chafin. When the marching miners had begun definitely to turn back towards their homes, Sheriff Chafin undertook to serve warrants upon 42 men at Sharples who had held up and disarmed members of the state constabulary on August 12, fifteen days previous. The sheriff, according to his own testimony, had had those warrants for several days, but the time chosen to serve them was after night and with an armed force of about 130 men. Sharples was in the heart of the troubled area and in Union territory. Just at the time the miners had been dissuaded from their first march and had begun returning to their homes and reports had come out of this territory that the trouble was over, the descent upon this town at night to serve these warrants could hardly have had any other effect than to start afresh the threatened trouble."

If this is so obvious to the senatorial committee it must have been equally so to Governor Morgan, Don Chafin, and other distinguished citizens who were coal operator partisans. Our theory as to why the Sharples incident occurred has already been given.

As the news spread of the Sharples raid the miners began their march all over again, a fact of which the authorities of Logan County were immediately made aware from a dozen sources. From the nonunion side Don Chafin and his men, possibly 2,000 in all, including deputies, state police and anyone else who could be pressed into service, marched toward Blair Mountain. From the Union side the miners, some with machine guns captured from coal company stores (again, why did these peaceful industrialists maintain such arsenals?), also directed their steps over rutted roads and grassy mountain paths toward the same destination. On August 28, according to the same William M. Wiley before quoted,

> "The Logan Operators' Association passed a ringing resolution, which was telegraphed to the Charleston Chamber of Commerce, who had a meeting, and a committee from the Governor (was sent –Ed.) to Washington to explain to General Bandholtz just exactly what the situation was and to put up to the federal authorities the dire necessity for troops."

This "ringing resolution" and action bears out and still furthers our theory as to the origin and reasons behind the Sharples incident.

As we have said, Don Chafin was notified from many sources that the miners had turned back after the Sharples raid, and were proceeding toward Logan

County. But a very prominent gentleman had the honor of being the first to notify the "law-and-order" sheriff of Logan. His name, along with his own explanation of his telephone call, will be given in the next installment of this series.

1/31/1953 (Fifty-second)

The gentleman who first informed Sheriff Don Chafin that the miners had resumed their march toward Logan was seen recently on television by millions of viewers. He presided at the Republican national convention at which General Dwight Eisenhower was nominated for the office of the President of the United States, with Richard Nixon as his running mate. He is a Republican national committeeman. His name is Walter Hallanan.

His explanation of the matter is given below in a letter to UMW Attorney T.C. Townsend, wherein he politely refuses to testify as a defense witness for William Blizzard in one of the murder trials which grew out off the Armed March.

"I take it that you had the subpoena issued for me in connection with the testimony of Sheriff Chafin of Logan County that he had been given information by me as to the resumption of the march. I recall that you mentioned this matter once before to me and I was perhaps not entirely frank in replying to your question and may have given you the wrong impression. I recall that you said something to me concerning it one evening in front of my house....

"The facts are these, as I recall – I happened to be talking to Siegel Workman of Madison from my home one night about midnight while the trouble was going on. I think I had called him with reference to some political matter, then in the course of the conversation he mentioned to me that the miners had resumed their march toward Logan County. I had been in the Governor's office earlier in the evening and knew that it was the impression that the miners were returning to their homes. After talking with Workman I called Governor Morgan and told him what I had learned from Mr. Workman. I felt it my duty to give him this information under the circumstances. He in turn asked me to call Sheriff Chafin at Logan and give him the information that I had received from Mr. Workman. I called Sheriff Chafin and told him the source of my information and what I had learned. I really had supposed that he knew of the resumption of the march before that time, but later on when I saw him in Huntington he told me that was the first information he had received concerning the miners turning again toward Logan County.

"I am very sorry if there has been a misunderstanding in the matter. I had intended to talk with you fully about it before the Lewisburg trial was called. You probably have the wrong impression from your former conversation with me as to my knowledge of the matter.

## Hallanan Is Shy

"I, of course, would like to avoid any party (sic) in the trial because I have a naturally (sic) antipathy to appearing as a witness. However, I am writing you fully so that you may know just what facts I would have to testify to if called as a witness. If you should desire me after having received this further information, please call me on the phone or write me...."

With the hope that "everything is moving along nicely," Hallanan closes his letter.

It is interesting historically that Hallanan played this role in the Armed March, but not of great moment. For before the morning sun of August 28, 1921 had wiped the dew from the courthouse lawn Chafin had received ample confirmation of Hallanan's midnight telephone call. Every able-bodied man who could be lured, persuaded, bought or coerced into joining Chafin's forces of "law and order" was mobilized into a small army and marched toward Blair Mountain. We say "coerced" advisedly, for Chafin's methods of recruiting soldiers were in some cases similar to his methods of combating unionism. We offer this affidavit as proof of our contention:

"This day, G.P. Armstrong personally appeared before me, S.M. Foster, a justice of said county (of Boone –Ed.) and being by me first duly sworn says: that he is by occupation a timberman and in the month of August 1921, he was cutting timber for a lumber company in Logan

County and when the deputy sheriffs tried to make him fight against the invasion of Logan County, he went out of the lumber camp and hid in the woods for three days, and came back to work and worked up until September 21, 1921, when he ran into some deputy sheriffs names unknown, knowed (sic) only were sheriffs by their badges, about dark and (one) of them said, there is the damn son of a bitch who would not fight against the damn rednecks and the deputy sheriffs told him they believed he was a damn redneck and that they were going to kill him and when he started to run, one of the deputy sheriffs knocked him down with a pistol and three or four of them beat him and kicked him until he went unconscious (sic) and he come to himself at 2:30 the next morning and went into the hills and the next day he came down to Jeffrey in Boone County and further says he would not go back to Logan County as knows they would kill him."

Being "drafted" in Logan County in 1921 involved something more than a letter of greetings!

## Fabulous Logan County

There is so much that should be told of Logan County. We fear that we have already endlessly bored the reader through our anxiety for thorough and incontrovertible documentation. We shall linger no more, therefore, upon the peculiar system of government in that area and era, nor shall we speak of the unbelievable harshness of men such as Chafin and William H. Coolidge, chairman of the board of directors of the Island

Creek Coal Co. We can not refrain, however, from noting that Coolidge was from Manchester, Massachusetts, and he got in on the ground floor in Logan County in 1901, buying 30,000 acres of coal land.

He was a director in at least 20 corporations, more than he could remember, and his net profits for one year ran to $2,200,000.

Coolidge, needless to say, was more than a little arrogant in his testimony before the Kenyon committee. When he had finished, he asked Sen. David I. Walsh, also of Massachusetts, if it hadn't been "unfortunate" that he had answered questions the way he did. "No, sir," replied Walsh, "I will tell you what, I have claimed there were persons like you for 10 years and nobody would believe us, and you have exhibited yourself, and I am delighted with it, if you ask me."

Incidentally, we note that we have referred to a Republican in this installment. With fine impartiality we shall point out that in 1921 Logan County was a Democratic stronghold.

But we leave these interesting asides, and revert to the armed men who were heading toward a collision on Blair Mountain.

2/3/1953 (Fifty-third)

As has been related, after the Sharples incident of August 27 the miners resumed their march toward Logan, Don Chafin was warned that this was the case, and the two opposing forces began to line up on opposite sides of the Coal River-Guyandotte River watersheds. It was deadly serious business and both sides were well-armed, but organization in both "armies" was somewhat helter-skelter, as is shown by the fact that no one to this day seems to know, even within some thousands, just how many men were involved.

Governor Morgan sent W.E. Eubanks to Logan County to take charge a day or so after he had been informed that the miners were still on the move. Eubanks was a traveling salesman, a member of the West Virginia Legislature, and a colonel in the National Guard. When asked how many men he commanded at this time Eubanks replied that "It was estimated at from 2,500 to 4,000." Neither did he know the size of the force opposing him, saying that it was supposed to be from 5,000 to 8,000 strong, but he didn't know exactly.

The confusion on both sides of Blair Mountain must have been enormous. The Union men and their sympathizers poured in and around Clothier and Sharples, using every type of transportation, just as they had in the initial part of the march. Men not accustomed to military ritual, and excited anyway, gave some highly original variations on "I Come Creeping" when replying to a challenge. But so long as the idea was about right they were permitted to pass. On the south side of Blair Mountain the antiunion forces set themselves up with nurses and doctors and commissaries and flung out a battle line between 15 and 18 miles in length.

One observer described the action of the next few days when he said that each group went up its respective side of the mountain and both shot at the top. A great deal of shooting went on, that is certain. The operators had a number of machine guns, and the miners had captured at least one themselves, with a miner operating it who had been a gunner in World War I. Eubanks, the traveling salesman colonel, judged that his side fired between 500,000 and 600,000 shots and he supposed the miners "wasted as much as we did." Eubanks had a weapon the miners did not possess, however. This was the airplane. The coal operators hired aviators W.F. Denim, Earl Halloran and R.S. Haynes to "observe" for them. At least Denim and Halloran claimed that they did nothing but observe. Haynes, however, admitted that he dropped two types of bombs on the miners, one explosive and the other designed to cause nausea and vomiting.

### Lawyer Represents Client

It is not known whether or not Haynes succeeded in killing or maiming any coal miners, but he certainly made attempts, later describing how the miners scattered and took to cover when the bombs were dropped. For his contribution to "law and order" Haynes was paid $400 by the coal operators, who must have congratulated themselves that they lived in an age which boasted such efficient weapons for use against coal miners.

Aside from the general barrage, each side sent out patrols. The three men that operators admit were killed on their side (and in this case there is no reason to doubt their estimate) met their deaths as a result of patrol action. How many coal miners were killed will never be known, as the miners through their years of struggle did not permit the opposition to learn of their casualties if they could prevent it, and the same policy evidently was followed at Blair Mountain. It appears, however, that they had far more men killed and wounded than the coal operators. The brutality of the Logan deputies has been pointed out, and it was again shown in some of the fighting at Blair Mountain. For instance, one miner killed, a Negro, was shot 11 times. Is it not clearly evident that this butchery sprang from pure sadism, with racist overtones, but it is not difficult to believe.

Among prominent Charleston citizens who were on Blair Mountain, supposedly shouldering a gun for the coal operators, were Ben B. Brown, a lawyer, and George L. Coyle, a merchant. Brown, in courtroom testimony, spoke proudly of his part in the affair. "I had a verbal commission (from the governor)," he said, "and I left my work just as did old man Putnam in the Revolutionary War." Brown was not quite accurate here, as he had not left his work, but was merely continuing it as attorney for the coal operators. It must be said that Mr. Brown was more zealous than the usual run of lawyers in defending the interests of his clients.

There was a great deal of shooting done around Blair Mountain, that is certain, to cause so little loss of life. The reason for this seems to be that the miners made no real concerted push toward Logan in an attempt to crack the enemy lines during the days of active battle from Aug. 31 through the first two or three days of September. Had they done so there would have been heavy loss of life on both sides, although the miners would have won. That they were confident that they could defeat Chafin's army is shown by the remarks of Phil Murray when he reported on the West Virginia situation to the 28<sup>th</sup> consecutive and 5<sup>th</sup> biennial convention of the UMW:

**Estimates Are Elastic**

> "I visited the battle front, met with large numbers of the citizens' army, discussed every phase of the so-called insurrection with them, and am satisfied in my own mind that if Federal troops had not arrived in the State of West Virginia, as it was self-evident to any casual observer that the outcome was inevitable, as the citizens' army was making steady advance into the camp of the enemy."

There is little reason to dwell in detail upon some of the shootings that went on between small groups of miners and deputies. It is sufficient to note that there was a good bit of this, and that John Gore, an assistant of Don Chafin's, was killed, along with two other deputies named Cafago and Muncy. When asked for the correct password by a Union patrol they answered instead "amen." A battle ensued in which they were killed. How many were really killed and wounded in the Armed March, as we have said, will never be known. Coal operator Walter Thurmond told the Kenyon Committee that he had heard estimates of from 300 to 500. As the chairman of the committee pointed out, this was quite an elastic estimate. All estimates as to detail of the Armed March must remain elastic. It was that kind of battle. Eye witnesses who were not participants were not welcome, as we shall show in our next installment.

# Chapter Ten: Deputies Shoot Reporters

2/4/1953 (Fifty-fourth)

The situation in West Virginia during the closing days of August and early days of September, 1921, had developed into a shooting war between coal operators and coal miners, and sympathizers of both sides. As Phil Murray pointed out, the miners were not alone in their battle:

> "The general impression has been created by the Governor that this moment of protest, or 'invasion' as they call it, was confined to members of the United Mine Workers of America. Nothing could be further from the truth. As a matter of fact, and from my own personal observation, I know that the men who were on the firing line, fighting for abolition of the guards and Baldwin-Felts system, consisted of miners, railroad men, merchants, doctors, ministers of the gospel and almost every element of the citizenry of those communities and throughout the state."

The miners were not made to feel better during their march when they received news that C. Frank Keeney, their District 17 president, and Sec.-Treas. Fred Mooney, had been indicted on a murder charge in Mingo County. What the miners felt that this meant is related by William Petry, UMW organizer:

> "That meant that they, too, were to be done away with, like Sid Hatfield and Ed Chambers. Keeney and Mooney disappeared. Where

they are I don't know, but I'm assured they are safe from the hired gunmen at present."

In miners' parlance, the Union leaders were "hiding out," an indication that they also were firmly convinced of just what fate the operators desired for them. Petry amplifies his statement concerning the murder charge: "As a matter of fact, Keeney and Mooney were 250 miles away attending a state labor convention when the killing of a mine guard (with) which they are charged took place in Mingo county."

Leaders of other unions supported the UMW marchers. For instance, here is a statement of James Lord, then President of the Mining Department, American Federation of Labor:

> "This cry from Mingo county is the cry of the disinherited and the oppressed, that had run out all down the vistas of time, and will never be stilled until this country, and every other country, is in reality and in fact, a government of the people, for the people and by the people."

Such was the feeling as the firing went on near the Boone county – Logan county line. As we pointed out in the last installment, non-participants, such as newspaper men, were not precisely welcomed by either side. The miners were aware of the fact that they had seldom received a friendly press, and West Virginia coal operators were afraid of out-of-state reporters over whom they had no control.

Some little noise was made in the press over the fact that a group of Washington, D.C. and New York "war correspondents" were fired upon and actually shot while covering the West Virginia scene near Blair Mountain. That one reporter was wounded seems borne out by the facts; but there is evidence to show that the coal miners were not the culprits, despite editorial intimation to the contrary and the undoubted fact that the miners had no reason to love many gentlemen of the fourth estate. Here is the story as given in the Sept. 10, 1921 issue of the newspaper, *Labor*, published in Washington, D.C. The story is under the byline of Clint C. Houston:

> "A party of Washington and New York newspaper correspondents had a narrow escape from the rifle fire of Morgan's army. They were traveling along a mountain ridge on their way to Logan, seat of Logan county, when bullets began to sing all about them, coming form the point where Morgan's men were located. Boyden Sparkes, of the *New York Tribune*, received a scalp wound and was hit in the leg. Miss Mildred Morris, of Washington, representing the International Press Service, received a sting on the head by one of the bullets.

> "The corresponding were rescued from their perilous position by two miners one of them was shot in an ankle while guiding the party to a place of safety. When the correspondents reached the line held by the state police they were arrested as spies, but were finally released by showing military passes signed by General

Bandholtz, of the War Department, who had arrived on the scene ahead of the Federal troops.

"The 'defenders' who fired upon the correspondents were under the command of Sheriff Don Chafin, of Logan County, who has long been a tool of the coal operators..."

The Boyden Sparkes referred to as receiving a scalp wound wrote an article describing the dispersal of the Union miners which we shall quote as fully as possible, despite the fact that Sparkes obviously did not have the background to understand the coal miners of West Virginia. For the article is well-written and unconsciously revealing in many ways.

## Federal Troops Intervene

Governor Morgan, as soon as he heard that the March had started again after the Sharples incident, immediately got in touch with President Warren G. Harding who in turn summoned General Bandholtz for a conference. Bandholtz had returned to Washington on Aug. 28, saw Harding on the 30th, and was ordered back to West Virginia, arriving at Charleston Sept. 1. The General then wired the Adjutant General to send Federal troops at once to the Mountain State. By the second day of September there were 170 troops at Madison, and by the 3rd 700 soldiers around that town and Jeffrey, with smaller groups scattered elsewhere. There were, in all, between 1,500 and 2,000 troops in the coal fields, plus a number of bombing and observation planes. Gen. Billy Mitchell, of later "airpower" fame, was on the scene in case the opportunity presented itself to test his theories as to the effectiveness of the newest military weapon.

It is clear that the federal men were in many cases sympathetic toward the miners, although individual sympathies would have meant nothing if there had been a showdown battle between them and the coaldiggers. There would have been slaughter. One man, who said he was a pilot in the armed forces in 1921, told this writer that he was ordered to fly a bomber to Charleston from an airfield in Virginia, and that he jettisoned his bombs in the James River. General Bandholtz himself manifested anger over the Sharples incident, blaming the coal operator deputies and state police for being responsible for the second phase of the Armed March.

The coal miners were angry men, but they were a long distance from being fools. They surrendered to the soldiers without the latter being required to fire a shot. Their plight, however, after they returned home, was far from a happy one, for the troops left the coal fields within a few days without any sort of change in the status quo being recommended by federal or state officials. As a writer for the *Charleston Gazette* recently put it, in the usual newspaper fashion, "local authorities again took over administration of law and justice" in the affected counties.

After we give the story of Boyden Sparkes concerning the surrender to federal troops, we shall speak more fully of the sort of "law and justice" the miners received after the Armed March. The miners and their leaders were, in fact, left to the tender mercies of their enemies.

The exhaustive investigation by the Kenyon Committee might as well not have occurred, insofar as remedial action by federal or state governments was concerned. The miners in West Virginia remained under industrial autocracy.

2/5/1953 (Fifty-fifth)

As we have said, we are going to quote at length from an article which appeared originally in *Leslie's Weekly*. It was written by the newspaper man who was shot, according to the evidence we have given, by the Don Chafin forces on Blair Mountain. We use it not because we consider the analysis in line with sound thinking. We don't. We consider it an authentic eyewitness account of the surrender of the miners to the federal troops in Sept., 1921, at least on one front. And there is the added reason that it points out certain of the Logan coal operator attributes with some accuracy:

"JACK DALTON VERSES BILL BLIZZARD – IN THESE TWO LEADERS ARE PERSONIFIED THE CONFLICTING IDEALS THAT HAVE LED TO CIVIL WAR IN WEST VIRGINIA.

"(By BOYDEN SPARKS)

"(Editor's note – Mr. Sparks, the author of this article, was sent down to the scene of hostilities in West Virginia as the staff correspondent of a New York newspaper, in the course of a thorough investigation of the conflict, including interviews with the leaders of both sides, he exposed himself to rifle fire and came away with bullet wounds in the leg and scalp. He insists, however, on a strict neutrality of attitude, since both sides shot at him.)

"In one of the old melodramas that toured the country before the movies came along to provide daily thrillers the hero through clenched teeth would shout: 'Now then, Jack Dalton, gimme them papers.'

"Then came the awful struggle on the edge of the precipice. So it was something of a surprise to discover that Jack Dalton is still cast in the role of villain in West Virginia's mine war, or at least that part of it which raged along the Logan – Boone County line until the federal troops forced a temporary suspension of hostilities.

"Jack Dalton is the principal owner of the largest nonunion coal operation in West Virginia. He is president of the Main Island Creek Coal Co., which is operating about 27 mines on its 27,000 acres of Logan County coal land. It has other property in other counties.

"It was with the intention of forcing the unionization of those mines that a red-badged army recently sought to invade Logan County from the neighboring and unionized County of Boone. To that mob, or army, if you would have it so, Jack Dalton represents 'privilege' and 'the interests' and 'Wall Street,' and yet he used to be a miner himself. His career, in fact, suggests one of Horatio Alger's boy heroes and is complete justification for those who argue that America offers every youth a chance to get to the top.

## Very Fancy Diggings

"Bill Jones was the first man down there in the West Virginia hills to mention Dalton to me. Jones is the general superintendent of the Main Island Creek Coal Co. I had gone with him to Omar, the center of their operation, to see for myself how nonunion miners are treated by their employers. All shooting had stopped two days before.

" 'You'll sleep in our president's house,' said Jones, easing his six-shotter into a fresh position on the front of his khaki breeches. 'He is in Huntington now, but the house is open.'

"We mounted the steps of a large frame house with a pyramidal roof. On one side were the railroad tracks. Across the muddy street was the rambling Young Men's Civic Association, a clubhouse conducted by the company for their employees. Unlocking the door, Jones led the way through a deserted lower floor to a large bedroom upstairs. It was furnished in golden oak.

" 'Dalton's a great guy," said Jones. 'He used to be a miner himself. Came up here with $10,000 and opened up this field. We're getting out 40,000,000 tons a year.'

"I went into the adjoining bedroom. It was as large as an ordinary apartment house living room. The tub was enormous, and there was a wonderful shower. Here was a miner's long suppressed desire to be utterly clean and free from coal grime finally expressed in several thousand dollars worth of plumbing. I used both baths and then crawled into the massive golden oak bed with an armful of newspapers....

"I met him (Dalton) the following day in Huntington, at the offices of the Main Island Creek Coal Co., which occupy an entire floor of one of Huntington's tall, modern business buildings. He proved to be wide, stoop shouldered, clean shaven and dark. He is big, and when he shakes hands you feel the power of muscles developed digging coal far back inside of a West Virginia mountain. Dalton was in the room where his board of directors meet. This is furnished in mahogany. Maps of his companies' properties hang on the wall. Half a dozen of his executives were there. Each of them told me something about the depredations of Union miners. They whispered tragically of nationalization; of the winter suffering of the nation if ever the Guyan field is unionized and a general strike is called. Dalton merely listened. He puffed steadily at a black cigar, but sat impassive sphinx-like.

## Chafin King of Logan

"One of his executives, when the boss was out of hearing, said: 'He's a born trader. He'd rather trade than eat.'

"But I think that the important thing is that he used to be a miner, a nonunion miner, and that he is determined that his miners shall continue to be nonunion. When the unions are willing to use force to effect organization, Jack Dalton is willing to use force to prevent it.

"His weapon – and the weapon of the other coal operators in the field – is Sheriff Don Chafin and his deputies. And whatever you may think of the system, the coal operators pay their salaries, and the deputies make of Logan County a region utterly unhealthy for Union organizers and agitators. Be sure, however, that Jack Dalton cares little what you think.

"Chafin, whose mother was a Hatfield, a woman of the feudist clan, is called the king of Logan County. Yet, if there were no Chafin I believe that Dalton would have another king on the shrieval throne. Chafin is merely a convenient instrument, ready forged and tempered with Hatfield blood.

"So much for Logan County, where each miner deals independently with his boss. Across the ridge in Boone County it is different. There collective bargaining is the method of dealing between miners and operators; and, it may be said, the operators there sing in a different key. Some of them openly supported the miners' army when it mobilized there in the Coal River Valley.

"If there is a king in Boone County I should say it was Bill Blizzard. At least Blizzard was the dictator while the miners' army had a firing line that extended the full length of the Logan – Boone County line. Blizzard is a sub-district president of the United Mine Workers. His territory includes all of Boone County, and would include Logan if that county was organized.

2/6/1953 (Fifty-sixth)

(Today's installment continues the quotation from a magazine article describing the dispersal of one sector of the miners' Armed March of 1921.)

"Blizzard arose from the ranks in the coal mines to the leadership of his fellow miners. Ten years ago he worked in the mines of Cabin Creek and played an important part during the strike of 1912 and 1913. His work was recognized by the State Federation of Labor, and he was elected president of sub-district No. 1 (An error. It was No. 2 –Ed.). I first saw him when the Federal troops entered Madison. The miner's army – the rednecks – then confronted along the serrated top of Spruce Fork Ridge the hastily recruited defending army of Logan.

"The Coal River division, a section of the Chesapeake & Ohio, about 60 miles long, loading from St. Albans on the main lines (15 miles west of Charleston, W. Va.), south across Boone into Logan county, for two weeks had been operated as the miners dictated, except for one train a day, that carrying the United States mails. Even on that the miners had exercised a strict supervision over the passengers. It had been the miners' main line of communication with the world outside the valley.

"Up and down this valley foraging parties of armed miners had gone from store to store in the small towns, purchasing entire stocks of supplies with receipts promising payment from the United Mine Workers' organization....

"Order in Coal River Valley had been kept by armed patrols in overalls, distinguished by red bandana handkerchiefs knotted about their necks or bit of red cloth tied to their sleeves. Seven moonshine stills were found hidden in the hollows and destroyed. Blizzard knew that he could keep his men in hand only as long as he could keep them sober.

"It was through this region that Capt. John J. Wilson's command of 150 picked Regulars traveled by night to the scene of hostilities. The engine of the troop train pushed ahead of it three flat cars, two soldier lookouts riding at the very front. Those extra cars were intended as a protection against obstructions on the track or explosive mines. The train ran along steadily at 20 miles an hour. Forty-five minutes ahead of it, although Captain Wilson was unaware of it, there traveled a commandeered train loaded with miners going to the front.

## Prosecuting Attorney Upset

"Two hours after the start from St. Albans, the troop train entered Madison, unionized seat of Boone County, and with a normal population of 700. This night a number of its men were up on the Spruce Fork Ridge doing their best to kill other men who dwelt in the seat of Logan County. It was civil war; no less.

"As the train slowed down, the assistant prosecutor of Boone County swung aboard. His name was Hager, a lank, sharp-eyed little man, in a wrinkled suit of light summer 'store' clothes. His knitted tie, almost thick enough to deserve the title of muffler, flopped over his shoulder.

" 'We're glad you're here,' he said to the first soldier he saw. 'A commandeered train went through here on the way to the fighting at Blair just 45 minutes ahead of you. It's been just terrible.'

"If Prosecutor Hager had been a woman, his state of mind might have been diagnosed as hysteria. His breath came convulsively.

"The bugler sounded 'assembly.'

" 'Packs and guns!' Shouted a sergeant, 'fall in.'

"Buckling on their heavy packs, each rolled as neatly and smoothly as a stove pipe, and running their fingers in a final pat over each stuffed pocket of their cartridge belts, the Regulars dropped to the cinder-covered right of way. There they waited, immobile, while half their slender number was selected for guard duty. Outposts with machine guns were sent up and down the tracks. Sentries were stationed at five-yard intervals to 50 yards up the hillsides from the train. As the last of these took his post, Blizzard appeared and accosted Captain Wilson.

"'William M. Blizzard, sub-district president of the United Mine Workers,' he introduced himself. (An error here. Blizzard had no middle initial –Ed.). He was young, wiry, dark-eyed, cordial and convincing. He was short, almost undersized: Jack Dalton, physically, would make two Blizzards. Yet when both men were merely coal miners with numbered brass tags to identify them, Blizzard probably loaded quite as much coal as Dalton.

"The difference between them even then was mental. Where Dalton possessed the trading instinct, Blizzard was endowed – or accursed, as you will – with the spirit of the zealot. When Blizzard takes sides on any question I can imagine that for him the other side is effaced.

## The March Ends

"Blizzard wore a weather-beaten, black felt, narrow-brimmed hat, pulled low over his eyes. He did not wear overalls, but his suit appeared to have been slept in for a week. A necktie was knotted wrong side out against his soiled, white collar.

" 'Are you the general of the miners' army?' he was asked.

" 'What army?' countered Blizzard with a smile, and added: 'I guess the boys'll listen to me all right. I just told the captain here that if he'll send a squad of his Regulars up the line with me, I can get all our fellows out of the hills by daylight....'

"Captain Wilson searched Blizzard and discovered that he was carrying a pistol – 'toting a short gun,' as they express it in West Virginia.

"The Army officer asked him if he had a permit. Blizzard produced one signed by the sheriff of Kanawha County. Charleston is in Kanawha. Captain Wilson returned the gun.

" 'Does this mean you are going to allow only men with permits to keep their guns?' asked Blizzard. Captain Wilson said that those were his orders.

" 'The men on the other side of the ridge will keep theirs?' " 'If they have permits, yes.'

"Blizzard's blue eyes flashed. For a moment he ceased to be the diplomat.

" 'Know what that means?' he demanded. 'Our boys'll be unarmed and those Baldwin-Felts thugs will just shoot 'em down whenever they please.'

"He thought a moment. Then he spoke to a man standing near. This individual trotted away to crank a flivver, and a few minutes later Blizzard was on his way up the line. What he did when he arrived can only be surmised, but when the Regulars moved on up to Sharples at daybreak a few hours later, the miner fighters were coming out of the hills. Their guns had been hidden, probably far back in the black recesses of old coal mines. Their red badges had been snatched off. They were simply a swarm of stubbly-faced men getting out of the hills and back to their homes as quickly as flivvers could take them. But it was Blizzard who started them out."

Thus ended West Virginia's Armed March of miners, the newspaper's penchant for the dramatic. Allowing for omissions from the above that are merely opinion, an opinion that we consider absurd. The description remains intact.

2/7/1953 (Fifty-seventh)

The end of the Armed March, however, was just the beginning of trouble for the coal miners. The operators seized upon the march with great eagerness as a legal means of eradicating the United Mine Workers of America from the face of the earth. That they wished to take no chances of failure is shown by the fact that somehow or other they had their own attorneys to prosecute the miners in trials growing out of the march. A.M. Belcher, for instance, was the prosecuting attor-

ney. He had once been a UMW attorney, but had turned
renegade years before and was now a faithful operator
tool. Another operator attorney was John Chafin, a first
cousin of Don Chafin. That something was rotten in the
State of West Virginia was not merely a Shakespearian
metaphor, and it wrinkled noses all over the United
States, as we shall presently show.

Just how the operators managed to get their at-
torneys, retained by them on a yearly basis, to prosecute
William Blizzard for treason against the State of West
Virginia is not now known.

## Logan's Heavy Hand

The evidence may have been destroyed, or it may
exist in the Governor Morgan files at West Virginia
University. But we print below a letter which will give a
hint. It is addressed to UMW Attorney T.C. Townsend
and is dated July 2, 1923:

> "Dear Sir:
> "I gave Mr. Keeney a note to you in regard
> to some evidence which I accidentally ran across
> after leaving there which I believe would be very
> valuable in showing the powerful influence
> wielded by Logan County with our Chief Execu-
> tive. Thinking that Mr. Keeney might have over-
> looked this matter I am writing you.
>
> "The Attorney General told me that he
> would gladly testify and exhibit the correspon-
> dence between he (sic) and the Governor in re-

gard to his request to represent the State in these trials growing out of the Armed March.

"I seen (sic) these letters and was very much surprised that the Chief Executive would commit himself in writing as he did. He refused to appoint the Attorney General to represent the State on account of the Prosecuting Attorney of Logan County objecting and so stated in his letter.

"I wish you would please ask Mr. Houston to send me a typewritten copy of the statement I got from Edgar Combs as I did not get a chance to get it before I left there. Trusting that all is well with you and that e'er another week rolls by the jury will have came (sic) in with a verdict of ACQUITTAL.

"Sincerely yours,
"/s/ P.D. Burton."

But we are a little ahead of our story. It will be recalled that a murder indictment was brought against Fred Mooney and C. Frank Keeney, as a result of a Mingo County killing, while the Armed March was still going on, and the two men went into hiding for a brief time. It developed that they had gone only as far as Columbus, Ohio. In late November, 1921, they voluntarily returned to Charleston and surrendered to the Governor at the State House. Blizzard, who had for a time been hunting rabbits on Cabin Creek, also surrendered, and all three were confined in Kanawha County jail.

Meanwhile, in Logan County and elsewhere, miners were being arrested and jailed in wholesale lots. James M. Cain, then a young reporter for the "Baltimore Sun," and later the author of *The Postman Always Rings Twice* and other novels, described the situation in a contemporary article:

> "Echoes of the last shots (of the Armed March –Ed.) had scarcely died away before the Logan County Grand Jury was convened in special session. Men were indicted by the hundreds for the murder of John Gore, for insurrection, for violation of the 'Red Man Act,' for conspiracy. Then the regular session of the grand jury was held in October and more were indicted. It was not until the January grand jury, however, that the idea was conceived of indicting men for treason. No sooner said than done, however, so that when the January grand jury was over, 543 men had been indicted in all, whom it was proposed to try and if possible to convict. At the rate the Blizzard trial went, it would have taken exactly 50 years to try all these cases, assuming that the trials are run off one right after the other without any delays incidental to the election of a new judge every six years and the employment of new attorneys as each generation goes by."

## Home for Christmas

It goes without saying that Keeney, Mooney, and Blizzard were charged with a multitude of sins sufficient to keep them behind bars, if convicted, for an inconvenient number of years. Through their attorneys, and through the bars of the Kanawha County jail, they learned of the imprisonment of their fellow miners in Logan. They decided that their presence in Logan might boost the morale of the miners confined there, so Keeney telephoned Chafin on Christmas Eve that they would surrender to him, but would like to spend Christmas with their families. This was arranged with the proper authorities and so it was that the mine-union leaders had Christmas dinners with their wives and children in 1921.

On the day after Christmas the three men boarded a train for Logan and headed toward the county where no Union man had set foot without danger of mutilation or death. What treatment they would be accorded by Don Chafin they could not know, but they were aware of what was possible and it was not a pleasant prospect. Jail was certain, of course, but a good strong cell might be something of a comfort if a lynch mob got ideas.

Keeney, Mooney and Blizzard did not remain in Logan jail for long. Attorney T.C. Townsend was busy making bond arrangements and the men left the jail in January, 1922, after being paraded through a hostile crowd from the jail to the courthouse. As Blizzard was the only one of the three actually present during the March, he seems to have been considered the most desperate "criminal" of the group. For the bonds of Keeney and Mooney were fixed at $10,000 while $20,000 was required of Blizzard. This did not include a $10,000 bond posted in Kanawha County, plus a $3,000 bond covering the issuance of a pistol license.

During the next two months there was much legal maneuvering and at length a change of venue from Logan to Jefferson County was granted. This, of course, was important, for expecting a fair trial in Logan for a Union man was like expecting Hell to flow with cooling waters.

2/10/1953 (Fifty-eighth)

The coal operators now felt that their opportunity for eradication of the UMW had come. And the odds certainly appeared in their favor. For it was without doubt true that some thousands of armed men had rebelled against coal operator rule, which was conveniently garbed in the formal cloak of the state government of West Virginia. The operators had their own lawyers as prosecuting attorneys, they had money, and they had, by and large, a friendly press; although this last was not 100% true, as will be shown.

In attempting to convict the District 17 leadership and other miners of treason to the State of West Virginia the operators were overreaching themselves, but the move was logical. That is, they felt that they had strong cases under, say, the "Red Man Act," which is a repressive old law now obsolete as to original purpose, against individual members of the UMW. The statute has been quoted elsewhere in this work, and pertains to so-called "conspiracy." It has proved a convenient weapon against the coal miners in the past, so much so that it yet remains a part of the Code of West Virginia.

But the operators wanted to do more than merely send a dozen or a hundred Union men to jail, which they might have done with much less expense (for they paid the bills of these trials supposedly conducted by the State). What they wished to do was prove that the United Mine Workers of America was an organization guilty of treason. If they could succeed in this there was no telling where the decision might lead, even on the national level. It might well result in a Supreme Court order dissolving the Union, with implications that all other unions were similarly suspected, in which case the West Virginia coal operators would be blessed by all right-thinking employers everywhere. It will be remembered, too, that this was not purely a local affair, as we have already pointed out with our references to United States Steel and the network of outside capital. The treason trials at Charles Town are thus an important landmark in United States labor history.

It was late April, 1922 that miners and coal operators began their trek toward the apple orchard country which surrounds Charles Town. The focal point was the old courthouse in which John Brown was tried and convicted of treason, which must have been a comforting thought to the defendants. On April 22 a train arrived carrying about 200 miners who had been able to secure bail, and April 23 a special train carrying 250 coal operator witnesses and attorneys steamed into the little station. It is hardly necessary to give the names of the "prominent and important" people who in part composed this group but we will note that they were headed by Gov. Ephraim F. Morgan.

## The Slaves Appear

On this same train were UMW members who had been thrown into jail and had been unable to secure bail. It appears that these men were arrested at the time of the Sharples raid on August 27, and, held without bail, had been lying in Don Chafin's jail ever since. There were nine of them, and they were marched from the train station to the town jail "completely surrounded by armed guards, handcuffed, locked in pairs, then shackled to a heavy iron chain." The Charles Town residents who witnessed this barbarous treatment, perhaps dubious before, were now willing to believe the stories the miners had been telling of conditions in the southern part of West Virginia. The operators at times were stupid in publicity matters.

The miners' worst enemies could not say this of them, for publicity had always been a prime weapon in their struggles, and they were old hands in the game. The operators had generally possessed enough brute force, plus newspaper editors afflicted with blindness characterized by green spots before the eyes, that they felt they could safely ignore public opinion. Not so the miners. They made the most of this operator's "chain gang" incident, and with telling effect.

And they had been busy, without any doubt, ever since they knew of the change of venue from Logan County. This writer is fairly certain that miners were sent to the Charles Town area with their pay statements and those of others, armed with arguments to show that their wages, certainly, were not the prime reason for the high price of coal. And to the farmers of the area they pointed out that they and the miners were, after all, simple working men whose interests lay in common with theirs, despite the coal company propaganda which sought to keep them apart.

How had the 200 miners arrived in Charles Town, when their train had come in two days before Governor Morgan with the nine chained men? It is interesting to note the contrast. All the miners had been furnished with pink lapel ribbons bearing the following words: "United Mine Workers of America Defendant." Their people who had arrived beforehand, their advance agents, so to speak, had organized a reception committee, which met them at the station. Word as to the arrival of the train had been noised about, so that a large crowd was in attendance. The reception committee marched the miners to a public hall over the fire department, where speeches were made and many of the citizens of Charles Town learned that these supposed revolutionists were after all not very different from themselves. On the following day they formulated a Resolution as follows:

### The $90,000 Team

"Resolved, that we, the defendants in the Logan case, in meeting assembled express our most sincere thanks and appreciation to the mayor, the business men's association and the citizens of Charles Town in general for the cordial reception tendered and their genuine hospitality in securing for us suitable accommodations at hotels and private residences and for the many other courtesies extended; be it further

"Resolved, that copies of this resolution be presented the mayor and the business men's association and given the press."

The miners were out to make friends and they passed up few opportunities. The 200 men, with their wives and children, divided into three groups and attended church services at the Presbyterian, Methodist and Baptist Churches. The miners formed a baseball team to play the Charles Town boys, and they were rather careful not to beat the hometown team too often. The composition of this baseball team is probably one of he most interesting on record and was as follows, including name, charge of crime committed, if any, and bail set:

Dewey Bailey, center field, treason, $10,000.

W. Lacey, third base, defense witness Joe Rhodes, shortstop, murder, $1,000. Okey Burgess, second base, murder, $2,500. William Chapman, catcher, defense witness.

A.C. McCormik, left field, murder, $5,000. Cecil Sullivan, first base, murder, $1,000. William Blizzard, right field, treason, murder, etc., $33,000. Okey Johnson, pitcher, treason, $5,000.

J.A. Neff, first base, treason, $5,000 (substitute). Frank Stump, catcher, murder, $2,500 (substitute). Ray Williams, fielder, murder, $2,500 (substitute). Bert Adkins, shortstop, murder, $2,500 (substitute). Frank Snyder, manager, treason, $10,000. Dee Munsey, umpire, treason, $10,000.

This team, which had never played before, beat the Charles Town nine in the first tilt, 7 to 3. The proceeds went to a hospital fund. These miners were rather clever players.

2/11/1953 (Fifty-ninth)

But the munching of popcorn and the yelling of a baseball crowd could not eradicate the grim facts that the coal operators were attempting to stretch the necks of many individual members of the UMW, and through perfectly legal process, annihilate the United Mine Workers of America as an organization.

The trials at Charles Town took place against a rather grim national backdrop. As we have indicated briefly, hard times had come to workers all over the United State in mid-1921, a depression which was a harbinger of the debacle of 1929. Millions were unemployed, among them some 242,000 coal miners. The Republicans had come to power in 1920, and it was their fate to hold the reins of power during the period of the worst economic cyclical crisis in world history.

On April 1, 1922, the UMW in both the anthracite and bituminous fields called a national strike, four months after UMW President John L. Lewis had announced his now famous "no backward step" policy. The essence of the policy was simply that the Union would not bind its members to live as did the nonunion miner, and that there would be no wage reductions. The

1922 strike was a lockout in the sense that the coal operators refused to negotiate or discuss a new wage agreement. It was a violent and bitter struggle even in West Virginia, where so much Union strength was tied up in court battles.

For instance near Cliftonville, W. Va., in July, 1922, there was the old situation of mine guards and evictions of miners, and "transportation" men to take the jobs of strikers. This industrial witches' brew culminated in a battle in which seven Union men, 13 strikebreakers and the county sheriff were killed. The UMW won victory at the national level in about 5 ½ months, insofar as the unionized districts were concerned. In John L. Lewis' words: "The mines reopened with wages and working conditions intact."

**Treason Charges Preferred**

The above sketches briefly the national scene during the trials of the miners who had participated in the Armed March. The State of West Virginia (represented by coal operator lawyers A.M. Belcher. Charlie Osenton, and John Chafin, among others) decided that 24 of the miners, including District 17 and Subdistrict officers, organizers, members of the executive board, and Frank Snyder, editor of a labor paper called the *Federationist*, published in Charleston, would be tried on treason charges. The defense (headed by Harold W. Houston and Thomas C. Townsend) of course filed a demurrer, which was overruled by Judge J.M. Woods, who based his action on a decision of one Judge Story in a Rhode Island case in 1842. William Blizzard, president of Subdistrict No. 2 of the UMW, was selected as the first defendant, and a jury, consisting of 10 farmers, one merchant, and a miller was finally selected.

Both John L. Lewis and Philip Murray were present at Charles Town, the latter as an important defense witness. The trials, it might be noted, were a heavy drain on the Union treasury, estimates of the cost running from $1,000 to $2,000 a day. The proceedings got off to an exciting start with charges by defense attorneys that company gunmen, well-armed, were seated in the courtroom, and the refusal of the operator-attorneys to divulge names of their intended witnesses. One of the first witnesses to testify for the coal operators was Gov. Ephraim F. Morgan. He did not, however, make an impressive witness against the miners, from such evidence as may be procured at this date.

In fact, the one-sided West Virginia industrial situation was eliciting comment from the national press. The *New York Tribune* said: "In his testimony in the West Virginia 'treason' trial Governor Morgan made the extra-ordinary admission that a private government, whose army consists of the notorious 'mine guards,' exists in his state, and that though opposed to it he is powerless to end it.

"If this condition exists it would seem that the treason prosecution should be against the organizers and maintainers of this private government rather than against the citizens of the state who went on the warpath to suppress it."

**Private Operator Government**

The Washington, D.C., *Daily News* commented:

"So far as the law is involved, some coal miners are on trial at Charles Town, West Virginia, on a charge of treason. At the same time, however, the State of West Virginia itself is on trial before the bar of public opinion throughout the entire United States. The state might be indicted in this court of public opinion on several charges, and one of them would be contempt of justice.

"That the coal operators appear to be the real government of West Virginia has been charged for years. Investigations have shown that they wield an extraordinary power in all three branches of the state government. Moreover, it has appeared from time to time that in the state constabulary and the so-called mine guards, the operators have a privately-owned and privately-operated army.

"The attitude of sheriffs toward coal miners was shown, to the amazement of the country, when the indicted miners were brought to Charles Town in manacles and chains. Then when the trial of the miners started the country witnessed the astounding and shocking spectacle of the regularly elected prosecuting officials of the state stepping aside to permit the hired lawyers of the coal companies to take charge of the prosecution and conduct the case.

"It is reasonable to assume, in the light of this spectacle, that the hired lawyers of the coal companies not only produced the indictment themselves with the expectation of doing what they now are doing – prosecuting the cases.

"It looks as if the entire machinery of government in the state of West Virginia had been turned over to the coal operators, to be used as the operators see fit to use it, in their private war on the coal miners of that benighted state. West Virginia may earn the title of The Outlaw State."

West Virginia was not, of course, alone among states in being bossed by huge capital combines, but it was certainly a murderously horrible example.

# Chapter Eleven: A Witness Squeals

2 /12/1953 (Sixtieth)

The "treason" trial of William Blizzard continued at Charles Town during the early days of May, 1922, but there was comparatively little information given that was not already common knowledge in southern coal fields. Nor did it appear that anything new would develop despite a reputed 1,600 witnesses summoned by both sides. The coal operators did not charge, in either this or a later murder trial, that Blizzard actually shot anyone, or was present when anyone was shot. The allegation was that as a leader of the miners he was responsible for their acts and was, therefore, guilty of murder and treason against the state.

In the treason trial they hammered steadily at this point, although the procuring of witnesses for the prosecution, except for state police, military men, Don Chafin, and their own coal operators representatives, was not an easy task. Just how they got witnesses was interesting, this writer is certain, although at the moment their procedure is rather difficult to prove. We shall cite a statement which may give a clue. However it was done, the operators found a star witness in one Ed Reynolds, of Dana, Kanawha County, who swore that he, along with Blizzard, helped lead the Armed March. The star dimmed somewhat when defense counsel Harold W. Houston put the following question, and received the following answers:

"Where you ever at Fayetteville?

"Yes, sir. I was in jail there.

"You were arrested, were you not, for obtaining money – about $600, under false pretenses?

"Yes, sir.

"Who had you arrested?

"Mr. Keeney, the president, and Mr. Mooney, the secretary of District No. 17, United Mine Workers."

Without making any charges that Reynolds was paid well by the coal operators to testify in their behalf, we merely comment that Reynolds was evidently not above taking money under false pretenses. The other major witness for the State of West Virginia was John (or Jack) Brinkman, a carnival employee who said that he was pressed into service by the miners and made to take part in the Armed March. He said that he had seen Blizzard not exactly praising the Lord, but very definitely passing the ammunition to a group of miners.

This was the most criminal act with which Blizzard was charged by any witness, unless swearing at Federal officers, while not in the presence of such officers, might be considered a hanging crime.

That Blizzard did this was testified to by Dick Benton, then Sunday editor of the Huntington, W. Va., *Advertiser*. Also a prosecution witness was Charles E.

Frampton, a reporter for the same newspaper. Just who had strong ties with the "free" press in Huntington was made pretty obvious by this trial.

We have said that the prosecution seemed to have trouble getting witnesses, aside from people from their own ranks, and we have intimated that it was possible that they had great persuasive powers or they would have obtained even fewer. We quote briefly from a statement made in Lewisburg, W. Va., by Charles F. Basham, a miner that the operators tried to talk into being a witness against Blizzard in a murder trial also growing out of the Armed March. If the operators followed such policies there it is not unlikely that they did the same at Charles Town.

"Q. How much money did you receive and from whom?

"A. I received the first $20 from Belcher (chief counsel for the operators –Ed.). I received the second money, $25, from A.M. Belcher, by check. I received the next money from J.A. Scott, $50 – no, $30 it was, before we started to Berkeley Springs. When we got to Berkeley Springs he gave me $10, J.A. Scott did. When we got back at Charleston, on the next day, he give (sic) me $30 more. I went up there again in a few days and he wanted me to go to Logan. I said, 'Yes. I will go over to Logan if you furnish the finance.' He sat down and wrote me a check for $50. I didn't go that day. I went up Cabin Creek and I come (sic) back in two days. Belcher give (sic) me $20. Scott give (sic) me $25 in Logan. When

I come back the next check was $50 and the next was $75 and the last one was $50. Last Monday evening he wired me $25.

"Q. What was the money for?

"A. For me to have a good time on, I reckon. To tell you the plain truth, he was giving it with the expectation of hiring me to swear to suit them. When I am out on the ground walking around I will talk any way to a man but when I am on the stand swearing I won't."

"Q. Who was Belcher?

"A. The attorney.

"Q. Who is Mr. Scott?

"A. That is J.A. Scott, financial agent and, I suppose, paymaster for the Logan Coal Association, for he had always been the man that paid me."

## Miners Exhibit Bombs

It is plain that the operators were not above using methods of suasion which might have been frowned upon by presiding Judge J.M. Woods.

Blizzard's defense counsel was clever and alert. For instance, the prosecution put Adj. Gen. J.H. Charnock on the witness stand and asked if he had any of the rifles the miners were carrying when they surrendered to federal troops. In an obvious attempt to impress the jury, Charnock had three rifles brought in, whereupon he proceeded to snap triggers and manipulate bolts until he was sure that jury and audience were convinced that the miners had been possessed of deadly weapons in good operating order.

The defense immediately topped Charnock's exhibition. It was admitted by the state forces that they had dropped explosive bombs on the miners from airplanes, and it seemed that one of these bombs had failed to explode. Fred Mooney, Sec.-Treas. of District 17, in the middle of the courtroom removed this dud from a suitcase and handed it to Charnock. The latter was directed by defense counsel to take it apart to see what was in it.

The whole courtroom, including jury and judge, was tense. For the bomb was an ugly looking home-made contraption, as an eyewitness describes it: "It consisted of an iron pipe about six inches thick and two feet long, with caps screwed on each end and a foot-long detonator sticking out of one of the caps."

Charnock obediently began to twist the ends of the bomb, until one of them loosened and came off. The Adjutant General poured out the contents of the bomb on the floor for the benefit of the jury.

2/13/1953 (Sixty-first)

When Adjutant-General J.H. Charnock tilted the pipe-like bomb which the state had dropped on the miners, out rolled the following:

One ratchet wheel from some kind of machine.

Seven bolts, 15 nuts, an indeterminate number of screws, nails and minor pieces.

Several pieces of metal that looked like souvenirs from the Baltimore fire.

What looked like the hindquarter of a flivver, although it was afterward denied that any such thing was a bomb.

The vicious nature of this bomb, which the State of West Virginia had thought necessary to drop on its coal miners, made a perceptible impression upon the jury. Compared with it, and the knowledge that it had been dropped from a state-hired airplane, the clacking of rifle bolts seemed rather mild. The defense had scored a point.

Don Chafin himself testified, as did Elbert Gore, 22-year-old son of Deputy Sheriff John Gore who was killed on Blair Mountain, but they had nothing to add to the testimony against Blizzard, unless, as the coal operators contended, Blizzard could be held responsible for the acts of all miners who participated in the Armed March. On May 17, 1922, the State of West Virginia (read coal operators) rested its first treason case against the coal miners. If they were successful in hanging Bill Blizzard they would have an excellent chance of metaphorically stringing up the whole United Mine Workers of America, and were almost certain to eliminate the organization in West Virginia.

It was unfortunate for the coal operators that the principal defendant had to be Blizzard. For he was quite young, a family man with two children, and had the appearance of anything but a wild-eyed desperado. He underwent the trial by jury, along with that old American custom, trial by newspaper, with a cheerfulness which made some think that he had forgotten that his neck was at stake. This writer, however, is in a position to know that such was not the case. Here was the impression of Blizzard received by James M. Cain, then reporting for *The Baltimore Sun*:

**Treason, They Said**

"Blizzard is a young boyish-looking fellow, with a  rather boyish outlook, apparently. How he ever acquired the title of 'generalissimo of the insurrection' is a mystery. Charleston newspapermen say they got hard up for cut lines to go over a picture one time and stuck it on him. This seems about as plausible an explanation as any."

The coal operators based their case largely on the fact that men had assembled at Marmet, which constituted an overt act, and that Blizzard was responsible for all acts of those who participated in the March thereafter. Defense attorneys denied that the charge of treason was allowable in the case, that no overt act of Blizzard had been shown, and that in the Aaron Burr case the idea of "constructive" treason was killed for all time. A "constructive" crime is one in which no overt act on the part of a defendant is alleged: it needs to be proven only that defendant is a member of a group which "conspired" to commit a crime, whereupon he also is supposedly as guilty as if his hands were dripping with blood.

The defense moved to dismiss the treason charges for the reason that no treason existed. T.C. Townsend, last of four defense attorneys to speak in argument which consumed most of two days, ended on this note:

> "The big question involved is whether we are going to turn back the hands of the clock 200 years, resurrect the tyrannical doctrine of constructive treason and constructive presence, and furnish a ready tool for the hands of one class with a powerful backing which wants to destroy another class. This case ought to stop now, because the state has miserably failed to make even a semblance of a prima facie case of treason."

Judge J.M. Woods, however, refused to dismiss the treason charge. His remarks, in part, were as follows:

> "If war is levied by citizens of this state against the state, without aiming at entire overthrow of the government, I think those guilty of levying the war may be guilty of treason.

> "The aim does not have to be entire overthrow of the state in all treason.

**Judge's Ruling Adverse**

> "An attempt to coerce the state government by force of arms would be treason. The evidence naturally has taken this wide range in establishing the body of proof in this case.

"The evidence before the jury is sufficient for their consideration, I believe, to prove an act of levying war.

"The constitution of this state recognized levying of war as an act of treason….

"It matters not whether those who opposed the armed marchers of Logan County were formally enlisted in the state militia or not, because that conflict was only part of an act of treason."

The judge's ruling made matters look not very bright for the young coal miner defendant from Cabin Creek. However, Judge Woods did limit the discussion of overt acts of Blizzard to Logan County, where the indictments were returned. It is rather odd that Judge Woods made no mention in his ruling of what was obvious to so many both within and without the borders of West Virginia, that to rebel against the coal operators was to rebel against the state government for they were one and the same. Carrying the situation to its logical extreme, any coal miner who refused to abide by a decision of his boss was also refusing an order from the state government, and thus liable to prosecution. There was naked industrial tyranny in West Virginia, plain for all to see; that Judge Woods fails to note this fact is merely one example of many cases of judicial blindness.

The United Mine Workers of America was to have other headaches than the treason trial and the national coal strike, both back-breaking burdens. For on the same day, May 19, on which Judge Woods made his adverse ruling quoted above, a suit was filed in Federal Court in Charleston, W. Va., asking $1 million in damages as a result of the alleged shooting up of the Willis Branch Coal Company during the 1919 strike. An attempt was also made to attach the property of the union, valued at about $150,000, in Charleston and Beckley. The coal operators were giving the UMW no rest, pouring in blow upon blow in an attempt to kill the organization which had the colossal effrontery to give their employees the right of collective bargaining strength.

2/14/1953 (Sixty-second)

Defense witnesses were called after the adverse treason ruling of Judge Woods, among them one Roy Roberts, a *Charleston Gazette* reporter who testified that he knew where Blizzard was from Aug. 24 through Sept. 1. Later than that he could not swear to, but assumed that he saw Blizzard at an even later date in the Charleston area, for he was assigned to cover the Union headquarters. This is hardly important, except to show that if you catch a reporter young enough in life and early enough in the newspaper business, he may still be a pretty nice person. Roberts at the time was 21 year of age.

In accordance with the ruling of Judge Woods, limiting consideration of an overt act to what occurred in Logan County, the matter seemed to resolve around just why Blizzard was on Blair Mountain Sept. 2 and 3, 1921, if he was there at all. If the operators proved that he was present he still stood an excellent chance of acquittal if he could establish a reasonable alibi for his being in Logan at that time. But Army General H.H.

Bandholtz was not of much help on the witness stand, in fact injuring the miners' case by reading form the *Charleston Gazette* his statement about leadership carrying with it "responsibility for acts of subordinate," a contention heavily emphasized by the prosecution.

W.R. Thurmond, president of the Logan County Coal Operators Association, admitted on the witness stand that the operators had paid $15,000 to finance the treason trial against Blizzard, $1,000 of this money, he said, was for attorney fees, and the rest for witnesses. Judge Woods excluded the jury from the room while this evidence was being given, and it was not admitted into the record. Woods maintaining that it didn't make any difference who was financing the trial, if Blizzard was guilty. Thurmond said that it was the hope of the operators that they would be able to get some of their money back from the state.

## Murray Takes Stand

Philip Murray took the stand and stated that the UMW as an organization had opposed the March, but that he had no use for coal operator "desperadoes" who were responsible for the incident at Sharples.

"Do you call state troops desperadoes?" demanded A.M. Belcher, prosecution attorney.

"I call the troops who maliciously and deliberately murdered our miners desperadoes no matter who they represented," said Murray.

After five weeks of questioning and cross-questioning, both sides, judge, jury, and general public were growing weary of litigation. On May 25, 1922, defense and prosecution rested their cases. Final arguments were made and the jury was left to make a decision. Coal Operator Attorney C.W. Osenton made a bloody closing speech, demanding the life of Blizzard, and intimating that the prosecution of Chief Counsel Harold W. Houston, presumably also on treason charges, was to occur in the immediate future.

The brilliance of Osenton's oratory was somewhat obscured when, at a high point in his tirade, a juryman's chair broke and one of the 12, good and true, tumbled into a cuspidor.

Coal Operator Attorney A.M. Belcher attacked Attorney General E.T. England, whom he said was "against the state," meaning, of course that England could not stomach the high-handed methods of West Virginia coal operators.

Perhaps 500 people crowded the old courthouse in Charles Town where John Brown had been hanged for treason in 1859, as the jury deliberated the fate of Blizzard, the fate of the other defendants, and the fate of the United Mine Workers of America. For the conviction of Blizzard would be the first explosion in a chain-reaction of coal operator thrusts at the miners and their union. A large burden of responsibility lay upon the shoulders of the jurymen who retired for about two hours and then shortly before 5:30 p.m. on Saturday, May 27, announced to the tense crowd that they had been unable to reach a decision.

The jurymen retired again at 7:30, after a short recess, and at 9:37 they once more filed into the courtroom. This time the foreman announced that they had reached a verdict. Judge Woods warned against any demonstration. The clerk read the verdict: "We, the jury, find for the defendant." Every person in the courtroom rose to his feet, but there was complete silence, broken only by a defense motion that the wording of the verdict be changed to conform with the law. But legal technicalities did not matter to the raw-nerved crowd in the Charles Town courtroom. The verdict was clear. Blizzard was acquitted.

## Operators Spurn Defeat

Judge Woods adjourned court until 10 o'clock Monday, and the pent-up feelings of five grueling weeks could be restrained no longer. Cheers resounded throughout the courtroom. Blizzard's mother, wife and children clung to his neck, while the young defendant, all smiles, shook hands with friends until his hand was sore. He later headed a parade, complete with drum corps, which marched through the streets of Charles Town.

The following comment from *The Nation* magazine was typical of the opinion of the liberal press:

> "The acquittal of William Blizzard, charged with treason in connection with the march of the miners in West Virginia last summer, is a welcome sign of the probable collapse of the entire prosecution. The fact that Blizzard was picked for trial first has been accepted as an

indication that the case against him was the strongest, and its failure to stand up before a jury confirms the impression that there never was any justification for charges of treason as a consequence of the unhappy events of nearly a year ago. The sham and animus of the proceeding is further illuminated by the testimony of W.R. Thurmond, president of the Logan County Coal Operators, that his organization financed the prosecution to the extent of at least $15,000. The ruling of the judge that this fact had nothing to do with the guilt or innocence of Blizzard may be technically correct, but it warrants the assumption of persecution rather than prosecution, and ought to jolt the citizens of even coal controlled West Virginia."

But it was not true that the coal operators had accepted defeat. One other miner, Walter Allen, was also tried at Charles Town on treason charges, and convicted on Sept. 16, 1922. He was sentenced to ten years in the penitentiary, but gave bond and appealed to the State Supreme Court. While decision was pending Allen apparently decided that his faith in courts of law was somewhat shaken, for he simply disappeared, forfeiting bond, and has not been heard from since. His case yet reposes in the Supreme Court files, and decision is still pending.

The Rev. James E. Wilburn and his son, John, were tried on murder charges at Charles Town in June, 1922, for the killing of Don Chafin's deputy, John Gore, on Blair Mountain. That is, they were charged with being in the patrol which fired on Gore and his party. The two miners were convicted and sentenced to 11 years each in the penitentiary. But, in the 1923 murder trial of Blizzard and other UMW leaders, growing out of the same incident, the Wilburns became stool pigeons for the coal operators. As a reward, evidently, their sentences were commuted to five years each by Governor Morgan, and they were later given full pardons by Governor Howard M. Gore. Which proves how great and kind are the hearts of the governors of West Virginia.

2/17/1953 (Sixty-third)

A series of murder trials during 1923 and early 1924 kept the District 17 officials and their attorneys busy. Again the State of West Virginia chose to put on trial William Blizzard, alleging that as a leader of the miners he was therefore responsible for the deaths of George Munsey and others on Blair Mountain. There was a change of venue from Jefferson County to Morgan County and then to Greenbrier County. Blizzard went to trial in Lewisburg, in the latter county, in mid-June, 1923, and after a month of litigation the jury was unable to agree and was discharged by Judge S.H. Sharp.

Blizzard was scheduled for another trial in August in Lewisburg, but grand jury charges of bribery of jurors in the first trial caused another change of venue, this time to Fayette County.

This time C.F. Keeney, District 17 President, had to face a murder charge, but was acquitted in March, 1924. Other trials were set for June, but they never occurred. The coal operators apparently felt that they were going to useless expense in attempting to convict the District 17 leadership of major crimes, for they dropped all charges against Blizzard, Keeney, and Sec.-Treas. Fred Mooney. Nor were any of the many other defendants ever brought to trial.

Without a doubt this sudden cessation of hostilities had behind it very good reasons. It may be that the operators knew that they would deal with the men from the local Union at Eskdale, on Cabin Creek. (Keeney, Mooney, Blizzard and others of the District leadership were all from this same area.) But whether the operators knew it or not, the end of an era was in sight. Gone were the days of District autonomy in the UMW. John L. Lewis had apparently decided that the International Union could better handle the vast miners' empire through a network of appointed District officials, and the effect of this new policy was soon to be felt in District 17. But more of this later. Let us revert briefly to this period of court battles.

## A 'Deliberate Distortion'

This time of the treason and murder trials – 1922 to 1924 – was one of real crisis for District 17 and West Virginia miners. It will be recalled that a national strike was in progress from April 1, 1922, and West Virginia miners were idle for many months. The expenses of this strike, plus the heavy expenses of the trials, were a real burden to the District. There are many references in Union reports of trips to Cleveland and elsewhere for the purpose of borrowing money. But the District weathered this storm, there being, on July 5, 1923, $43,184.77 in the treasury.

The UMW had its difficulties with the press during the time when the very lives of the District 17 leadership were at stake. For instance, here is a telegram signed by UMW Defense Counsel T.C. Townsend and Harold W. Houston, dated July 8, 1923:

"Frederick Roy Martin, Gen'l M'gr.
"Associated Press
"51 Chambers Street
"New York City.

"We hereby re-affirm and stand by the statements made in our joint telegram to you of July fourth to the effect that the reports of the Blizzard trial at Lewisburg, W. Va., as carried by the Associated Press were unfair and prejudicial to the defendant, and unwarrantably favorable to the pseudo prosecution. We are alone responsible for the sending of that telegram and for the protest, and have no notion or desire of retracting one word of it. Am writing you fully."

One or more of the same attorneys, under date of July 10, 1923, also wrote as follows:

"Hon. Herbert Phaler,

"Editor, *Charleston Gazette*,
"Charleston, West Virginia.

"My dear Mr. Phaler:

"I am enclosing you herewith a transcript of a portion of the evidence of Viars containing a portion of his direct and a portion of his cross examination. You will observe from this testimony that Viars went to Marmet to Indian Creek on Big Coal River, reaching Indian Creek about the 25th or 26th of August, 1921. On Saturday, the 27th of August, 1921, Viars returned to his home. He did not leave his home until Tuesday evening, August the 30th, 1921, and reached Blair late Wednesday evening. He remained in Blair on Wednesday night, and went to the mountains on Thursday.

## Newspaper Bias Shown

"On his return from the mountains on Thursday evening, which was September the 1st, 1921, he saw Blizzard. This was the only time he saw Blizzard in and around Blair. Compare this testimony with the article in the *Gazette* of Thursday written by your correspondent here, and you will see clearly that the article places Viars in Blair on August the 30th, and that he saw Blizzard on August the 30th in Blair. By his own testimony he did not leave his home until the evening of August the 30th, and did not reach Blair until Wednesday evening, the 31st of August, and did not see Blizzard until Thursday evening, September the 1st. The article further states that the ammunition which Viars secured from Blizzard was used in the battle where Munsey, Gore and Cafalgo were killed. This battle took place on the 31st of August, 1921, before Viars had reached Blair and before he testifies to seeing Blizzard in Blair. You can clearly see that the article is a deliberate distortion of the testimony."

Additional communication was had with the *Baltimore Sun* and H.C. Ogden of the *Wheeling News and Intelligencer*, in efforts to get unbiased coverage of the court proceedings. The coal company bias of the Charleston newspaper had long been the lament of the UMW, as, indeed, it is today. We have no record of UMW communication with the *Charleston Daily Mail*, and it may be that Union attorneys felt that protest was useless with the hopelessly biased '*Evening Wail*', as it was christened by the pro-labor *West Virginia Federationist*.

As to the charges of bribery in the trial of Blizzard at Lewisburg, this writer is unable to comment, except to indicate that he has in his possession a letter signed by Harold W. Houston, along with some rather interesting hand written statements relating to same which were evidently torn from a small notebook. Houston's letter concludes as follows: "You can trust the bearer of this note. Destroy it as soon as read." The handwritten notes indicate that an unknown party was attempting to sell the letter to A.M. Belcher coal operator attorney, for $3,000. They also indicate that some very well known West Virginia lawyers and politicians did offer this unknown party three one thousand dollar bills for the letter, although they suspected a trap. And it may have been a trap, for all this writer knows. The parties concerned are not likely to do much talking about it, so it must remain something of a mystery. It is mentioned merely to show that the coal operators apparently were not above spending a little money in the worthy cause of hanging members of the United Mine Workers of America.

2/18/1953 (Sixty-fourth)

While the leaders of District 17 were fighting off the attempts of the coal operators to hang them by their necks until dead, the coal owners were quite busy doing "publicity" work designed to show that all this silly talk about miners getting shoved around in West Virginia was merely "radical" poppycock.

To succeed in their purpose they desired something a bit more effective than the sometimes rather dry, although always helpful, reports of the state Chamber of Commerce, and the aid of the editors of the various local newspapers. The latter were doing well in pulling the wool over the eyes of the residents of West Virginia towns, but it was unfortunately true that national attention had been turned toward West Virginia by the Armed March and the consequent treason and murder trials. And this attention, as few remarks from conservative and liberal journals, was not of the most flattering type for the coal operator, who wailed that the honor of West Virginia was being besmirched.

For it has ever been true, and is true today, that the West Virginia coal operator identifies the interest of the state with his own private welfare. In 1921 and thereafter the coal operator was quite justified in this viewpoint, and could say, with Louis XIV, L'etat, c'est moi, that is, the operator could say so with regard to the

state governmental machinery. His welfare and the welfare of the people who worked for him were often a
long distance from identical, although you will never, if
you live to be a thousand and there is still coal left in
West Virginia, get him to admit this point.

Anyway, the West Virginia coal operator at this
time was worried about adverse national publicity. In
order to secure a "good press" and in order to continue a
tight grip over governmental affairs in the Mountain
State, a group of operators and public officials who
were hand in glove with them banded together to form
the American Constitutional Association. We have
briefly mentioned this organization in a previous chapter, and asked that it not be confused with the Constitutional League, an organization which the miners attempted to form in 1921.

## A Whitewash Job

The American Constitutional Association was a
forerunner of such groups as the present-day Committee
For Constitutional Government, America's Future, Incorporated, and other ultra-reactionary bodies whose
purpose seems to be to take away the liberty of the ordinary American with one hand while holding fast to
the American constitution and a hymn book with the
other. They do not like to be thus characterized and they
are hypocritical enough and clever enough to fool some
very good people, so their power is often rather awe-
some.

Nevertheless, it must be said that the American
Constitutional Association of this era was formed for

two purposes only: to consolidate and increase, if possible, the power of the coal operators in West Virginia, and (2) to hoodwink the more-or-less-gullible public into believing that there was not a selfish desire in their coal-dust hearts.

To accomplish this latter purpose they hired a bright young man named Phil M. Conley, who worked with what was called the West Virginia Publicity Commission but what was actually the publisher of a blurb sheet for the coal operators. We are going to quote a few of Mr. Conley's remarks from a release of the West Virginia Publicity Commission of Jan. 26, 1923. In this release Conley speaks of Mingo County, "bloody Mingo" the miners called it, and we hope that in this work we have shown the reasons for the appellation. It will be recalled that Williamson, the county seat, was the headquarters for Major Tom Davis and his numerous regular and "volunteer" state police who enforced martial law in 1920-21. The Lick Creek incident will be remembered, as will the killings at Matewan in which Sid Hatfield and Ed Chambers were involved.

## Mingo the Mild

It was Conley's simple task to eradicate these memories from the minds of his readers by the process of counter-propaganda. Like this 1923 release: "The term Mingo County conveys to the mind of the average person in West Virginia as well as to the average person in other states, a picture of industrial trouble, warfare, lawlessness and factors that make for uncivilized conditions.... Like most pictures described by people who are interested in only one angle, it is untrue....

"I was astonished at the report made by Mr. A.C. Davis, superintendent of schools and Mr. McCarty, principal of the high school.... Six years ago Mr. Davis started an innovation in West Virginia by introducing a course in Bible in his high school. The YMCA secretary taught the course the first year, and after that the three ministers in town were drafted as teachers....Here in a city that has been heralded throughout the United States as a place where civilization is at a low ebb is to be found a progressive up to date school system that compares favorable with the best....

"While Williamson has had a trade organization only six months, it is one of the best known commercial bodies in the State. Rarely a day passes but some report is made of what the Williamson Chamber of Commerce has done or is doing. Dr. W.W. Rosenheim, secretary, is a live wire man who believes in getting things done on a big scale.... The industrial controversy is apparently a closed chapter in the history of the County. Everyone regrets the publicity given the circumstances surrounding the efforts to unionize the field that have occurred in Mingo during the past few years.... Captain Brockus of the State Police (he of the Sharples raid – Ed.) said: 'Mingo is quiet except for the disturbances connected with the bootlegging industry. The lawlessness occasioned by the industrial troubles has been entirely settled.'

## A Special Detail

"I left Williamson feeling that here is a city of wonderful possibilities for development. With the progressive ideas possessed by her young business and professional men, there is no reason why in the near future this city located midway between Huntington and Bluefield on the Norfolk and Western Railroad should not become a real power in the State."

Thus did Mr. Conley perform his function of describing the beauties of peaceful, operator-owned, non-union Mingo County in 1923. But the American Constitutional Association had a special work for him to do. Before we go into detail on this matter we may as well list the names of the officers of the Association in 1923:

**President**, Edwin M. Keatly, **Vice-president**, Earl W. Oglebay, **Treasurer**, Robert L. Archer, **Managing Director**, Phil M. Conley, **Directors**, Gov. E.F. Morgan, Howard M. Gore (who, as 17th governor of W. Va., succeeded Morgan – Ed.), John W. Romine, Bernard McClaugherty, Dr. I.C. White, Milton Rouss, and W.M. Wiley.

In addition to attempting to hang the mine Union leaders and keeping the miners in servitude the above distinguished citizens felt that they should further explain their work to all concerned. Ordinarily they cared little about publicity one way or another but, as we have observed, the thickest of skins might have been penetrated by out-of-state criticism of high-handed operators methods in West Virginia. Under the editing of Phil

Conley a special booklet was issued by the Association. It was called *Life in a West Virginia Coal Field*:

2/19/1953 (Sixty-fifth)

*Life in a West Virginia Coal Field* was printed with the blessing of Governor Ephraim F. Morgan, who, in a forward, said:

> "An unbiased study of life in the coal fields of West Virginia by a gentleman of high standing and character of Mr. Conley merits the confidence of all persons who desire to know the facts relative to this subject, and is a refutation of many misstatements of propagandists sent into the coal fields by radical and irresponsible organizations."

The "radical and irresponsible" organization foremost in Morgan's mind was, obviously, the United Mine Workers of America. Surely Mother Jones never saw this pamphlet and its endorsement by Morgan, or she could not have lauded the Governor in her autobiography. Phil Conley does the best he can with the material he has to work with, but the publicity attempt does not seem wholly successful. The coal district covered seems to be the Kanawha Field, although the reader is not told that this area has been at least partially Unionized for many years.

Unionized or not, it may be a surprise to some to learn that in 18 coal towns studied there were 24 tennis courts. The public in 1923 had hardly been taught to think of coal miners as playfully scooting about in white trousers, burning up the tremendous amounts of energy

left to them after loading 20 to 30 tons of coal in an atmosphere of powder smoke, coal dust, mule stench and
constant danger. This writer's grandfather, for instance,
who in his last years wheezed like a wrecked old locomotive as his coal-filled lungs fought for enough air to
sustain life, who left a black splotch of coal dust on the
ground when he spat, never told stories of his prowess
with a tennis racquet.

## Why Be Discontent?

The truth was that these tennis courts, which Mr.
Conley pointed to with so much pride, belonged like
everything else in the coal fields, to the coal companies.
They were for the use of coal company officials, mine-
guards, company guests, and others who pledged allegiance to the men who sat at the right hand of King
Coal. Baseball, as the booklet truthfully states, was the
principal sport of the coal miner.

It is not necessary to go over the contents of the
association pamphlet in detail, except to show that it
does not succeed, despite the intent, in picturing the
West Virginia coal fields as some kind of sooty Eden,
ante Eve and the apple. In 58 towns, Mr. Conley says,
386 miners owned their own homes. There was a great
turnover in teaching personnel, and school buildings did
triple duty as churches and lodge halls. There was no
hospital in the entire field surveyed, the miners being
served by the six in Charleston and Huntington, if they
happened to still be alive when they reached these
populous centers.

This meant, among other things, that it was a rare miner's child who was born in a hospital. According to the survey there were 62 miles of "paved" road in the entire area, and 14 of the 58 towns included were inaccessible in winter. Four mining towns, with a population of 5,000, had one doctor and one nurse, and it should be remembered that the towns were scattered over mountainous rugged terrain. But this was nothing to be alarmed about, said Mr. Conley, but rather a point of pride. For, says he, "the fact that one doctor and one nurse could adequately serve so many people proves that a great deal of attention has been paid to the protection of the health of the citizens in the towns affected."!!

The terrible death toll, when the influenza epidemic of 1916 struck the coal fields, will probably never be entirely known, but it may without doubt be in some degree attributable to this rather odd medical situation.

**Absentee Landlords Hit**

Late in the same year in which *Life in a West Virginia Coal Field* was issued, there was held a special constitutional convention of District 17 which also had something to say about who was responsible for the reputation of West Virginia in 1923. "It is the absentee landlords who do not live in West Virginia but reside in Athens, Ohio, 'Millionaires' Circle in Cincinnati, the Bronx in New York, Boston, Mass., and elsewhere that are both directly and indirectly responsible for the blackened name of West Virginia. There is only one way to clear the name of West Virginia. That is to break the political stranglehold of John L. Dickinson. Wm. McKell, Isaac T. Mann, Edward Houston, Samuel Coolidge, Elbert H. Gary, John Laing, and others who are throttling civil liberties in this state while they strut from place to place with a Bible under one arm and a list of contributions to the foreign mission fund under the other, and believe me this is going to be some job to educate the masses sufficiently to break up the political corruption which has burned itself into the vitals of government in our little mountain state."

In the same year was launched in West Virginia, primarily by District 17 officials, a Farmer – Labor Party. It was doomed to a short life, largely for the reason that the entire body of labor in the state was unable to work together effectively. But the remarks on this subject of Secretary-Treasurer Fred Mooney at this 1923 convention are worth recording in any labor history.

## Labor Party Launched

"You have seen fit to inaugurate a political party known as the Farmer – Labor Party. This is a step in the right direction, but remember that Labor parties can become corrupt just the same as other political parties. Keep it clean. Select men and women to put into effect your policies whose integrity cannot be doubted, whose willingness to sacrifice reaches beyond their own personal ambitions, for the history of break-aways from established political parties are polluted with lynchings, tar and feather episodes, midnight rides, kidnappings, deportations, and even murder for those who dare to organize the workers and farmers for effective political action. You must not expect any immediate relief for if you do you will be disillusioned. It will take years of education and organization to accomplish effective political cooperative cohesion between the industrial laborer and the farmer because both have been taught by the 'Goose Step Universities,' colleges and schools to regard the other with suspicion. It has been hammered into both the industrial worker and the farmer by the subsidized press, church and Sunday School that one is the enemy of the other and that their interests are diametrically opposed. This situation can only be remedied by a slow and tedious process of education which will take years, but there is no better time to begin than now. Today is the day to begin, not tomorrow."

Many tomorrows have crept in their petty pace from day to day and a Farmer – Labor Party in America yet remains in the dream stage of 1923.

Rumblings of great portent were taking place in District 17 at this time, International Representative Percy Tetlaw had been sent into West Virginia by President John L. Lewis, and it is evident that in late 1923 Tetlow had assumed a number of administrative tasks in District 17. That this was a forewarning of a major change in the conduct of the affairs of the United Mine Workers of America is now apparent. That is, it was the beginning of the transfer of power from the hands of the district to the hands of the man from Luca, Iowa who had been elected UMW president in 1920.

This is not to say that this process began in District 17, but was rather part of a general UMW policy which became confirmed and final as the years passed. In District 17 it marked the end of an era.

# Chapter Twelve: W. Va. Operators Stall

2/20/1953 (Sixty-sixth)

The period from 1920 through 1924 was an extremely difficult one for District 17, aside from the famous treason and murder trials which so drained the district treasury. During this period there was not a time when the entire membership was at work simultaneously. Thousands of miners in West Virginia were forced to apply for exoneration from dues payments in order to maintain their membership. West Virginia was a battleground, as we have said before, and there was hardly a miner in the state who had not been battered physically or financially or both. When the great depression of 1929 struck America it was not a new thing to the miners in West Virginia. They had faced depression conditions since shortly after the first world war.

The 1922 strike had been won with the operators signing a contract incorporating a $7.50 daily wage for the men from the pits. But coal mining was an obviously sick industry, the major reasons being that the operators could produce more coal than was demanded by the market, and could do so with fewer men than were asking for work in the mines. For the UMW another serious matter was the fact that a large percentage of the mines in the country were yet nonunion. There were, in fact, enough nonunion mines to supply coal for the entire United States, an uncomfortable fact which had to be faced in the event of a national strike.

In early 1922 President Harding appointed a Bituminous Coal Commission to make a thorough investigation and report on this troublesome problem of just what was wrong with an industry which produced a mint of wealth and forced its employees to live in poverty, which was so efficient at the business of getting coal on top of the ground that it had cut its own throat in the process. They submitted in 1924, a four-volume report which was a great jigsaw puzzle of facts, but no key to the mystery.

The UMW had not been increasing its membership during these years, nor had it won major wage advances. The battle was one of survival, not growth, a fight on the negotiating level, to prevent wages from being cut. In an agreement at Jacksonville, Fla., signed Feb. 19, 1924, the operators of the Central Competitive Field agreed to extend the $7.50 daily wage scale for another three years. But getting coal operators to sign an agreement is one thing: forcing them to live up to it is another.

When April 1, 1924 came in West Virginia the operators felt sufficiently strong, or rather, felt that the weakened District 17 was so feeble, that they refused to honor the Jacksonville Agreement. They asked for a reduction of about 16 cents on machine and pick mining, and $1.50 a day on day labor. The UMW insisted upon the Jacksonville terms, and the men were again forced to strike. A parallel situation occurred in seven other districts, so that there were in early 1924 about 60,000 miners on strike throughout the country. And these strikers could hope for little help from the international Union for the simple reason that the treasury was not what it had once been. In West Virginia the situation was rather desperate, and a delegate convention of District 17 was held at Charleston, May 14 through May 16, 1924, in order to find some answer to the pressing problems of the strike. The district itself had hardly any funds, so that one of the more urgent problems was just how to cut expenses. On this the convention had something of a battle, for the recommendation of President C.F. Keeney was the abolition of the four sub-districts in District 17, thus eliminating the salaries of the officials and clerical help.

## Terrible Hardships Told

We shall understate the first reaction of the sub-district officials by saying that they hardly welcomed this suggestion with enthusiasm. It should be explained that District 31, in northern West Virginia, had not yet been formed, and District 17 covered this territory through its Sub-district No. 4. District 29, in the southern area, was formed after the 1912 strike, but had virtually ceased to exist. Its first president, L.C. Rogers, had turned renegade and given testimony against the miners and their Union in certain of the trials during the twenties.

It was not, however, the purpose of the convention, or within its power, to take action on the abolition of the sub-districts beyond declaring for a referendum vote of the membership. There was a big wrangle, the sub-districts declaring that the district itself could save money by cleaning up its own house and protesting that they had too little votes in the formulation of the Union policy they were called upon to implement.

This was a highly serious convention, as the delegates well knew, one of them stating that their decisions might mean the life or death of District 17. This statement was correct, for it was not long after this that the district changed. It did not die, of course, for it is exceedingly lively today, but its nature underwent changes. That this was a time of crisis in shown by the remarks of the chairman of the convention. And these remarks also show the sort of sacrifice it took to build the union:

> "There have been circumstances in Cabin Creek and on Coal River where these men have been on strike for two years and more. The men are naked. They have no clothes or shoes to wear. In some instances two heads of the family had to wear one pair of shoes....

## A Troubled Time

> "$3.50 and $4.50 per week has (sic) been paid to feed these people for two years, and they have gone naked, as they are not going to be able to take anything out of that amount to buy clothing with. That amounts to less than forty cents a week for each person. There is nobody here who would like to eat on forty cents a week. This money was for the assistance of our strikers and has been spent with discretion and has been paid in accordance with what we have in our treasury to pay out with....

> "...There are cases where two women have to wear one dress. One of them stays at

home in order that the other may go out. She goes behind closed doors until the other comes back. That is the situation that is prevailing.

"There are families on Cabin Creek and Coal River that are living under rock cliffs with not even a roof over their heads. They have only their household effects to protect them against the elements. Yet these men are standing pat and are refusing to break away from the miners' union."

Such was the struggle which built the United Mine Workers of America. But it was nevertheless true that some miners were not so tenacious in their support of the union. District 17 at its peak period prior to 1924 had 42,000 dues-paying members. In 1924 there were only 29,000 members in the district, and only 20,000 of these were paying dues. It was true that an indebtedness of a quarter of a million dollars, largely incurred because of the Armed March and consequent litigation, had been very nearly liquidated, but almost all of the district income was being paid out in strike relief, the difference going for administrative expenses.

The convention acted favorably on the submission to a referendum vote of the question of abolition of the sub-districts. When it adjourned, and the travel expenses of the delegation were paid, there was left a balance in the District 17 treasury of exactly $261.06.

2/21/1952 (Sixty-seventh)

On Jan. 15, 1923, Captain Percy Tetow was sent to West Virginia by UMW President John L. Lewis to assume charge of the executive and financial affairs of District 17. The reason given by Tetlow for this step was the fact that the district leadership was busy being tried on charges ranging from misdemeanors to treason and was therefore unable to function effectively. Whatever the measure of fact contained in this declaration, it is nevertheless also true that the arrival of Tetlow marked the beginning of the transfer of power from the district to the national level. This shift in authority did not come all at once. As late as May 15, 1924, Tetlow spoke at a District 17 convention in Charleston, giving a financial report, and explained his presence as follows: "I am only making this explanation because during the year 1923 I was in here and had charge of that particular work to assist the district, and my duties in that respect are over as your president has assumed the duties of the district immediately after he was acquitted at Fayetteville.

> "Consequently, I am only here in an advisory capacity to assist the district in whatever manner I can as a representative of the International Union."

## New District Leader

This is quite a modest statement in view of the fact that just one month and two days later Tetlow wrote a letter to Sub-district No. 2 head William Blizzard upon the letterhead of District 17, and on this letterhead Percy Tetlow's name is typed in as president and C.F. Keeney's name is X'd out. The letter follows:

"Office of President
"Charleston, W. Va.
"June 17, 1924.

"In view of the policy adopted by the International Executive Board, I deem it inadvisable to continue your Sub-district office after June 30, 1924. Will you kindly make arrangements to close all accounts of your office on that date and that no further obligations nor indebtedness (sic) will be granted after June 30th.

"I will arrange to have an audit of Sub-district accounts and such accounts will be taken over by the District Organization which will assume all obligation. (sic)"

"Trusting this will meet with your approval, I beg to remain,

"Fraternally yours,
"/s/ Percy Tetlow
"President District No. 17."

In another letter Blizzard was informed that he was retained as a District organizer.

It seems that the referendum vote on the abolition of the subdistricts was taken and their abolition approved, but this had not yet occurred on June 1, 1924, when sub-district and District 17 officers met again in Charleston and jointly signed a resolution which brought on a meeting of the International Executive Board June 12 to 14, 1924. At this meeting a decision was made to revoke the autonomy of District 17, effective June 17, 1924.

The content of the West Virginia District-Sub-District resolution, which led to this drastic action, is not at this time known. But we have shown the desperate plight of the miners in the Mountain State, and the increasingly difficult position of District 17, and it is probable that the local leadership thought it best to retreat somewhat from the scale set by the Jacksonville Agreement: whereas the "no backward step" policy of President John L. Lewis was well known. At the conclusion of the Board meeting which deposed the elected District 17 officials, replacing them with provisional appointees, Lewis said:

> "The International Executive Board had given profound consideration to the menacing conditions existing in District No. 17, United Mine Workers of America, as revealed from the testimony of the members of the District Executive Board and the several sub district officers. It is apparent that the integrity of the district organization is threatened by marked differences of opinion existing within its councils and that the declared policies of the United Mine Workers of America are being applied with insufficient vigor in that territory."

**Very Sad Days**

It appears that Lewis was alarmed over the loss of membership in the UMW, over the increasingly severe economic decline in the industry, and this centralizing step was an effort to wrestle with the terrible forces which were leading to the debacle of 1929, when bodies hurtling from skyscraper windows were an uncomfortably common sight. It was true that an era of seeming prosperity led the United States as a whole to the foolish optimism of "a chicken in every pot" philosophy. But the coal miner in West Virginia had not even the proverbial pot, let along the chicken. Not even the iron will and undoubted ability of John L. Lewis could cope with the forces of economic necessity.

Many of the enemies of Lewis have said that this revocation of autonomy led to the destruction of the UMW in West Virginia, prior to the great new days of 1933. But the welfare of trade Union members, willynilly, is tied to the economic well-being of the industry in which their members work. This is not to say that the owners of industry, though they were rolling in wealth, would permit more than a trickle of the profits to go to their workers. Their history proves that they will not, and that the grimmest sort of struggle is necessary before working people are able to obtain even elementary rights. But we are repeating the rather well known fact that it is impossible to get blood out of a turnip.

Whether a different policy on the part of Lewis could have wrung from the turnip some sort of substitute for blood is now an academic question. That the appointing of officials in 1924 to head District 17 did not help matters is obvious from a casual glance at the West Virginia scene a few years later. Paid-up membership in 1920-22 in District 17 was 42,000. Under elected district leaders it shrank in mid-1924 to about half that number. Under appointed district leaders from 1924 to 1927, it further diminished to a probable 1,000 members. Just prior to the election of Franklin D. Roosevelt there were a few hundred members, at most, in all of West Virginia. The 1930 miners' convention reported 512 UMW men out of a potential 100,000. The iron-studded club of economic depression was more merciless toward trade-union than toward the large capitalist. And many were the small business men who sold apples on the same corner with their former employees.

# Chapter Thirteen: An Era Ends

2/27/1953 (Conclusion)

The coal operators had won a complete victory in West Virginia. Through injunction, through supine and active government accomplices, through far-reaching court-action, through pistol and blackjack, the coal owners in the 1922-32 period virtually extirpated the United Mine Workers of America from West Virginia. Unionization in the coal fields of the Mountain State was thrown back to the 1897-1900 level. Percy Tetlow, District 17's newly appointed president, told yet another congressional investigating committee in 1928 that 50,000 people had been forced from their coal company shacks from 1922 through 1925, their crime being that the family breadwinner was a Union man.

"The Chairman: Where are those people?

"Mr. Tetlow: God knows.

"The Chairman: Are they still about there?

"Mr. Tetlow: Everywhere.

"Senator Bruce: Of course many of them went back as nonunion laborers?

"Mr. Tetlow: Yes, they have gone back to work on a nonunion basis.

"Senator Wheeler: You mean they had to do that or starve?

"Mr. Tetlow: Yes"

Mr. Tetlow, with his repetitions of "Everywhere," sounds somewhat like Poe's Raven, and indeed America's foremost tragic poet could have found inspiration for the most gloomy maunderings, had he been alive and in the neighborhood. The UMW membership in West Virginia shrank to nothing, the deposed District 17 leadership, or part of it, from time to time began rump organizations which had no real permanency, and the country as a whole skidded toward such poverty as it had never before seen. There is little need to detail political organizations which from time to time dipped an inquiring finger into the West Virginia pie. They were several and all had some sort of following, but not until the spring of 1933, with the National Industrial Recovery Act and its Section 7(a) which guaranteed the right of collective bargaining, did the United Mine Workers of America, like the mythical Phoenix, arise from its own ashes in an all but miraculous rebirth of power. But these days of the twenties and the early thirties were the end of an era in the epic of Struggle and Win, Struggle and Lose. Few could then see the shining future when pressing all about was the bleak present, made more bitter by memories of a brilliant past.

# Postscript

The historian finds convenient heading under which to block off and isolate for study certain segments of the human comedy, and this is a necessary process, for otherwise the vast panorama of man's fighting, loving, struggling existence would be too complex for comprehension. The boiling inferno of the life of humankind, however, with its many-sided social relationships in continual flux, never ceases and this of course holds true in our little study of a small segment of humanity, the coal diggers of West Virginia.

Because of the well-defined break, the temporary defeat of 1922-23, we end our story of Struggle and Lose, Struggle and Win, at that time. The story of the rebirth of the United Mine Workers of America, of roaring mass meetings in which the West Virginian reaffirmed his right of collective bargaining, of a Keynesian Federal Government under Franklin D. Roosevelt, of the horrible drift toward World War II, of all this and more, must be told at a later date. A great deal has been told, of course, in many thick volumes, but not so much from Labor's point of view. And Labor must tell its own story.

What has become of many of the men mentioned in the foregoing pages? Death has overtaken many, oppressed and oppressor alike. One of the UMW attorneys in the Charles Town treason trials died a Republican and near-millionaire. Another died a comparatively poor man and a Communist. Fred Mooney recently put a bullet through his head, after having been a small businessman for years. Other District 17 officials of the Armed March days are beaten old men, working as flagmen on State Road Commission jobs or as clerks in West Virginia liquor stores, or, apparently, at nothing at all.

Of the top District 17 men of the twenties, William Blizzard alone has somehow lived to pull through to continued high-ranking position in the West Virginia UMW. He is currently District 17 president, a few years away from retirement.

It is not necessary to tell anyone of the current power, numerical and financial, of the United Mine Workers of America. The name of John L. Lewis is as well known as that of any breakfast food, which, in our rather peculiar way of assessing recognition, is solid assurance of national fame. The UMW is seemingly impregnable.

## What Lies Ahead?

What of the future? Unless the past is a key to the future the study of history is a profitless exercise. This writer pretends to be no seer. However, he wishes to advance certain opinions, which will be tested with the passage of time. Today the UMW stands on the verge of another era in unionism in the United States. The retirement of John L. Lewis from the Union scene, through death or otherwise, is bound to occur within a few short years. Due to the UMW structure, in large part, this will have a telling effect upon the Union, for men of the caliber of Lewis, with the years of prestige behind a name, are not easily found. A successor to

Lewis, who could not walk several yards in the Iowan's shoes without moving a foot, is not at the moment in sight.

## A People's History

Men of strong will and great ability are not so often likely to have others of equal strength as cohorts. It seems not to bc of the nature of strength and ability to invite partners into the limelight. Witness Franklin D. Roosevelt, and witness the debacle of the Democratic Party since his death. This is not to say that with the death of Lewis a similar debacle will result for the UMW. It will likely not. Such historical parallelism is far too pat and simple to be convincing. But there is coming a period of crisis for the UMW, and the death of Lewis may be a part of that crisis. Our national economy at this time, while appearing strong, is much like the pre-1929 economy. The seeming flash of health is the unnatural rosiness of the tubercular patient's anxious face.

The UMW will be forced more and more into the political battles which are so obviously a part of the economic struggle. This may eventually take the form of a Labor Party.

A final note. Some readers, some scholars, may protest this writer's method of departing from academic "objectivity," and rooting enthusiastically for the coal miners. That is too bad, but we have no apologies. We want our writing to be read, not grow musty in the library of any elite coterie. This is a people's history, and if it brawls a little, and brags a little, and is angry more than a little, well, the people in this book were that way, and so are their descendants. The people in West Virginia haven't had a chance to get their lively history between covers very often. "History" is ordinarily that dull subject which tells about who was governor, when, and what a fine fellow he was, and the great things all the great people did. Well, in this book we told about a lot of the little things the great people did, and a lot of the great things the little people did. We hope it hasn't been as boring as the average historical tome. We have tried to give an idea as to the lusty history of the coal diggers of West Virginia. We hope that we have in part succeeded.

## Appendix 1 – Original Document Images

All document images from the William C. Blizzard Collection archived at Appalachian Community Services, unless otherwise noted.

HAROLD W. HOUSTON
ATTORNEY AT LAW
KANAWHA NATIONAL BANK BUILDING
CHARLESTON, W. VA.

August 9th., 1921.

Mr.Everett Early,
Secretary Burial Fund,
Local Union 2887,U.M.W.of A.,
Blair, West Va.

My dear Everett:-

It is of the utmost importance that this matter be brought to the attention of your local officials at once.

My information is that you have a considerable sum in the local burial fund. I would suggest that you appropriate at least $600.00 at once. You, and the others on the inside, will, of course, understand that it is to be used for the purchase of necessary equipment for the Mingo enterprise. It must not fail this time. The boys need guns, etc. Act at once. You can trust the bearer of this note. Destroy it as soon as read.

Fraternally yours,

HW Houston

Houston was Union attorney for many years, including the trials following the events on Blair Mountain.

**From the William C. Blizzard Collection of the West Virginia Division of Archives and History**

| | | | |
|---|---|---|---|
| Dewey Bailey, C.F. | *line up* | Treason | $10,000 |
| W. Lacey | 3 B. | Defense Witness | |
| Joe Rhodes | S.S. | Murder | $1,000 |
| Okey Burgess | 2 B | " | 3,500 |
| Wm. Chapman | C. | Defense Witness | |
| A.C. McCormick | L.F. | Murder | 3400 |
| Cecil Sullivan | 1 B. | " | 1000 |
| John Phipps | R.F. | Defense Witness | |
| Okey Johnson | P. | Treason | 5000 |
| *utility Players* | | | |
| J.G. Neff | 1 B. | Treason | 5000 |
| Frank Stump | C. | Murder | 5000. |
| Ray Williams | C.F. | " | 2500 |
| Bert Atkins | S.S. | " | 2500 |
| Frank Keeney | R.F. | Treason | 20000 |
| Wm. Blizzard | 3 B. | " | 20 000 |
| Frank Snyder | Mgr. | " | 2000 |

Above note likely written by team manager Frank Snyder, listing players (i.e. defendants), their position, along with partial list of charges against them with bail amounts. The team played in and around Charles Town to aid local charities — and influence the jury pool.

The letter below is from C.A. Lively, son of the Baldwin-Felts detective/spy who murdered Sid Hatfield and Ed Chambers. Written to author William C. Blizzard, son of the leader of the miner's march on Blair Mountain (Bill Blizzard). In its postscript Mr. Lively revealed his astonishing view of the conflict.

Mr William Blizzard.

Dear Sir.

In answer to your letter concerning the late C.E. Lively I think I may be able to help you some. My recollection of some things in matewan vague I remember the Resturant my Father ran used as a Cover for His operations He was supposed to be a good friend of Sid Hatfields C,E seem to Think duplicity was an honorable Trait, He would sign men up for the union And Then Turn These mens name over To the Felts Dective agency when He was in one of His braging moods. He usualy refured to the union men as Reds. And any offe Them were Killed was one less Red to deal with.

I know up until I was 12 I was Terrified of my Father, He had a split personality and was a diffrent person from one day To The next,

The scrap book and gun you speak of are in the possision of paul Lively my younger brother the only photos I know of were of news papers clippings except some Taken in Denver an missouri. there were two photos af albert and Le Felts Two Brothers of Toms who were shot in mingo County the gun

you speak off is a 38 special Smith and Wesson
it belonged to either Albert or Lee Felts I do not
know if it was used to shoot Hatfield or
Chambers, several times I would butter my
Father up how brave He must of ben He would
Through out That Chest and brag That They drew
first. I cannot see Hatfield or Chambers drawing
as my Father had swore out the warrant to get
Hatfield into McDowel County as He stated
Hatfield and others had braged They were going
over the McDowel Co. and shoot up those scabs
houses, He had allso stated when Albert and Lee
were killed Hatfield signed His Death warrant
previous my Father had testified against
Hatfield in Williamson W. Va (Mingo Co) Against
That is when He blew His Cover. Hatfield was
supposed to have taken some men and Ambushed
some Baldwin Thugs, He did not bother to go
back to matewan for the family, The union men
Came to our Home and Told my mother That
The Children and Her had nothing to fear from
Them They helped to load some Things on The wagon
to take to The Train station to be shiped when we
left. excuse I am writeing this in a hurry
trying to make The evening pickup.
    I have a passion micro Recorder I was

intending to try and see Gladys after the fourth. She is in bad shape and I am concerned for her. If I can make it I will try and contact you

yours Truly
Charles A Lively

P. S.

I know your Father was on the right side, as it helped to defeat Industrial Feudealism in this Country.

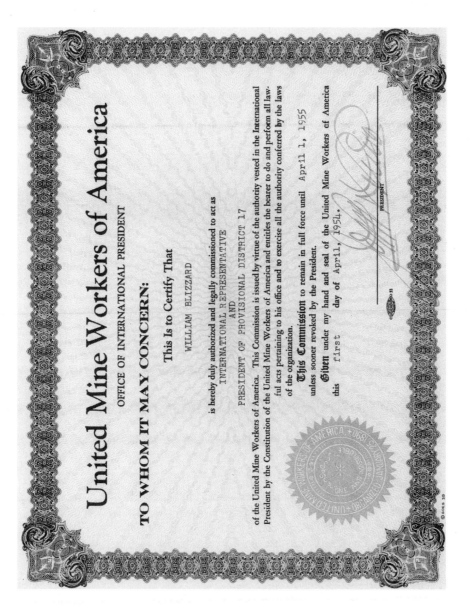

# United Mine Workers of America

## OFFICE OF INTERNATIONAL PRESIDENT

### TO WHOM IT MAY CONCERN:

This Is to Certify That

WILLIAM BLIZZARD

is hereby duly authorized and legally commissioned to act as

INTERNATIONAL REPRESENTATIVE
AND
PRESIDENT OF PROVISIONAL DISTRICT 17

of the United Mine Workers of America. This Commission is issued by virtue of the authority vested in the International President by the Constitution of the United Mine Workers of America and entitles the bearer to do and perform all lawful acts pertaining to his office and to exercise all the authority conferred by the laws of the organization.

This Commission to remain in full force until  April 1, 1955  unless sooner revoked by the President.

Given under my hand and seal of the United Mine Workers of America this  first  day of April, 1954.

PRESIDENT

February 11, 1955

Mr. John L. Lewis, President
United Mine Workers of America
United Mine Workers' Building
Washington 5, D. C.

Dear Sir and Brother:

Since October 1919 it has been my privilege
to work with the United Mine Workers of America, the greatest labor union in the world,
led by the outstanding labor leader of the
world.

I hereby request you to permit me to retire
as of March 31, 1955. You will recall that
I suggested this to you in Washington on my
visit there last Monday. I have also expressed this desire to Secretary-Treasurer
John Owens. I will appreciate your acting
favorably on this request.

Whether my life span be long or short, I will
always say that I have worked for the greatest
Union in the world and the greatest boss.

Sincerely yours,

William Blizzard

WB:cb

Bill Blizzard's letter of resignation

to UMW president John L. Lewis

# United Mine Workers of America

JOHN OWENS
SECRETARY-TREASURER

TELEPHONE
METROPOLITAN 8-0530

UNITED MINE WORKERS' BUILDING

## Washington 5, D.C.

February 18, 1955

PERSONAL AND CONFIDENTIAL

Mr. William Blizzard, President
District 17, U. M. W. of A.
Post Office Box 1313
Charleston, West Virginia

Dear Sir and Brother:

President John L. Lewis has referred your recent
letter to me.

Effective April 1, 1955, we are placing you
upon a disability salary of $500.00 per month payable
twice a month. This arrangement will continue in effect
until such time as you are eligible to qualify for a pension
under the United Mine Workers of America Pension Plan.

We take this opportunity to express our appreciation for the many years of service you have rendered the
United Mine Workers of America. Your labors in behalf of
our Organization and its members have assisted materially
in bringing it to its present magnificient place of leadership in the field of organized labor as well as the attain-
ment of the many benefits enjoyed by our members.

With best wishes,

Sincerely yours,

Secretary-Treasurer

FEB 23 1955

O:hwc

cc: President John L. Lewis
Vice President Thomas Kennedy

William C. Blizzard wrote the following chronology in prep-
aration for a lecture given at WV Tech in Montgomery, W.Va.
It was likely written when he was an instructor for Antioch
College in Beckley, W.Va. during the mid 1970's.

## (ARMED MARCH CHRONOLOGY)

*6, 1917*
*p·11, 1918 - -*
*World War I:*
*april 6, 1917*
*Nov. 11, 1918*

Some         and Facts on the GREAT ARMED
        Chronology
MARCH OF ~~EXSEX~~ 1921.

~~TXMEW~~ Times were still good in 1920, but
had changed drastically in 1921.  Coal that sold for
$14 a ton in September, 1920, sold in March of 1921 for
$2.50 a ton.

Living costs in 1920 were 143 per cent over
what they had been in 1913.  Miners in 1920-21 working
three days a week in many places.  Wildcat strikes in
Illinois and ~~KXX~~ Kansas (Farrington and Howatt); *see below*.
with the Garfield and Wilson commission awards.

Lewis 40 years old in 1920, when he took over Union.

1919--W. Va. gets state police.

Sept. 6, 1919--Miners in Kanawha Valley start a march to
Mingo, after hearing reports of miners being mistreated
in that county.  Supposed to have been 5,000 to 6,000
men in march, gathered at Marmet.  At request of Gov.
Cornwell, Keeney stopped them, but perhaps 900 marched
as far as Danville.  Keeney spoke to miners at Madison.
At Danville, miners were brought back home on trains at
state expense.  State billed union, but never paid.
Big prelude to 1921 MARCH.

Nov. 1, 1919--A great soft coal strike, the first under
John L. Lewis leadership.  He was acting president, Frank
Hayes the actual president.  For ~~XONNXXXNN~~ some time before
Lewis took office the miners had asked for nationalization
of mines, many still favored it, but Lewis did not emphasize.
Miners asked for 6 hour day, five-day week, and 50 per cent
increase in wages.  Truth was that miners could produce
all coal needed in peacetime by working two or three days
a week.  Wages ~~BS~~ had been frozen during WWI at $5 a day.

Dec. 1, 1919--Garfield award became effective, giving ~~kx~~ the
miners a 14 per cent increase.  Miners not satisfied, continued
to stike.
Dec. 7, 1919--
~~XXIXXXH XHH~~ Lewis and Wm. Green call off strike after
conferring with Wilson, Lewis making his famous statement
that he would not fight his government, "the greatest government on earth."

Dec. 10--1919--Miners' convention where settlemnt was
ratified, accepting 14 percent Garfield award, but with
Wilson's promise to appoint an impartial commission to
investigate and make further adjustments.  This at Indianapolis.

Jan. 6, 1920--Miners held another convention at Columbus
to further consider and agree to accept findings of the yet
(more)

XXXXX --2

unheard from Bituminous Coal Commission.  Robert H. Harlin,
president of the Washington State miners, wanted to amend
the resolution X of acceptance so that miners XXXX could
vote on whehter or not to accept Recommendationsof BCC.
He was steamrollered.
                    (Lewis and others had been held
on contempt of court charges X in connection with 1919 strike).

March 10, 1920--Wilson's Bitum. Coal Comm. gave the miners
a 27 per cent X increase, effective almost immediately, over
the rates of Oct. 31, 1919 and the 8 hour day, which they
had already in CCF.  This included the 14 percent awarded
the miners in Garfield award, so was only a further 13 percent
increase.

Along about this time, or a little later, District 17 began
attempts to organize Mingo County.

Early May, 1920--Miners in Mingo join union and are locked
out and evicted as fast as they do.   2,700 or 2,800 men affected.

Wednesday, May 19, 1920--About one dozen Baldwin-Felts men
come to Matewan to evict six men from their homes belonging
to the Stone Mountain Coal Corporation.  Did evict and came
back to Matewan about 3.30 pm.  X Mayor C. C. Testerman had
issued a warrant for their arrest for violating a town ordinance concerning the carrying of weapons.  BF told Hatfield
he was under arrest and had to go with them to Bluefield.
He did not XXXXXX resist, but goes toward Matewan railroad
station.
                    Mayor Testerman protested, and XX BF men said
no bond could be posted; then Testerman said the XXX warrant
was no good.  According to Hatfield, A Felts brother shot
Testerman, and shooting immediately became general.
Seven of the Baldwin men were killed and two citizens of
Matewan besides Testerman.  Albert and Lee Felts killed in
this battle, leaving Tom Felts alive.

June 15, 1920--Miners congregate on Cabin Creek with a
threat of a march on Mingo, but the march doesn't materialize.

July 1, 1920--Official strike call went into effect in
Mingo, after 2,700 men had been locked out

Aug., 1920--"Anse" Hatfield shot and killed on the porch
of a XXXX hotel in Matewan.  He had testified before the
grand jury against Sid Hatfield.

Aug. 29,1920--War Dept. sends federal troops into Mingo
near Williamson.  Equipped with rifles, machine guns, trucks,
and a one-pound cannon.
Nov. 4, 1920--XXXX Troops leave.

                    (more)

*morgan*

--3

Nov. 27, 1920--Gov. proclaims a state of insurreciton.

Nov. 28, 1920--Gov. has troops called back, and asks Wilson
for martial law. Wilson refuses. Troops stayed through
February 15, 1921.

Nov. elections give landslide to repubs, nationally
and locally, but almost one million votes to Gene Debs in
pen.
Feb. 16,1921--
xxxxxxxx--Fed. xxxx troops leave Mngo.

Shortly thereafter, govs. of both W. Va. and Kentucky
ask for return of federal troops. Harding in now, since
March 4, not quick to act. Many battles in Mingo.

Among Mingo battles about May, 12, 13, X and 14, are those
at Merrimac, Sprigg, xxxx McCarr, and Blackberry City. Mooney,
Keeney and Workman indicted for killings in these battles
on Aug. 20, 1921. *1921*

June 26, 1920--Keeney xxxxxx *had sent* telegram to 71 xxxxxxx coal
companies in Mingo and Pike counties, asking for a meeting
to negotiate wage agreements. All refuse xxxx except for
19 tiny "wagon" mines in Mingo, two year contracts. Fed.
mediators arrive in Williamson, but no ops show up.

May 19, 1921--Morgan declares martial law, but as national
guard had during WW I been incorporated into army, there
was no military force to enforce it. Men arrested for
being caught with or reading the UMW Journal. Morgan had
drafted enough men to police the county, two military
companies of 35 men each.

June 14, 1921--Lick Creek battle with killing of miner
xxx Alex Breedlove by state xt police and xxxxxx enrolled
militia. *On sam day a subcommittee of the Senate Education
[?] Labor committee began hearing, came to Williamson Sep 18.*

July 19, 1921--Philip Murray visits Williamson, is insulted
by police, militia, followed everywhere, harrassed.

August 1, 1921--killing of Sid Hatfield and Ed Chambers
on Welch courthouxse steps. (insert materdal from book).

August X 7, 1921--This a Sunday. Mass meeting of miners
on capitol grounds. Submit demands to Gov. Morgan. Said
Z. T. Vinson, coal-op attorney to subcommittee on Education
and Labor: "I see no reason to go on and keep on insisting
that we shall recognize their union when we have so positively
stated that under no circumstances will we do it, either
xk through this honorable committee, thpough the President
of the United States, or any other tribunal." Morgan refuses.

--4

August 16 17, 1921--Morgan refuses the Aug. 7 demands.

About August 20--Miners begin to assemble at Lens
Creek, as they had in 1919. Mother Jones on Aug. 23
announces good news coming in a speech.

Aug. 24, 1921--Mother Jones returns to Marmet, says President Hardinghas promised to help miners, advised men to
go home. Showed them what purported to be a telegram from
Harding. Keeney, Savory Holt, andothers say it is
a fake, to pay no attention. The Armed March starts
that night.

Aug. 26, 1921--General Harry H. Bandholtz arrives in
Charleston at 3:05 a. m. Awakens gov., who, at 4 a. m.,
says he wants troops. Calls in Keeney and Mooney
at 4:55 (with Houston) K and M leave at 5:30 of 26th
in a car, headed up coal river. About 11:30 Band. got
word from K and M that miners had been stopped at
Racine and were being notified to stop elsewhere.
Asked state authorities for transportation for miners, but
were ignored (not like 1919)

                                    including William Blizzard
August 27, 1921: Bandholtz and others/go to Marmet and
Racine, see miners returning, go back to Washington that
night. At midnight the Sharples incident and March resumes.

Aug. 31, 1921--Proclamation by President Harding giving
men until 12 noon, Sept. 1, 1921, to return home. John
Gore, Charles Munsey, and John Caffago killed on
Blair . Gore had been pres. of Local 12 at Blair during
the 1919 march, had helped to turn that march back.
Later accepted a commission from the operators as a deputy
sheriff and was expelled from the UMW for 99 years.

Sept. 1, 1921--Bandholtz and staff arrive again in Charleston,
at 11:30 a. m., half hour before time given by Harding expires.
Conferred with Morgan and Phil Murphy, sent Ford, an attendant,
up Coal River by way of St. Albans. Ford reports that
miners do not intend to comply with Harding's proclmation,
so Bandholtz sends telegram to War Dept. asking for troops.

Setp. 3, 1921--Fed. troops arrive that eve. in Charleston.
(Kenyon committee had been investigating, arrives
on Sept 18 in Williamson for on-the-spot inves.)

Ben Brown, a lawyer, and George Coyle, merchant, both of
Charleston, fought for operators on Blair.

By Sept. 3, 700 fed. troops around Madison and Jeffrey,
and perhaps 2,000 in the coal fields, plus federal bombing
and observation plans and Billy Mitchell. March ends.
Quote Sparks.

By William C. Blizzard and Wess Harris

William "Bill" Blizzard was born, appropriately enough, above Paint Creek in rough and tumble 1892 West Virginia. At the age of ten, when so many of his city counterparts were in school, he began working in the mines with his father, Timothy. As a young teenager, striking miners would often camp in his yard and more than once his mother, Ma Blizzard, would send him out to hunt game to feed the hungry strikers. Raised to be a miner's miner, he detested men who smoked in the mine – not because of safety concerns, but out of a dislike for time wasted and coal not loaded. A Union man from a Union family, he would become a UMWA sub-district president while still in his 20s and would go on to orchestrate the massive Armed March of 1921. Leading the famed Red Neck Army of 10,000, he wore a coat and tie throughout those dangerous ten days. Bill Blizzard was a class act. Coal miners could be (can be) a hard drinking lot, but all knew not to offer Bill a drink. Organizing requires a clear head.

Bill was blacklisted from the mines after the Armed March and would never again dig coal. Along with several hundred vets from the Red Neck Army, he was put on trial for his life after the Battle on Blair Mountain. Bill would continue to lead the men and designed a host of jury moving tactics that may well have saved his life and the lives of his men. The UMWA stood by Bill during the treason trial in Charles Town but afterwards John L. Lewis was bent on centralizing power and local heroes were not much in demand. The miner's hero was told from above that he was no longer employed. Even so, he would advocate for the Union before the West Virginia Legislature throughout the 1920s and beyond. Bill spent much of the 1920s at a variety of jobs. Pulling fresh fish from the Kanawha River to serve with Rae's highly regarded pies, the Blizzards ran Wright's Restaurant at a time when Union support was not something oft found in public.

In the early 1930s, his beloved Union needed capable organizers. Bill, champion for and hero to the men of the mines, was called back. He knew the creeks; he knew the hollers; he knew the hearts of the miners. For his dedication he consistently won grudging agreements from the coal companies and the admiration of Union families. Blizzard's hero status from Blair Mountain and the Trials insured his success as an organizer but he received little credit for his efforts. John L. Lewis had need for such a talent but no liking for anyone who could emerge as a potential rival. While Bill and his cadre of leaders hardened on Blair Mountain did the heavy lifting (most notably Charley Payne, lifelong friend who would serve with Bill until his retirement), Lewis installed Pennsylvanian Van Bittner as head of District 17. Lewis missed no opportunity to credit Bittner at the expense of Blizzard. In the August 1, 1933, *UMW Journal*, Bittner is mentioned no fewer than six times while Blizzard is ignored (see Corbin's anthology, final entry). Yet Bill Blizzard was the chap who made the huge gathering of miners happen. Van Bittner was hardly the type to inspire the miners. He was from out of state, preferred to ride in a Cadillac (with a driver!), expected his staff to call him Boss or The Boss, and kept a mistress in a Charleston hotel. Bill drove his own Chevy.

Bill would eventually move up to become President of Provisional District 17. Provisional meaning PROVIDED John L. Lewis wants it to be a district! Yet even heroes ultimately see their days move into twilight. Bill would retire in 1955. His final letter to John L. Lewis makes it clear that while they may have had private differences, Bill Blizzard was a man loyal to the Union: "Whether my life span be long or short, I will always say that I have worked for the greatest Union in the world and the greatest boss." Much had been accomplished.

Sadly, Bill Blizzard is given scant attention in the history books – and what is written is often grossly inaccurate. Many of his achievements were left to the great tradition of oral interpretation. Everyone seemed to have a Bill Blizzard story though they were careful to whom it was passed. The people of West Virginia choose their sides like someone picking out a coffin. Once committed, owners rarely change their minds. Perhaps that is the greatest testimony to his import. You either loved or hated Bill Blizzard, with a passion. In 1939, when L.U. 6113 complained of being lied to by a district rep, Bill Blizzard stood with the men and sent a letter supporting their position. He was also willing and able to communicate with his fists when the situation merited – such as an incessant heckler at one of his

speeches. The phrase "knocking some sense into someone" was played out before a stunned but supportive
crowd. Abraham Lincoln once said, "Everything for effect." Bill was that kind of leader. Sometimes nonverbal
communication helps to create a better environment for
civil debate.

Bill was a highly intelligent analyst of the world
into which he was born but, lacking all but a minimum
formal education, he was no intellectual. He was an
avid reader of newspapers and labor journals, and his
library held favorites such as Jack London rather than
tomes of the professional academes. He would prefer
hunting and fishing to reading of the latest government
scandal. He scorned those fond of theory and spent little
or no time with such works.

Colorful Sid Hatfield is far better known to our
school children by way of textbooks and even a Holly-
wood movie. Make no mistake, Sid was the miner's
friend and died for it – but Sid poses no contemporary
threat. The economic and political powers of today are
not anxious to have Bill's story told. What is it about
the image of Bill Blizzard that worries them? Maybe it
is his strength of character, his ability to organize even
in the lion's den, or his simple message: "We are miners, we are Union, we are our own protectors."

Harvard Law educated H. John Rogers has
deemed Bill Blizzard, "arguably the seminal West Virginian of the first half of the 20$^{th}$ century" and yet even
the West Virginia Labor History Association waited until 2006 to induct him into the Labor History Hall of

Honor. Bill Blizzard was both sui generis and the archetypical West Virginian: honest, tough, and independent. He was a thinking man's worker and a working man's thinker.

Bill Blizzard physically departed this world from a Charleston hospital in 1958. But perhaps Bill, like Joe Hill, did not die but went on to organize.... Perhaps Bill was so important because he was – IS, one of us.

# Appendix 3: Relevant Literature Review

Many sources exist for those wanting to learn more of the Great West Virginia Mine War – 1890 to the present. No attempt is made here to create a complete bibliography. A limited sample is offered below, selected based on their importance to understanding not just events but the creation of the history/myths of those events. Readers are encouraged to form their own opinions.

**The Good Stuff**

Biggers, Jeff. *The United States of Appalachia* (Emeryville, CA, Shoemaker & Hoard, 2006.)

Biggers offers a solid, readable account of the import of Appalachia to our nation's development. Within that context, he grasps the significance of the miner's rebellions and Blair Mountain, but sadly fails to note Bill Blizzard as the grassroots leader so critical to the Union's ultimate success. The entire work serves well to shake stereotypes; it is an excellent place for students to begin...

Corbin, David Alan. *Life, Work, and Rebellion in the Coal Fields* (Urbana and Chicago, U. of Illinois Press, 1981.)

Long the "go to" book on the early mine struggles, this is a must. Well documented factual account that dispels myths of idyllic company towns. Corbin makes clear his lack of information regarding the leadership on Blair Mountain (p.218) and offers only minimal coverage of the trials.

Corbin, David Alan. *The West Virginia Mine Wars, An Anthology* (Martinsburg, WV, Appalachian Editions, 1990.)

Although a strong collection, it unfortunately misses the import of Bill Blizzard. Mooney and Keeney "guided the state's miners through the Mine Wars." (p.64) His final selection of the August 1, 1933, *UMW Journal* article on the Historic Convention is also misleading. John L. Lewis, no friend of Bill Blizzard, credits Van Bittner no fewer than six times while ignoring Blizzard. WCB repeatedly made clear in interviews that 2500 miners would not have attended without the organizing clout of Bill Blizzard.

Giardina, Denise. *Storming Heaven, A Novel* (New York, Ballantine Publishing, 1987.)

Provides a better understanding of events that most "non-fiction" accounts. Not to be missed.

Keeney, C. Belmont "Chuck". *'Son of the Struggle,' Goldenseal Magazine,* (Summer 2006.) Charleston.

Offers a glimpse into the wit and wisdom of WCB.

Jones, Clarence Edward "Red". *Memories of a Coal Miner,* Unpublished manuscript. (Appalachian Community Service archives.)

Wonderful recollections important for providing a "smoking gun" that Bittner sold out the miners by ignoring their hard won contracts (p.33).

Mooney, Fred. *Struggle in the Coal Fields,* Edited By J.W. Hess (Morgantown, WVU Library, 1967.)

Written in the late '20s this work is a solid primary source. Mooney was an enemy of Bill Blizzard (once planned to kill him on a hunting trip – Bill was warned by Keeney). He dispels the oft repeated myth that he and Keeney managed events on Blair Mountain. "We kept in touch with developments through the press reports and by messenger until September 16" (p.99.)

Readers are reminded that this was an age before emails and "wireless".

Payne, Charles. *Oral History, Special Collections,* (James E. Morrow Library, Marshall U, Huntington, 1978.)

Charley "Tuck" Payne was a lifelong friend and colleague to Bill Blizzard and he has been virtually ignored by the history books. At various times, both he and Bill saw fit to slug Raymond Lewis, John L.'s kid brother. Charley got the "one pounder" cannon when Bill died.

Payne, Dale. *Pictorial History of Cabin Creek v. 1 & 2* (Fayetteville, 2008.);  Payne, Dale, and Perry, Marlene. *The History of Eskdale,* (2007.)

Excellent windows into the region, these entries are available from Dale Payne, Rt.3, Box 75, Fayetteville, WV, 25840.

**Standard Fare**

Savage, Lon. *Thunder in the Mountains (*South Charleston, Jalamap Publications, 1984.)

Long the most readable account of the struggles, Savage makes much ado of Sid Hatfield while down playing the role of Bill Blizzard. He announces that Blizzard could not have led the March since he was acquitted at trial (p. 120). He ends his work quoting the Union marker on Sid Hatfield's grave (p.144) but fails to note that the marker was likely placed between 1945 and 1955 when Bill Blizzard was President of District 17. Bill most certainly saw to the placement of Sid's marker as well as identical ones for Woodrum, Estep, and Chambers – all of whom he knew.

Shogan, Robert *The Battle of Blair Mountain* (Boulder, CO, Westview Press, 2004.)

Shogan clearly tries to be sympathetic to the miners but simply failed to do his homework and thus offers nothing new. He failed to interview William C. Blizzard and insists on referring repeatedly to the Red Bandana Army. Readers must wait until page 184 of his 228 page text to find mention of Blair Mountain. He includes three photos of Sid Hatfield but none of Bill Blizzard.

Sullivan, Ken. ed. *The Goldenseal Book of the West Virginia Mine Wars* (Charleston, WV, Pictorial Histories Publishing Company, 1991.)

A collection of articles from the magazine. Most significant perhaps for the article on the deaths of Estep and Woodrum and their grave markers (p.25-32). The Hazel Dickens tune *Coal Miner's Grave* is about Estep's murder and neglected gravesite. (Ed. note:  The site is currently maintained by students from around the country.)

**Oops!**

Brecher, Jeremy. *Strike* (San Francisco, CA, Straight Arrow Books, 1972.)

Although this labor history work is considered a classic, it fails to mention the Battle of Blair Mountain and Bill Blizzard. Blair Mountain was the largest armed insurrection since the Civil War.

Davidson, Shae Ronald *The Boys'll Listen to Me* (Huntington, WV, Masters thesis, Marshall U, 1998.)

Space does not permit a full review of this work. Suffice it to say that Davidson's claim that Bill Blizzard and Van

Bittner's "close friendship" (p.66) is completely wrong. Extensive interviews with William C. Blizzard revealed otherwise. WCB would never concede that his father would so much as join Bittner for a cup of coffee if it were not job related. Davidson lists Blizzard's greatest victories as "his support of free and reduced hot lunch programs in the public school system and his backing of the UMWA's hospital program" (p. 103). This thesis somehow missed that Blizzard avoided the hangman and organized West Virginia for the Union!

Lee, Howard B. *Bloodletting in Appalachia* (Morgantown, WV, WVU, 1969.)

The following is a 1969 review of this work by William C. Blizzard:

"In his foreword, Lee asserts, 'I have no bias or prejudice in favor of or against either group,' meaning coal miners or coal operators. Unfortunately, his book does not bear out his assertion.

"Although Lee condemns the Baldwin-Felts detectives (and the Don Chafin organization) that ruled the coal fields with armed force and, implicitly, the coal operators who hired such killers, the total effect of *Bloodletting in Appalachia* is that of an anti-labor tirade. Lee's loathing, hatred, and contempt for such Union leaders as William Blizzard and Mother Jones is unsubtle and obvious.

"Of Mother Jones: '(a) profane and vulgar labor agitator. She possessed no qualities of leadership.'

"Of Bill Blizzard (in his role at Widen): 'He imported the goon squads, frequently visited their camp, and made numerous speeches to the mob.'

"Lee reveals that William Blizzard was a field

leader of the Armed March of 1921 and the leader of attempts at Union organization at Widen in the fifties. To labor historians, this revelation is about as startling as the news that George Meany leads the AFL-CIO.

"Lee usually refers to gatherings of Union miners as a 'mob'. In one case, where many miners were 'foreigners and unable to speak the English language,' they are referred to as a 'mongrel mob.'

"The author repeats many personal conversations and alleged quotations throughout his book. There are few advantages to being 90 years old, but one is evident: Not many of your old associates are around to dispute the accuracy of your memory.

"A factual inaccuracy on page 115 of *Bloodletting in Appalachia* should be noted. Lee writes that 'In 1933, when the miners were unionized nationally, E.C. Townsend was made general counsel for the union, and he persuaded Lewis to name Blizzard as president of the union's District 17, with headquarters in Charleston.'

"In fact, a man named Ben Williams was appointed District 17 president on Nov. 19, 1932, and was succeeded in late 1933 by Van A. Bittner. Bittner held the post for more than 10 years.

"William Blizzard was not appointed District 17 president until Nov. 1, 1945, serving until 1955.

"*Bloodletting in Appalachia* poses as an objective, unbiased account, but is in reality an attack upon the UMW of A and, inferentially and specifically, organized labor in general."

*Picturing West Virginia, A Century of Collecting by the West Virginia State Archives* (Charleston, WV, West Virginia Division of Culture and History, 2005.)

This picture book includes the well known photo of Bill Blizzard batting during the Charles Town trial. The caption reads, in part, "During the trial, Union members, coal company officials, and journalists played baseball." Upon seeing the caption, WCB most forcefully commented, "My dad would never play ball with the operators! They were trying to hang him! They wanted to make me an orphan!" 'Nuff said.

Sullivan, Ken. Ed. *The West Virginia Encyclopedia* (Charleston, WV, West Virginia Humanities Council, 2006.)

This work claims currently two printings but an honest account would admit to two editions. Following complaints, some changes were made in the entry for Bill Blizzard but they can hardly be called corrections. Suffice it to say that both editions claim that during the Battle of Blair Mountain, Mooney and Keeney "managed events behind the scenes". See the entry regarding Mooney's book above for a primary source refutation of this fiction.

Zinn, Howard. *A People's History of the United States* (New York, NY, HarperCollins Publishers, 1980)

Howard Zinn, icon of People's History and Labor History, missed the big one. No mention of Blair Mountain, the largest armed insurrection since the Civil War. No mention of Bill Blizzard. Zinn's work is rightfully a classic "must read" for students of American history. It is also a loud reminder that the people's history can easily be forgotten if the people do not insist on remembering.

PM Press was founded at the end of 2007 by a small collection of folks with decades of publishing, media, and organizing experience. PM co-founder Ramsey Kanaan started AK Press as a young teenager in Scotland almost 30 years ago and, together with his fellow PM Press co-conspirators, has published and distributed hundreds of books, pamphlets, CDs, and DVDs. Members of PM have founded enduring book fairs, spearheaded victorious tenant organizing campaigns, and worked closely with bookstores, academic conferences, and even rock bands to deliver political and challenging ideas to all walks of life. We're old enough to know what we're doing and young enough to know what's at stake.

We seek to create radical and stimulating fiction and non-fiction books, pamphlets, t-shirts, visual and audio materials to entertain, educate and inspire you. We aim to distribute these through every available channel with every available technology.

PM Press is always on the lookout for talented and skilled volunteers, artists, activists and writers to work with. If you have a great idea for a project or can contribute in some way, please get in touch.

PM Press
PO Box 23912
Oakland, CA 94623
www.pmpress.org